Reading
the
Torah
Out
Loud

Other Fortress Press books by Marc H. Ellis

Practicing Exile
The Religious Odyssey of an American Jew
2001

O, Jerusalem!
The Contested Future of the Jewish Covenant
1999

Unholy Alliance
Religion and Atrocity in Our Time
1997

Reading the Torah Out Loud

a journey
of lament and hope

Marc H. Ellis

Fortress Press   Minneapolis

READING THE TORAH OUT LOUD
A Journey of Lament and Hope

Cover image: Prayer at the Tomb of the Patriarchs, Hebron, West Bank.
 Photo © Gyori Antoine/Corbis Sygma
Cover design: Josh Messner
Book design: Jill C. Lafferty

Library of Congress Cataloging-in-Publication Data
Ellis, Marc H.
 Reading the Torah out loud : a journey of lament and hope / Marc H. Ellis.
   p. cm.
 Includes bibliographical references and index.
 ISBN 978-0-8006-6210-3 (alk. paper)
 1. Judaism—20th century. 2. Jewish ethics. 3. Holocaust (Jewish theology) 4. Arab-Israeli conflict—Moral and ethical aspects. I. Title.
 BM565.E388 2007
 296—dc22
                                    2007008149

Manufactured in the U.S.A.

11 10 09 08 07 1 2 3 4 5 6 7 8 9 10

Contents

I am reading the Bible, page by page.

Dietrich Bonhoeffer

For my son, Isaiah Dylan

(Little-man, I-man)

writer, cartoonist, guitarist, Bible reader, baseball pitcher

ADONAI TIRES

THE WATERS OF MERIBAH

IN THE LAND OF MILK AND HONEY

Preface

In this volume, I ask the reader to join me in seeking and articulating an authentic religious stance for our newly globalized yet highly conflicted situation. Each of us must do so from his or her own context, and I do so here. I begin in mourning over the end of a certain kind of Judaism and in search of an alternative of integrity. I hope that by working through my own Jewish roots and identity, and by tracing signal encounters in my religious odyssey with religious figures and movements in my life, I can begin to voice a post-Constantinian Jewish identity that can be instructive for fellow Jews, for Christians, and for other persons of conscience searching for a prophetic, faithful footing today.

I have always been drawn to the prophetic as the essence of what it means to be Jewish. But increasingly I am drawn to the prophetic as the center of the human journey, as the building block of meaning in the world, as the one way of speaking about God that can make sense in a seemingly godless world.

Emerging in the ancient time of the Israelites and then carried in the Torah, the five books of Moses, and by Christians and Muslims who adopted our journey, the prophetic is clearly alive in the contemporary world. How else can one explain Martin Luther King Jr., the varieties of liberation theology in Latin America and beyond, or even the witness of Jews of Conscience who persevere in their attempts to assert justice as the center of what it means to be Jewish, including and especially in the complex arena of Israeli power and Palestinian suffering? I feel that the survival, indeed the revival, of the prophetic voice in our time is of utmost significance as an antidote to its loss in much of Jewish life.

The prophetic seems to have a life of its own. Once it is in the world, even the communities that claim it, Jews first and foremost among them, have difficulty taming or defeating the prophetic, and it often turns to witness against them. The primary purpose of the prophetic may be precisely the witness it gives against the very people who claim it. If so, that witness began very early. One need read only one of the Prophets to understand the point. For every verse of forgiveness and consolation, ten speak condemnation.

Within the prophetic, at the core of the Prophets, is a mourning that, while surrounded by violence and condemnation, penetrates beyond both. Mourning is loss and grief, an acknowledgment of some squandering of possibility and hope. As human beings we have to build a world around us that is meaningful and future-oriented. Mourning is the sense that this world building is for no purpose, a construct that does not hold.

Perhaps we as humans are caught between the sense of purpose and the sense of purposelessness. We use our imaginative and tangible power to ward off what we know to be true—that hope has its limits.

The world seems to run on power, a separation of those who have and have not, a desire to shut off the voice that unmasks the charades, the pretense to innocence and self-righteousness. Perhaps this is what my encounters with Jewish establishment figures, some of which I relate in the following pages, are really about. Not Israel or the Palestinians or even the definition of what it means to be Jewish, but the call to mourn the squandering of the Jewish ethical tradition.

Though specific rites vary, mourning per se is not particular to any culture, religion, or time. We often see progress as the great theme in history, a linear progression that we assume is there despite the violence and atrocity that accompany it. Mourning is another persistent historical theme. But mourning, unlike progress, is difficult to discuss as an abstraction. Behind the public rite of mourning is a personal sensibility that cannot be defined outside the individual, that is almost impossible to share with others, even our most intimate companions, and ultimately cannot be assuaged.

Mourning is a brokenness of the world as we receive it and as we construct it. Though we must somehow piece that world back together in order to continue living, it is never the same world we remember from earlier.

In these pages I try to face the diminishing of the ethical witness of Judaism and Jewish life in light of its willing participation in the cycle of violence and atrocity. I do so in a dialogue that weaves the personal and the collective. We are defined by how we live within a tension of solitude and solidarity, and no doubt the Jewish journey I share in these pages is only one way of living this tension. To the reader, Jewish or not, I leave my reflections as a spur to your own. It is one testimony of one Jew at the end of Jewish history as we have known and inherited it.

This book is also an exploration of the prophetic beyond Jews and Judaism, how it lives and breathes in our time. Hence my lived dialogue with radical Christians—among them Dorothy Day, who lived and worked among the poor in New York City for almost fifty years; James Cone, an African American theologian who writes passionately about African American life in the welter of white-dominant Christianity; and Gustavo Gutiérrez, a Peruvian Roman Catholic priest and founder of Latin American liberation theology. Their religious and political projects have touched me at a deep level. In short, they have become part of my own struggle to be faithful as a Jew. Without their struggle, even their failures, and their diverse spiritual disciplines, I would be less than I am.

The prophetic is part of the Jewish heritage. It is also part of the global ecology with people from different traditions and geographies grappling with the questions of injustice, justice, violence, compassion, and reconciliation. The prophetic tradition among the peoples of the world is complex and needs exploration.

Often the prophetic is thought through analytically; other times a personal witness is recorded. In my life both aspects are part of my journey, and I have come to believe that the prophetic can only be understood in the complex interplay of the person, the community, and the world. At the least, a journey can shed light on this complexity in a way that either personal testimony or theoretical writing cannot.

The interplay is with the Constantinian forces of our time and through the life lived in contested commitment. How often have we thought through an important aspect of our life and commitment, perhaps the turning point, by experiencing the limitations and possibilities of others who also struggle?

Many of us have been called into the rooms where self-appointed leaders of our communities pronounce judgment on dissenters, lecturing them about the rights and wrongs of religious, cultural, and political life. Some people, especially the leaders of empire and those who serve it, make a life of pronouncing judgment on dissenters. It is an age-old story repeated daily in courtrooms and institutions—legal, military, and religious—that span the local, national, and international scene.

What do we say to these judges? Are we alone in their courtroom? Are others with us, people from our birth communities and people from other communities quite unlike our own? Is God with us?

My own journey ends in an unexpected place, at least for me and perhaps for you, at the Torah. It is here that I find the strength to confront the judges of my own tradition, who seek to hand over the prophetic for death and burial.

The religious establishments of our day preserve the power to do this and may, at least for now, feel it tangibly even as they are snubbed and mocked for tactics and sensibilities that contradict dialogue, freedom, and humanity. However, they will never subsume the power of the indigenous formative reality, the prophetic, that set the Israelites and later much of the world on a search for justice, compassion, and peace.

There are other texts and traditions that provide strength for me and others. Yet it is my sense that the indigenous prophetic of Israel must be grappled with. Where else could these other prophetic sensibilities, many now completely shorn from religious impulses, mature, retain grounding, even reach a new and better understanding of the world we live in and the call on our lives to be faithful within the world?

The prophetic will outlast the judges and will ultimately judge them. This judgment is on the horizon. It is unlikely to happen in my lifetime or in yours, which means God is before us, calling us to commitment here and now. The judgment will come later. *After*.

In these pages I share with you my own fate and that of so many others—and it may be even your own. That fate is connected with a God who was and is, a God who can be found in the traces of our lives and our fidelity. My hope is that my testimony will encourage others to stand and speak at the end of their own histories. It is my sense that a fuller understanding of the prophetic in our time is urgent and will, in and of itself, provide strength and solace.

I have found this strength and solace in the testimony of others. Theirs is a testimony to the prophetic. I can only hope, in a small and humble way, that mine may be as well.*

---

*Because this book is primarily about my journey as a Jew in the world rather than a scholarly treatise, I have decided that an extended bibliography of the sources I have cited will serve the reader better than footnotes.

1

A Time to Mourn

The Golden Age
of Constantinian Judaism

It was in 1970 that I first heard Auschwitz discussed as a seminal event in Jewish and world history. From that moment on, the death camp assumed the most prominent place in my young and evolving sense of individual and communal destiny. As a Jew born into the post-Holocaust world, I found urgency in my own identity.

The absolute horror of Auschwitz almost overwhelmed me. It also enervated me. In a world of death, life assumed a heightened sense of vulnerability and value.

Two decades later I traveled to Auschwitz for the first time. By this time Auschwitz hardly stood alone as it had, more or less, when I first encountered it in my early intellectual pursuits. A theology—even a religion—had developed around Auschwitz. These reflected a consciousness about Jewish suffering, specifically in the Holocaust, and the need for Jewish empowerment, exemplified in the state of Israel.

Recently, Norman Finkelstein, a professor of political science and a Jewish critic of Israeli policies toward the Palestinians, referred to reflection on the Holocaust as an industry. In this industry, certain assumptions about Jewish suffering are codified and promulgated as an ideological and political package. Jews are seen as perpetually innocent and suffering, even as the Holocaust industry itself belies incredible power. It also seeks to hide the culpability of Jews in the present time. In Finkelstein's view, the presentation of the Holocaust to Jews and the world is not about the Holocaust at all. Rather, it is about the projection and protection of Jewish and Israeli power beyond the norms of accountability, criticism, and sanction.

Yet the situation is much deeper than Finkelstein's industrial model. Though the sheer output of literature and institutionalized memorials stand as a testament to Finkelstein's view, it is more appropriate to think of the Holocaust and Israel as a new religion with its own rituals and liturgical language, linked to the Judaism of the past but in important ways supplanting and transforming it. Unlike Rabbinic Judaism—developed in the Common Era and featuring a more pacific and prayer-oriented spirituality —this new religion is highly politicized and empowered.

For most of today's Jews, and also for many non-Jews, to name Auschwitz is to name Israel as well. The connection between the two— Auschwitz leading to Israel, and Israel justified by Auschwitz—is assumed, a recognition that needs no explanation. An inverse dialectic reigns: any need to explain the link between Auschwitz and Israel is cause for suspicion. Since they are conjoined in thought and emotion, to question one is to question the other.

In this system of thought, criticizing Israel is almost the equivalent of denying that the Holocaust occurred. While this is especially true within the Jewish community, it carries over into public policy discussions, especially in the United States. Over the years, the one special exception to criticism on human rights violations is Israel. The standard that applies to other nations, apartheid South Africa, for example, is rarely applied to Israel. Indeed, the way the discussion is framed it cannot apply. How can Israel, as heir to the Holocaust event, and Jews, with their tradition of ethics and civil rights, be involved in racism and exclusion, seizing another people's land and creating a refugee population?

This lack of accountability is sustained by the ecumenical dialogue movement, with a background stemming from new interfaith understandings between Jews and Christians after the Holocaust. Post-Holocaust Christianity has acknowledged where anti-Semitism led. This prompted a reevaluation of Christian doctrine and practice, especially as related to historic Judaism and contemporary Jews. Jews demand this reevaluation and rightly so, but over the years the Christian reevaluation has not been followed by a similar movement in the increasingly powerful and now culpable Jewish community.

For some reason, what applies to Christians—a critical sense of their own history and place in the political and economic world—is rarely seen

as applicable to Jews. The ecumenical dialogue is now a deal wherein Christians continue to evaluate critically their personal and communal lives while Jews deflect criticism of Israel or the way American Jews use their newfound power.

The ecumenical deal between faith communities is even more important in the political arena. Here Israel is always different; most criticism of Israel is seen as a form of anti-Semitism. That is why the facts about Israeli expansionism and brutality in relation to the Palestinians are mostly buried and their exposure carries harsh repercussions.

Beginning in the 1960s, many Jews carried on an assertive and celebratory conversation about Israel in the public realm. Since the 1990s, there has been a peculiar silence about Israel. Though the bond between Auschwitz and Israel is firmly entrenched, the world is changing its attitude toward Israel, especially with regard to its oppressive policies toward Palestinians. Even in the post-9/11 world, where the discussion of Israel has again resurfaced, a growing number of critics of Israeli policy are met only with lectures on the need to fight terrorism. The moral terrain regarding Israel has largely been abandoned.

Jews are changing in their own attitude as well, choosing sides in what seems to be an escalating split within Jewish consciousness and values. Some Jews feel that any power needed to secure Israel's future is justified. Other Jews are becoming more and more critical of Israel's expansionism and use of force against the Palestinians. Still, because of the historical pressures of anti-Semitism and community demands for unity, many Jews choose silence. The stakes in this quietly evolving divergence are becoming higher.

Today, neither Auschwitz nor Israel sheds much positive light on the Jewish future. Pondering Auschwitz leads Jews in many directions, as does support and dissent in relation to the state of Israel. However, these directions invariably lead in a circular pattern, always returning to a destabilized, increasingly disturbed center.

Years ago, Israel Shahak, a Holocaust survivor and critic of Jewish religion, suggested that the circular pattern itself is a dead end, that Jewish religiosity is a "burden" that must be shed for Jews to be free of superstition and the desire to exclude others from their communal and public life. Like the Holocaust industry that Finkelstein analyzes, Shahak sought to unmask contemporary normative Jewish sensibilities for what they convey and the politics they engender. In his view, many of these sensibilities emerge from a Jewish religiosity that is archaic, discriminatory, and dangerous.

For Shahak, Judaism in its classical and contemporary forms is self-deceptive and degenerative. Instead of breaking with exclusion and injustice, Judaism, with its strong sense of "chosenness" and mission, enshrines both. It is this very particularity that deceives Jews into believing that they are different and better than others; this in turn forms the very heart of Israeli policies that favor Jews and discriminate against Palestinians.

Finkelstein believes that only by exposing the Holocaust industry can Jews and others come to a true understanding and action with regard to Israel's abuse of political power. Shahak believes that only by discarding Judaism can Jews and others come to grips with the need for a new and just arrangement among Jews and Palestinians. Going further than politics, Shahak sees Jewish history and religion as burdens that must be shed.

What of the Holocaust and Israel? Are these also burdens that must be shed?

Many have experienced what Finkelstein and Shahak analyze—the use of classical and contemporary Judaism, including the ritualized and empowered use of Holocaust and Israel—as instruments to silence dissent. Who can argue with Shahak when he refers to some purveyors of contemporary Judaism as "patriotic liars"? He writes so ironically with reference to Judaism and Jewish intellectuals: "Religion is not always (as Marx said) the opium of the people, but it can be so, and when it is used in this sense by prevaricating and misrepresenting its true nature, the scholars who perform this task take on the character of opium smugglers."

Patriotic liars and opium smugglers exist in all religions and ideologies. They are necessary for certain kinds of institutional life to defend, promulgate, and extend their power. Who can listen to the public faces of religion and politics without noting the twisting of "fact" and "necessity"? The justification of America's invasion of Iraq, the decades-long cover-up of pedophilia in the Roman Catholic Church, the use of Islamic rhetoric to justify the death of innocents—all are examples of lying for the sake of a greater cause, realities that people and institutions deem larger than the crimes they try to explain away.

Institutions need patriotic liars and opium smugglers to aggrandize their standing in the world. Individuals also benefit from representing these institutions. The individual's quest for meaning sometimes comes in arguing for something larger and more significant than daily life. What better way to find our significance than speaking up for our religious and ideological formation that struggles against "evil" in the world? Identifying with this struggle also provides an expected place in the normative community structure. Patriotic liars and opium smugglers achieve a status boost through their participation, becoming known in the community for defending understandings and policies they usually know little or nothing about.

Within the Jewish world, these are not just Jewish intellectuals, though they are crucial in framing the public debate about the Holocaust and Israel. There is an array of Jewish institutions beyond the academy engaged in mobilizing Jews through Holocaust memorializing, political fundraising, lobbying, and Israel-centered diplomacy. These efforts move beyond an industry or a clique of opium smugglers. They form an interdependent complex of formal and informal religious and political understandings that are now part of the fabric of intellectual, spiritual, and institutional life in America and beyond.

Does this interdependent and powerful network, driven by Jews but with a multitude of non-Jewish enablers, mean that all is compromised, lost, fraudulent, or in need of a violent exorcism?

The problem is multifaceted and deeply embedded. It cannot be analyzed through a simple political prism. If indeed the question is historical, political, and religious, involving ancient particularities, events of mass death, and modern political states, varying angles of vision must be brought to bear.

Beyond the immediate politics of the Holocaust and Israel, I do not believe that Jewish particularity is only and always fraudulent or even primarily so. From ancient times to the present, discussions surrounding Jews have featured at least some of these charges of fraud, conspiracy, and misplaced superiority. Though much of this has been brought to Jews from outside, Jewish history is replete with internal Jewish discussions on these same themes. When coming from the outside, this criticism is characterized, and for the most part accurately so, as anti-Semitic. Coming from the inside, though, the charge, for the most part inaccurate, is self-hate.

The question is thus joined. Can there be a healthy Jewish particularity, a particularity that is critical, self-examining, evolving, and open to Jews and the world? If so, can such an affirmation survive the Constantinian impulse of the Judaism of our day?

Like the Constantinian Christians of old, Constantinian Jews have made their deal with power and the state. To get what they want, status and power in America and Israel, some Jews employ the protection and power of the state. All the while, that power is disguised under the banner of innocence.

Particularities are not easily jettisoned. Context is important, and sometimes primal sensibilities override the most prescient intellectualism. There is a place for rejection of Judaism and a Jewishness that involves culture and peoplehood. There is also room for those who find the struggle for Judaism and Jewishness essential to their being.

For those who see Judaism and Jewishness as essential, the battle lines are drawn with increasing clarity. There is a burgeoning and triumphant Constantinian Judaism. But there is also a new and deepening movement of Jews of Conscience, Jews who break with the tenets and alliance of Constantinian Judaism. These Jews envision a Judaism beyond complicity, confronting dislocation, settlements, denigration, and political assassination.

Still, a demarcation between "bad" and "good" Jews is too simple. What if many Jews seen as good—that is, Progressive Jews—are also part of the problem? What if they, even as they argue for human rights for Palestinians and an end to Israeli occupation of Palestinian lands in the West Bank, help frame the public discussion so as to achieve, more or less, the same thing their ostensible foes, Constantinian Jews, want? If this is true, then Progressive Jews could be seen as the left wing of Constantinian Judaism.

The civil war among Jews about Jewish identity is not simply between those who seek to unmask Judaism and those who embrace Jewish particularity. It is not even between Constantinian Jews and Progressive Jews—a tension often portrayed in the media and in scholarly studies. The real struggle lies beneath and around these blocs. The struggle has reached a level where the very question of particularity is obviated by an aggressive power that uses even dissent to frame the limits of debate.

As Jews, we have arrived at a place of violence and complicity, in Israel but also in Europe and America. Though romanticizing the past is always a danger, the contrast with the years of my youth in the 1950s and early 1960s casts a decidedly unfavorable light. In the America of that time, society was opening up to Jews and Jews were open to others, especially African Americans. In Israel, a state had been established and at the same time was in an experimental phase. What Israel would become was very much in contention.

The violence against the Arabs in Palestine was already a fact. How else could a state with a Jewish majority be created when the majority of the people living in the land were Arab? In my childhood this violence—a violence that can only be accorded the contemporary label of "ethnic cleansing"—was virtually unknown to American Jews. Though it was known to the Israeli Jews who had themselves committed these acts to take control of the lands they now inhabit, there seemed to be limitations to the violence.

In the long sweep of Jewish history and in light of the recent mass killings of Jews in Europe, it seemed from a Jewish perspective small recompense to banish what appeared to Jews to be a relatively unorganized Arab population in exchange for an established Jewish political presence in the world. Little did American Jews, or Israeli Jews for that matter, know how much this violence against Arabs would come to infect Jewish life, promoting an imbalance in the ethical sensibilities the Jewish people have carried with them.

From our vantage point today, it is clear that Jews were naive about the exercise of power and its effect on the very values that we held—and hold—dear. The documents declaring Israel's independence and the consciousness that grew up around the Holocaust and justified the creation of Israel are clear in their bold assertion of innocence in suffering and in power. So many years later and with the knowledge that contradicts these claims, we still proclaim this innocence with a vehemence that demonstrates a supreme anxiety about the very claim.

The choice, though, is not to go back to a time in history when Jews were innocent and without power. Clearly the Holocaust and Israel do not, in and of themselves, provide Jews in Europe and America with a future. It is not clear whether either provides a future for Israeli Jews. Israel as the hope for worldwide Jewry was always illusory, recognized as such by the majority of Jews who, when the choice of the West was presented again after the Holocaust, largely remained in Europe or went to America in the post–World War II era. The number of Israelis who leave Israel each year exceeds the number of Jews who move there, and it is fair to say that most Jews who can leave Israel and live comfortably in Europe and America increasingly choose to do so.

This desire of Jews to live among others in open democratic societies should hardly surprise us. And at the same time, is the failure of Jews to live up to our own myth of innocence an indictment peculiar to the Jewish people? Jewish history seems on the verge of collapse as the symbolic invocation of the Holocaust and Israel loses its validation for Jews within and outside of Israel.

At the outset these seem like political questions, or at least moral and ethical ones. They are. But the returning, or perhaps better stated, the turning that is called for moves within and beyond these categories. In the end there is a deeply personal dimension to Jewish identity, and in a sense the personal may be primary. Yet we also know that the personal lies both within and beyond the person.

In our beginnings, the world is large, to be explored, ingested, changed. As we grow older, the world becomes smaller, partly because of our exploration and because of a narrowing of our focus. Such limitation can be avoidance; it can also be a concentration of attention, the culling of the necessary from the extraneous. And while such a diminution of what we once held in greater value may appear to be a capitulation, it can also represent the grasping of our destiny.

In many ways this very assertion of a particular destiny relating to Jews and Jewish history has defined the Jewish journey for better and for worse. On the one hand, such an understanding has led to group cohesion, achievement, and survival. On the other, Jews have often stood out among the peoples, making them targets for prejudices and grievances.

Almost alone among the ancient peoples, Jews have survived and are vibrant as communities today. Yet the celebrated survival has been at the cost of great suffering. Jewish destiny bears at least two faces, the one of particularity and the other of universality, and too often there has been an intense competition between them. At some points, even recently, which face would win out has been in doubt.

Though the external world has had its say and indeed helped shape Jewish identity and purpose, Jewish destiny has always been defined internally. Here too are a variety of faces, the face of the collective to be sure, but also the face of the individual. In Jewish life both have had their way and their say, sometimes in unison, often in conflict. The individual, like the collective, has an interior life, but it is fashioned in a certain way. Though it is malleable and instructed by the generational context, its broad parameters are set out in advance.

In Whose Court Are Jews of Conscience Called?

In the court of the powerful, too frequently, some Jews enter the halls of academia to inveigh against Jewish professors who they claim are self-hating, anti-Semitic Jews because their work includes criticism of Israeli policies, especially as regards Palestinians. The crime they outline is simple: any Jew who argues that Palestinians have been and are today being wronged by the state of Israel is to be banished. I myself have been "called in" for such discussions.

It is a fascinating case study in the attempt to use economic, political, and religious roles to stifle dissent. Many Jewish groups today define themselves as Jews primarily through their unqualified support for Israel. Their standing in the surrounding predominantly Christian community is demonstrated and solidified by such support.

In many areas of the United States, religious affiliation is a means of asserting a fundamental identity. Though historically Jews have been suspect in relation to Christian understandings of salvation, the two groups have often bonded around certain forms of racial politics and piety. This sometimes included agreement on a position about slavery and, after slavery, racial segregation. After all, the Christians who are empowered share whiteness with their Jewish neighbors, and though this has changed in relative terms, many parts of the United States are still, for all practical purposes, segregated.

Of course the Jewish community is itself diverse. Though various groups claim to represent all Jews, there are in fact Jews who think differently, who are horrified and embarrassed by such behavior. Often this diversity is found through back channels and in secretive ways. Unknown to the leaders of the community and often in fear of them, some local Jews refuse to sign petitions against Jewish dissenters. Still others voice their support through anonymous phone calls in the early hours of the morning.

The claim of Jewish leaders to represent all Jews is contested, as are the demands they make. The interrogators betray an anger of their own that assumes a new direction in their patent antipathy toward Muslims, Arabs, and Palestinians.

The term "racism" is never used in such discussions. Yet it is inherent in the arguments made that Arabs have no ethical sensibility or understandable political discourse. Jews have a right to be free and to fight for freedom. Arabs, especially the Arabs of Palestine, have no such rights. In fighting against Israeli occupation, Palestinians fight against Jews, Judaism, and Jewish history. Who can fight against the state of Israel, a compassionate democracy that represents hope in a dark region of the world?

In their view, such a struggle can only be fueled by an irrational hatred of Jews. And what Jew can support such a struggle except one who is full of self-hate? Christians who associate with such a Jew are thought to be encouraging anti-Semitism. They are showing their true colors as Jew haters, as they once were more openly. This Jewish "truth squad" presents a syllogism. It is difficult to argue against the logic once the premise has been accepted.

In these encounters over the years, something inside me broke. What broke was the wall I had placed around myself to defend Jews and the Jewish community even as I critiqued the actions of Israel and Jews in America. I engage controversy in criticizing the war Israel has conducted against the Palestinians, but in my work I also declare war on those who speak of Jewish economic conspiracies, the Jewish political lobby, and Jewish control of the media. While it is important to fight both wars, in retrospect I think the latter has kept me and others from facing a more difficult reality.

There is of course no Jewish conspiracy, and Jews are not taking over the world—people with these views are anti-Semitic. However, power used by Jews to promote their interests is a reality. Though each community seeks its own interests and uses the power it can garner to pursue them, and therefore Jews should not be singled out for this behavior, to me this recognition represents a signal moment.

When I hear these accusations of self-hate and anti-Semitism, I feel that I am experiencing the end of Jewish history as I have known and inherited it, a Judaism centered around the ethical and acting for the "other" who is displaced and marginalized. In its stead arises a Judaism that purposefully and forcefully excludes an "other," a precept and call to action that patently subvert all that I was taught as a child.

At the time I began writing this book, I had spent more than two decades speaking publicly on the issues of Holocaust, Israel, and Palestinians. Though I have focused on the issues of memory and politics, what interests me most is the question of Jewish identity—what in fact it means to be Jewish in our time. As the collapse of Jewish identity becomes clearer to my own understanding, I realize now that my very discussion of Jewish identity has been an attempt to shore up what ultimately cannot be saved—at least as it has been known and inherited.

I also realize that what cannot be saved internally is difficult to discuss externally. At least I can no longer do this. To do so is simply to build another wall to protect an identity that is suspect within the fold of normative Judaism. To do so is to name a Jewishness in the world in order to bolster my own sense of the continuation of a form of Jewishness I have difficulty affirming.

I am not alone in wondering what it means to be a Jew at this very moment in our history. In my travels I have met countless numbers of Jews in this very same situation who express this ending by refusing affiliation with Jewish institutions and taking action on behalf of those who suffer, including and especially the Palestinian people.

These Jews of Conscience are journeying forward at the end of Jewish history, journeying into an exile that is unremitting, without reward or solace in contemporary Jewish life. As Jews of Conscience continue their exilic journey, many Jewish establishment figures—from officials in Jewish organizations to rabbis, to everyday Jews living in towns and cities, to university academics in Jewish and Holocaust studies—often denigrate this witness through charges of treason or self-hate.

At the dawn of the twenty-first century, Jews of Conscience are, almost to a person, relentlessly secular and atheistic. While this is not disengaged from a trend in the Jewish world that began centuries ago when Jews declared their independence from the power of the priests and the rabbis, opting, at least in their minds, for a secular freedom over the backwardness and oppression of the church and synagogue, the trend is accelerating today. Even those who come from religious families or through their own life experience have recovered elements of Jewish religiosity are now leaving mainstream Judaism, severing whatever tenuous connections they once had. This includes people in the Jewish renewal movement of the 1980s and 1990s who criticized the Jewish establishment for formal worship without spirit and for neoconservative politics that betrayed the ethical center of Jewish tradition.

The Jewish renewal movement seeks to creatively reinvigorate the connections of textual reading, ritual, and justice in the hope that this minority movement will one day become the next Jewish establishment. The movement's argument for peace in the Middle East, however, is often phrased around Jewish suffering in the Holocaust, the innocence of Jewish empowerment, the Jewish need for security. In short, in relation to Palestinians, the Jewish renewal movement is too often patronizing and self-centered.

This became apparent when the challenge of the al-Aqsa uprising began in September 2000 and the limits of Jewish dissent were clarified. When Jewish Israelis died in greater numbers and when Palestinians took up arms and began to target Jewish settlers on the West Bank, full-page newspaper ads calling for Jewish unity in light of Palestinian "aggression" caused renewal Jews to question their dream of reforming the Jewish community from within. Their creative attempt to transform Jewish life, rescuing mainstream Judaism from irrelevancy and restoring ethics to the center of Jewish life, had come to an end.

During the last decades, holding on to Israel until the end has been, at least subconsciously, a holding on to Jewish life. But does this Jewish life have a future as a force of difference and justice? Without a sense of distinctiveness, even a secularized sense of chosenness, it is difficult to understand the choice of Jewish life when so many other alternatives are possible. The irony is that Jews who practice the most ancient Jewish understandings are exiled from contemporary Judaism. I speak of the free prophets roaming the land, emerging from the palaces and the countryside, speaking to God and the powers of the earth and to the diverse multitude, before Judaism and the synagogue and the canon, before the Torah came into being and the Talmud was compiled, before the decorum and status of the modern synagogue, before the Holocaust and Israel.

In my own life I have witnessed these free prophets, in the Jewish world and beyond. Two American Catholics, Daniel Berrigan and Dorothy Day, are among them. Gustavo Gutiérrez, the Peruvian father of liberation theology, stands in this line as does James Cone, the African American theologian. Indeed, the twentieth century is full of such people, Jew and non-Jew alike. One thinks of Martin Buber, Mahatma Gandhi, Martin Luther King

Jr., Thomas Merton, and so many others who, while moving within their own particular traditions and communities, transcended them as well.

A community has come into being—and perhaps it has always existed—that emerges from and breaks through particularity and by so doing pays tribute to its context and a reality beyond context. We might call this the broader tradition of faith and struggle, a community made up of people from all time periods and places who witness to a possibility beyond themselves and their traditions. It could be that the covenant has been with them too, prompting and encouraging their own commitments, accompanying them in trial and tribulation, in exaltation and exile.

Jews, Palestinians, and the Evolving Liturgy of Destruction

Today a liturgy of destruction pervades Judaism and Jewish life, from the fall of Jerusalem and the Babylonian exile recorded in 2 Kings and Psalm 137 to the rabbis in the ghettos of Nazi Europe, Kalonymus Shapiro and Zelig Kalmanovitch among them, who announced the end of Eastern European Jewry with a resolve and dignity that comforted those suffering and decried barbarism and atrocity.

One of its chroniclers, David Roskies, understands the liturgy of destruction as a peculiarly Jewish response to catastrophe. Drawing from stories and memoirs, Roskies identifies the rehearsal of catastrophes and persecutions as reconfirming the covenantal relationship between Jews and the God of History. By the middle of the twentieth century, in the vastness of the Holocaust, the literature of destruction had become so vast that no single volume, ritual, or mural could encompass that history.

The struggle with God embodied in the liturgy of destruction and deepened in the Holocaust is ever present in the writing of Emil Fackenheim. For him, God's Commanding Voice at Sinai is silent in the Holocaust and therefore silent after the Holocaust. Rather than God's voice, today Jews hear the Commanding Voice of Auschwitz.

The Commanding Voice of Auschwitz demands survival in the face of the threat of annihilation and the end of the Jewish tradition of martyrdom. There are to be no further events of destruction for the Jewish people, the Holocaust being the last addition to the liturgy of destruction. In Fackenheim's view—but surely this is shared by almost all contemporary Jewish intellectuals, theologians, and leaders—the task of the present generation is to consign the Jewish liturgy of destruction to a history that bears no repetition. This is precisely the lesson of the Holocaust itself: Jewish suffering and the historical patterns of Jewish tradition and life, which allowed or even encouraged suffering, are over. Never again.

For Fackenheim and others, the Commanding Voice of Auschwitz demands support for the creation and maintenance of the state of Israel. Paradoxically, this support reopens the tradition, expanding it in a novel and unexpected way.

The victory of Jewish soldiers and the defeat of Arab enemies within the context of Israel represent, only initially, the struggle against the liturgy of destruction. However, as in all victories, the vanquished return. While it once seemed that Israel heralded the liturgy's end, this initial optimism has been mitigated by a protracted and seemingly endless conflict without an apparent victor or a new direction to take, even for Jews. Judaism and the Jewish tradition have been irrevocably changed, including the Jewish liturgy of destruction and the place, indeed the very definition, of martyrdom in Jewish history.

History bears this out. Jews have historically been divided by the Zionist question and have held differing opinions on Israel and the Palestinians. On the margins of this heated discourse, unbeknownst to most Jews, are a growing sensibility and literature that point to the return to the land as a catastrophe for Jews and, within that catastrophe, a possibility for the healing of past wounds inflicted on Jews by a hostile world. Even from the origins of the state of Israel, Jews have recognized this dual sensibility of catastrophe and possibility. Understandably, and perhaps predictably, Jews have seen both aspects within the Jewish liturgy of destruction and the archetypes of destruction—exile, martyrdom, and redemption.

Since the Palestinian uprising of 1987, an inclusive liturgy of destruction has evolved featuring Palestinians at the center of Jewish history. Indeed, Palestinians have become the engines of Jewish history. In short, the Jewish soldier who, witnessing the expulsion of Palestinians from their native villages in 1948, invoked the image of the expulsion of Jews from Spain in 1492; and the Jewish Israeli soldier who witnessed the beating of Palestinian teenagers by the Israeli Defense Forces in 1988, in which the soldiers' wooden clubs were broken, and who wrote an article on this experience titled "The Night of the Broken Clubs"—both refused the new history of Jewish empowerment as false and misleading if built on the suffering of others.

Something greater is occurring as well. On the heels of the Holocaust, the very epitome of loss and destruction, another perhaps even more significant dispossession is occurring—that of the ethical and moral compass, thus allowing the liturgy of destruction to emerge in the first place.

This is not the first loss in Jewish history, as the mourning at the origins of the rabbinic period attests. The rabbis come into their own authority within loss, the loss of Jerusalem in the first century of the Common Era, symbolically a greater dispossession from the clear and unequivocal presence of God. Throughout the Hebrew Bible, questions flow from God's actions and God's history. Within Exodus, God initiates actions with no humanly known culmination. All is up for grabs. Will Pharaoh let the Israelites go? Will the Israelites actually inherit the land? Even then, finality is elusive as the journey in the land is itself fraught with the temptations of idolatry and the political embrace of injustice. Here the prophets make their appearance, and again history is charged with charisma and suspicion. Will the journey of the Israelites end in bankruptcy, and will God, who has invested so much in this people, denounce this failure?

The rabbis came to power when judgment seemed distant. In the rabbinic period, the God who announced failure through the prophets—in disturbing, raging, and often violent declarations—is absent. Jerusalem falls, the temple is destroyed, and a new era of Jewish history begins. The rabbis must come to grips with the loss of God; they deal with what God has left behind in text, law, and story, in the teachings of God broadly considered. The trajectory of history is behind them, or at least its consideration must be bracketed. The rabbis are the new leaders of the Jewish people. Without cosmic force or authority, they supplant God.

This may seem arrogant. However, the rabbis assume their leadership with the humility of the defeated and bereft. They are limited to discerning the design they did not author and one that seems, at least historically, to have failed. Their focus is restricted to salvaging the remnants of the chosen and, more, the remnants of the promise. The genius of the rabbis is that, as they mourn an end, they develop a system of reflection, commentary, and prayer that transforms mourning into a studied agnosticism that reinterprets the promise.

The *kaddish*, the Jewish prayer over the dead, is typically rabbinic in its tone and substance, for God's great power is extolled, the coming of God's kingdom is invoked, and history itself is banished. The expectation is messianic rather than historical, and the dead, while enfolded in peoplehood, are individualized. The *kaddish* never mentions death.

Contesting Post-Holocaust Jewish Identity

The American experience doomed the rabbinic system. At the close of the twentieth century, varieties of that system had replanted themselves and a renewal of the synagogue in its variety and substance was under way. This renewal, however, was a demonstration of Jewish ethnicity and religiosity as counterpoise in a Christian culture. Whereas in Europe, for the most part, Jews grew up surrounded by Jews in areas cordoned off from the majority population, in America, Jews increasingly participated, were accepted, and flourished in the broader society and cordoned themselves off only for religious training and worship. In the main, the Jews of Europe did not live segmented lives; in America most Jews would have it no other way.

Thus the public school/Hebrew school reality I experienced as a child. Being American and Jewish was the natural soil of the Jews of my generation. Though it was seemingly a split identity, we experienced it as a seamless one. There were indeed discordances. By day we learned of America and its perpetual dawn, the ever new, the shining light, the hope of the world. In the evening and on weekends, we learned about our ancient heritage and the commitment to that heritage through struggle and suffering.

Ours was less a learned rabbinic than a popular variant that stressed the fundamentals of text and commentary rather than a close study of them. Hebrew was taught to be read at our religious services, and the Torah portions we read at Bar Mitzvah ceremonies were often memorized. No one I knew could read the Talmud, and, if memory serves, few had seen a page of the Talmud or could define its place in Jewish life.

What did we learn? We learned that our Jewishness was precious, that we had a history that predated America, that we were special and different from others. How was this difference to be understood? Mostly, we knew the difference because Jews are for justice, because Jews are good; we question and think where others do not. The "other," the Christians, were not lectured about or explored, nor were the assertions about our quest for justice or our inherent goodness. Things were as they were. We accepted our difference without reflection or probing.

For the most part, the 1950s and early 1960s saw a healthy joining of America and Jews where the two worlds were neither separated nor united. Indeed, the juxtaposition led to a rigorous questioning of world views, a borrowing and merging between the two, and a dual sense of identity, Jewish and American. In short, we were American and different.

Popular rabbinic forms integrated into America could hardly afford mourning as a central teaching or the practice it evolved to deal with life in the present. Jews had little to mourn in America, with the last barriers of anti-Jewishness coming down. "Is there a better place for Jews to live on earth?" Jews often asked. To live in America is to break free of religious constraint. Could the rabbis' interpretations and rulings govern a Jewish life lived in the American mainstream? Jews refused to mourn or to be regulated by Jewish authorities. Freedom was the watchword, success in America the new bible.

Jewish identity, rather than learning or commitment in a traditional sense, flourished. This identity was a public one, increasingly integrated, like Jews themselves, into the mainstream. Jewish identity was found through Jewish comedy and food—the Yiddish expressions found on television, the bagels that could be bought in bakeries in local shopping centers. Increasingly Jewishness was embraced in the public realm as a sign from society that Jews and Judaism should be prized and celebrated for their contribution to thought and culture.

For the first time in modern history, Jews were reminded of their Jewishness in a positive sense from a non-Jewish culture. There was an understanding of being set apart as the way we Jews contributed to the broader world. That specific contribution was at the same time an integrating factor. The world was hearkening after and absorbing Jewishness. Instead of being a sign of contradiction, Jewishness was becoming an affirmation.

Now that there were fewer barriers, curious questions remained. Why should there be quotas for Jews at Ivy League universities? Why did Jews change their names in the 1920s and 1930s? I recall when my grandmother—at the Passover table no less—addressed my grandfather as "Abe" when we had always known him as "Al." The story came out that as a youth my grandfather, Abraham Goldstein, changed his name so he could secure a job with the federal government. Abe became Al, even at home. I thought it strange that this had been hidden from us. The idea that a Jew had to hide his identity to work in America was completely foreign to me.

It was at this juncture, as barriers began to fall, that the Jewish suffering in Europe during World War II became more widely known and was named as the Holocaust. In time this occasioned a return to the mourning that accompanied so much of Jewish history. This return came in a new form, empowerment, a triumphal mourning new in Jewish history. Little did we know that another twist was around the corner. This empowerment would ultimately occasion mourning rarely known before in Jewish history. This is a mourning that many Jews even today resist.

The Watershed: 1967

My early years did not feature Israel as central to Jewish identity for most Jews. Israel was a pioneering state, and though we were not drawn to live there (I do not remember a single reference to this possibility during my entire youth), there was certainly no prejudice against its existence. To our knowledge as youngsters, Jewish politics on this or any other matter hardly existed.

In a very short time, however, Israel changed everything for Jews in America, for Jews throughout the world, and for me as well. In 1967 Israel was less than twenty years old; the struggle for an independent Jewish state was still fresh in Jewish memory. With Israel's lightning victory in the Six-Day War (June 1967), Israel came to symbolize the emergence of the "new" Jew, proud and assertive, competing favorably, for example, with the emerging Black identity movement. If in the 1960s pride in being Black was emphasized, after the 1967 war pride in being Jewish was accented.

This represented a reversal in America that is hard to overstate, and if I had not experienced this myself as an early teen, I doubt that I would fully grasp it. Whereas earlier Jewish identity was often expressed in our being for others, now being for ourselves took priority. The months before the war saw fears in the Jewish community that the small Jewish state might succumb to Arab power and disappear. For most Jews this possibility had never occurred to them, and it dawned on many Jews that in defeat millions of Jews might be slaughtered. Most Jews did not think in a political or even military way about this possibility, for, after all, most American Jews had not thought about the creation of Israel in these categories. Israel existed as a Jewish state for the most part in the context of Jewish refugees after World War II.

This apolitical sensibility seems difficult to comprehend, especially for a community prized for its analytical thought and political savvy. The existence of Israel was humanitarian, and the idea of Arabs in Palestine before Israel became a state, or Palestinians after the formation of Israel, was largely absent from the Jewish imagination. In my childhood I cannot remember a discussion that pertained to Israel's origins or the effect its creation had on others. Before the 1967 war, discussion of Arabs was nonexistent; I never heard the word "Palestinian." During and after the 1967 war, this discussion changed considerably, and from that moment, when Arabs were discussed it was in a derogatory way, especially in relation to their military failures. These were linked to their backwardness, a condition that seemed perpetual, perhaps genetic.

With the overwhelming victory of Israel in June 1967—in six days no less—and the incredible conquest and unification of Jerusalem, the fears of American Jews regarding the war subsided. For the first time since the fall of Jerusalem and the rise of the rabbis, Jerusalem was in Jewish hands, conquered and now guarded by a Jewish army. And for the first time, perhaps in the history of the Jewish people, a Jewish military was celebrated by people around the world. In Europe Israel's victory was hailed as a victory for freedom, and in America, reeling from its seemingly endless entanglement in Vietnam, Israel was heralded as a power with the know-how and determination to beat back Third World nations.

For Jews, especially in America, there was a sigh of relief and more. We also celebrated our newly found power, relishing Israel's military victory as if we were the combatants. Most Jews in America came to the United States with horror stories about forced conscription into militaries that Jews ultimately fled, and the percentage of Jews in America's armed forces was perpetually low. Many of those protesting America's involvement in Vietnam were Jews. The irony escaped us.

Unlike Israeli Jews, American Jews were unlikely military heroes. In my childhood there was no mention—not once—of the importance of military service. As I reached draft age, discussion about my being a soldier began but only in light of my parents' determination that if drafted I would leave for Canada.

In victory Jews became soldiers in a way that was peculiarly modern and Jewish. When we discussed Israel's victory, which was often, all Jews were involved. In our minds, that involvement was hesitant and innocent. Israeli and American Jews mobilized only because the forces of evil threatened "us" with annihilation. "Our" victory against great odds was almost never ascribed to military superiority, technology, or affluence, as if victory in war could be the material stuff of combat. For us this victory was a morality tale of light against darkness, the civilized against the uncivilized, the suffering against those who would inflict more suffering.

Only evil people, cultures, and governments wanted to destroy the Jewish state, we thought. Only those whose ultimate goal was to destroy the Jewish people had animus toward Israel. We had seen this before in World War II. The world had not responded to the helplessness of the Jews then, and now we would take care of our own business. For Jews this was like the victory in World War II, a victory that the entire world could celebrate.

2

Politicizing the Holocaust

Richard Rubenstein
and Israel *After*

The naming of the Holocaust event—what we had known as the slaughter of Jews in Europe—was itself significant. Without a name, the horrific suffering of the Jews of Europe could only be understood within the rabbinic system and the liturgy of destruction. Mourning, as understood within both, would simply be extended, a new chapter in an ancient history. The explanation for the event would draw from the same theological resources.

Without a name, Jewish suffering was limited to Jews. The outside world could only peer in, if it wanted to and if it was interested. The naming of the Holocaust changed the perception of Jewish suffering from outside and also from within. The naming of the Holocaust was destined to become a power unto itself, ultimately dethroning the rabbinic system and changing Jewish life. It would also change the world around us, how we as Jews perceived the world and how the world perceived us.

"Holocaust": Danger to the Rabbinic System

Richard Rubenstein, whom I first encountered at the southern university I began attending in 1970, understood these changes as inherent in the event itself. He was struck not only by the sheer magnitude of Jewish suffering in the Nazi years, but by the method of the slaughter: industrialized, organized, bureaucratized.

Rubenstein, a rabbi and an academic, found the rabbinic discourse on suffering and God inadequate for the present day. The liturgy of destruction highlighted martyrdom, the choice Jews made to die rather than to capitulate to political or religious domination. The rabbis were caught in questions of theodicy and the silence of God. Some had proposed that, as a loving parent, God had chastised his own as a way of bringing them closer to the path and therefore to God. This was the traditional way the rabbis bridged the gap between the chosenness of the Jews and their suffering in history.

Rubenstein saw the death of six million Jews as a formative event that could not be explained or contained within the rabbinic discourse and the liturgy of destruction. Thus, in his groundbreaking book with the provocative title *After Auschwitz*, Rubenstein named the death of six million as the *Holocaust*, as an unprecedented alternative event in Jewish history. This event trumped the rabbis. Their answers were impotent. Too many Jews were murdered. Could any sin justify mass death?

The title now is almost a catchphrase, intoned regularly as a given of religious thought and reflection. In 1966, the notion that after Auschwitz everything is different, that somehow the political and religious universe has changed, was radical, controversial, subversive.

Rubenstein's teacher, Abraham Joshua Heschel, a prominent rabbi and professor at Jewish Theological Seminary in New York, understood the ramifications of Rubenstein's book quite well. By naming the Holocaust as a formative event, the entire rabbinic system was in danger. Judaism as a rooted but evolving system of religious practice and as the defining center of Jewish life could not survive that naming.

In many ways both Rubenstein and Heschel were correct. By the 1970s, the Holocaust was seen as formative. The rabbinic system was challenged to its very core. Though the architecture of the synagogues remained, a sea change in Jewish life took place. Only the edifice survives.

Since there was no course on the Holocaust at my university, I read *After Auschwitz* in Rubenstein's Sociology of Religion class. Though published in 1966, the book became important after the 1967 war, the event that marked Israel's twinning with the Holocaust. Still, Rubenstein's take on Israel in *After Auschwitz* is decidedly pre-1967, compared to the direction Jewish discussion would take on the Holocaust and Israel after the war.

The post-1967 discussion of both events represented a challenge to Rubenstein in a way that he could not have foreseen. Radical and controversial in naming the event of Holocaust as changing the direction of Jewish life, Rubenstein became even more controversial after the naming became accepted. Yet even as Rubenstein's analysis of the Holocaust as formative became accepted, his understanding of its meaning for Jewish life was attacked.

In a few short years, almost all Jewish thinkers understood that the rabbinic discourse on God and suffering was insufficient. The Holocaust as an event did change everything, including the liturgy of destruction. The rabbis had operated outside of history or had at least pretended to do so. The Holocaust was a reminder, a final wake-up call, that Jews are in history and that the community has to arm itself to survive that history. Patience—keeping the community together, lamenting the loss of Jerusalem and nationality, and existing as a minority surrounded by hostile majority populations—was not enough.

A change of direction was imperative. In fact, a change of direction had occurred mostly without our noticing or understanding it. Israel as a Jewish state had been created, and the decisive battle for its existence had just taken place. For many Jews, the 1967 war was a wake-up call that encompassed the Holocaust as well. It was this war that demonstrated the significance of the Holocaust and showed us, through empowerment, the true cost of our suffering. Could Israel be the response to the Holocaust that signaled a new age for Jewry, one that brought the past into the present while transforming it?

This was the essence of the debate between Rubenstein and Elie Wiesel in the early 1970s, a debate that mirrored the debate within the larger Jewish community. It was quickly affirmed that the Holocaust and Israel were central and formative for Jewish life, and because of this the relevance of the rabbinic as an intact system was relegated to history without much fanfare. The question then was what direction these events would take us as Jews.

Mourning, Martyrdom, and the God of History

Mourning was central to the rabbinic system. It would also be central to Jewish life as the new formative events of Holocaust and Israel were declared. The question remained as to how Jews would mourn the Holocaust and to what purpose.

Rubenstein saw mourning as limited and as part of the problem that led to the Holocaust. The point is empowerment and whether or not mourning limits the capacity of Jews to work toward this necessity. Rubenstein sees in Israel a refusal to mourn. Israelis turn their backs on mourning just as they turn their backs on Diaspora Judaism with its dependency on God and the historical political and military weakness of the Diaspora. For Israelis, and for Rubenstein as well, the two are linked. Rubenstein's empowerment sensibility sees the end of Jewish suffering as tied to the end of a particular kind of Judaism—a Judaism that believes in the God of History.

But who is this God? In my youth, identifying as Jewish and learning about our tradition were quite important, yet the question of God was almost nonexistent. My most vivid recollection is of a brief exchange I had with my father. One night I asked my father if he believed in God. My father's desk faced the wall; he quickly turned his head toward me and answered, "Of course." With that he turned back to his work, and I returned to my thoughts.

Rubenstein's break with the God of History was clearly important to him. He spoke bluntly of his journey in relation to God; at the same time, he called me to pursue my own journey. Those who responded to him also raised theological questions about God. Nevertheless, though the argument with Rubenstein was intense, I felt that the argument was not really about God. Rather, it was about the covenant that God had given the people Israel and whether or not that covenant had been breached.

How can a discussion about a covenant given by God not be about God?

Even then, this concept of covenant was difficult for me to grasp. The covenant was given by God at Sinai. There was also a sense that once given the covenant could not be revoked. In the rabbinic system the covenant remained, though the balance had shifted to the human because of the silence of God.

The differences between Rubenstein and his colleagues relating to the covenant and God are sometimes difficult to discern. Elie Wiesel, who was just coming into prominence then, wrote despairingly about God, at least the silence of God in Auschwitz. He also wrote critically about the Jewish community and its acceptance—or more accurately its nonacceptance—of the testimony of Holocaust survivors.

Though Wiesel's autobiographical *Night* was written before *After Auschwitz*, they came into the public mainstream at about the same time; Wiesel's later collection of essays published as *A Jew Today* in 1975 is in many ways an angry book, an anger with God matched only by his anger with the Jewish community because he felt that Jews had turned their backs on Holocaust survivors. Though beginning to discuss the Holocaust in public, Wiesel felt that American Jews in particular wanted to theorize about the Holocaust without dealing with the survivors and their needs on a personal level. Wiesel wondered if Jews were somehow ashamed of the Holocaust victims they so boldly invoked.

The anger in Wiesel's words was matched by Rubenstein's anger and their acrimony toward one another. I wondered then, as I do today, where that anger came from and why its public display so defined them, against the other, and also in their own persons.

I read Wiesel before his coronation in the Jewish world and beyond. His Nobel Prize was won years after the publication of *Night*, his anger forgotten with the coming of his almost statesman-like stature. Before achieving the status that allowed invitations to the White House especially during the Clinton presidency, Wiesel was an outsider and a rebel just like Rubenstein. This was also before the building of the United States Holocaust Memorial Museum and the enshrinement of Wiesel as the architect of Holocaust memory in the United States and the world.

Wiesel embodied what Rubenstein lacked, or, if you will, Wiesel highlighted what Rubenstein disdained, especially the narrative of suffering. Wiesel understood that narrative is central to Jewish life. Indeed, Wiesel's narrative was dramatic. So was Rubenstein's. What distinguished the two was Wiesel's sense of continuity even within discontinuity, asserting that the Holocaust may have changed Jewish life irrevocably. Still, Jewish life continued in this altered state.

For Wiesel, the 1967 war was part of that continuity even though it did not answer the questions posed by the Holocaust. Israel, while not an answer to the Holocaust, is also part of its legacy. Holocaust survivors play this role as well. Both Israel and the survivors define the Jewish witness in the world after Auschwitz, representing the fragments of Jewish life that remain. The covenant is in fragments, and so is God. Still, though broken, it remains. This was the power of Wiesel, affirming a future even in the ruins.

Wiesel could not understand Rubenstein's path except as a denial of all that had gone before. Rubenstein seemed to be retrospectively condemning all of Jewish history. Did this consign the Jews of the Holocaust and those before them who had struggled with the meaning of life and Jewish identity to oblivion? A subtext, though unstated, was a further question: Rubenstein's dismissal of the covenant seemed to bury the wrestling with God that had characterized Jewish history and Wiesel's own life. Without this struggle, Jewish life could not continue.

Rubenstein made it clear that the Holocaust reminds him, as it should remind others, that the human condition is not perfectible and that attempts at revolutionary change often betray Jews and the larger polity. Conservatism, albeit with safeguards for the dispossessed and limitations on the powerful, guides him after the Holocaust. This was true in America, where Rubenstein, though in general supportive of the civil rights movement, became increasingly suspicious of aspects of the African American struggle that moved beyond integration.

Though Rubenstein saw no future for Jewish religiosity, he did not believe in forsaking his Jewish identity. All people need a tribal identification to have some foundation in the world. With regard to Jews, the world always reminds us of our identification anyway. To be safe as Jews, we need to affirm this identification and the empowerment we strive for together.

For Wiesel, Israel is a dream in answer to the nightmare of Holocaust. Rubenstein sees it as a necessary recovery of tribal roots and a protection against the marauders of history that march against Jews with varying flags and ideologies. Rubenstein spoke out loud what Wiesel had only broached (and initially only in Yiddish and French), that after the Holocaust Jews have to protect themselves against violence. To do this Jews may have to advance against our enemies and, if necessary, wreak vengeance against our them.

Is this war against Jews a war against God as well? Rubenstein called the violence of Christianity against Jews understandable. After all, the central beliefs of Christianity clash with Judaism, and the charges of deicide against Jews are traditional, perhaps essential to Christianity. The old Israel had been replaced with the new Israel for only one reason, from the Christian point of view—because the original Israel had greeted the promised messiah with derision and violence.

If Jews resent this story and the violence that accompanies it, the only avenue for self-respecting Jews is to arm themselves against it, militarily if necessary. But blaming Christians for their own narrative is hardly feasible or even correct. Jews have their own story of being chosen by God, and that chosenness places Jews above others. Resentment is an obvious reaction to such a claim, and therefore Jews have themselves to blame as well. Jews can hardly argue against the Christian claim of replacing the Jewish Israel if Jews continue to claim chosenness vis-à-vis the Christian community.

One hears in Rubenstein's framing of Wiesel's approach to the Holocaust a continuing critique of chosenness found in the Bible. The very claim of chosenness incensed Rubenstein. The Holocaust was beginning to function as a claim of chosenness without God. Once chosen to be a light unto the nations, Jews were now chosen in their suffering. Perhaps this was the reason Rubenstein so adamantly opposed Wiesel's understanding of the Holocaust dead as martyrs. Wiesel proposes a new chosenness that can only lead, ultimately, to another round of violence against Jews.

Primal Loyalties

Though in my youth I never felt threatened as a Jew, I was aware of discrimination. During my youth my father was denied a position in an insurance company because he was a Jew. This position would have secured our financial future.

The letter informing him of this decision was couched in sympathetic language. Those in the company liked my father as a person and wished him well, even offering to write him a letter of recommendation for other jobs. My father saved the letter and many years later showed it to me. Reading this letter more than a half century after it was written, I have to say it strikes me as odd: liking my father as a person, thinking him quite capable for the job, they were, because of his religion, unable to employ him.

Jews were on the move in American society, yet the visible face of Jews on the public scene was minimal. Jewish political candidates were few and far between. To many Jews in America, low visibility and steady progress were preferred. Though overt discrimination was decreasing, the fear of being "too Jewish" in public remained.

The anti-Jewishness I learned existed was always linked with the oppression of Negroes. The old signs at the hotels in Miami Beach warned Negroes and Jews against applying for jobs. In the 1960 presidential campaign, my mother commented bitterly that Richard Nixon frequented Florida hotels that prohibited Negroes and Jews. In my mind, Negroes and Jews were together against these "others" who harbored feelings against both of us.

The civil rights movement was understood in my home as of great consequence. Popular culture was an important conduit of these new understandings. Television and newsprint brought images of an integrated society, a Jewishness integrated as well. On the music scene in the early 1960s were Bob Dylan and Simon and Garfunkel; Alan King and Carl Reiner, both Jewish comedians, were regularly seen on television. In the movies, Woody Allen soon emerged as the quintessential thinking filmmaker. There was a strong, though sometimes unannounced, sense of their Jewishness.

Comedians were especially important. They inverted negative Jewish stereotypes in a manner that raised those images to a level of respectability. On television we often saw Jewish and Black comedians, one after the other, and for me, as a young Jew, they represented the same perspective—the embrace of particularity as a way of entering the larger world. I wondered how long hatred of Jews and Blacks could continue when the entire country was singing songs sung by Jews and Blacks and laughing with comedians from both communities.

The relationship between Jews and Blacks in the civil rights movement was complex. Some Jews began to feel that the struggle of Blacks was impinging on the Jewish community, and the very identification of Jews with that struggle was thrown into question. Did the Jewish commitment to Blacks confirm Jewish identity or represent movement away from the Jewish community?

In the early 1960s, Rubenstein was part of this discussion. Indeed, his naming of the Holocaust as a formative event was crucial to the ongoing debate. Rubenstein was on the side of integration, as were most Jews, and he went, as a rabbi, with many other Jews to the South to help this process along. Soon he was disenchanted, not at integration per se, but at the growing demands made by factions of the civil rights movement under the rubric of Black Power. Rubenstein recoiled at these demands and the increasing critical analysis of Jewish participation in segregation.

The new discussions about Black separatism intrigued Rubenstein. They were also cautionary. Could the helping hand that liberal Jewish sentiment extended to Blacks be used to attack the evolving status of Jews in American society? Would the Black revolution, if it actually occurred, be detrimental to Jews and the Jewish community, as other revolutions in Europe have often been?

The community and its leaders were split on the issues of integration, not because they thought the cause unworthy. Rather, a worry was surfacing about the future of Jewish life. The commitment toward justice, the struggle for the rights of others in America, was seen as threatening to the obligations to our own people. There was also the question of whether commitments as Jews translated into commitment to the Jewish community.

A rabbi without a congregation, Rubenstein was the most outspoken among the religious studies faculty at my university and the most accomplished. He was also the most critical, to the point that some thought him to be embittered. What saved Rubenstein from a consuming bitterness was his capacity to explore beyond Judaism and Jewish life while remaining almost stereotypical in his Jewishness. Even as he complained and staked out his oppositional positions on contemporary Jewish life and the sociopolitical drift of American politics—convictions that could sometimes be expressed in one-dimensional ways—he allowed himself and others to explore diverse dimensions of religiosity and politics. Perhaps this was Rubenstein's saving grace.

Rubenstein's approach to the complexities of race relations shows this, as does his approach to the relationship between Judaism and Christianity. Rubenstein was repelled and attracted to Christianity, but, as was often the case, his final position was less interesting to me than his probing. *After Auschwitz* is clear on his more negative understandings of Christianity, holding it to be a rival religion that, at its essence, claims superiority to Judaism. The coming of Christianity meant the displacement of Jews, theologically and physically. Linked with earthly power and containing strong symbolic elements as well, Christianity defeated Judaism, relegating it to a despised and powerless condition, and then sought to abolish it. What saved Jews in Christendom was the Christian need to see their triumph realized in the defeat of the Jews. The Jews became constant reminders of Christian ascendancy and Christians' eschatological hope that when even the "blind" Jews saw the rightness of Christianity, the final days of world salvation would begin.

Rubenstein found false and misleading the ecumenical movements of the post-Holocaust era that sought to ameliorate or even suspend this "essence" of Christianity. Attempts to cleanse Christianity of its anti-Judaism may succeed in the short term, but because Jews and Judaism are essential to Christianity, they will ultimately return. So too the Christian attempt to distance itself from Nazism. Though it is clear to Rubenstein that the Nazis were not Christians, the Nazi ideology toward the Jews was impossible without Christianity. The Nazis capitalized on a hatred of Jews inaugurated by Christianity, and, since Christianity for better and worse is part and parcel of Western culture and society, anti-Semitism is, for Rubenstein, a permanent part of the landscape within which European and American Jews must live.

What is startling in Rubenstein is his refusal to blame Christianity or even, in the end, the Nazis for their views and policies toward Jews. In Rubenstein's view, while anti-Semitism is an ideology that Jews should struggle against, the logic of religions and ideologies must be carried out by their adherents. The Christian displacement of Jews is logical within the Christian framework of the old and new Israel. Nazi ideology is entirely consistent with this displacement. Jews are not only foreign; they resisted the society the Nazis sought to create. Jews strive against Christianity. After all, the differences of the religions are hardly trivial. Jews do reject Jesus as the messiah and oppose Christianity as the new Israel. Christianity does see Judaism as archaic and insidious.

Rubenstein finds the liberal attempt to cover over these essential dichotomies as ultimately useless. On the one hand, it does not prevent the recurrence of violence that emerges from these religious and ideological movements. On the other hand, it also deludes practitioners of these communities and disarms them of the need to defend against violence, thus preventing liberal Jews from recognizing and limiting the assault that is inevitable.

The caution that Rubenstein advises on the Black-Jewish dialogue is the same caution he advises here: primal loyalties trump modernizing sensibilities. The best way to protect one another from the violence that these primal attachments demand is independent power. Christians and Jews have a right to their communities, and both need to be protected from each other. Accommodation comes through mutual empowerment rather than an interdependent mutuality.

Both Christianity and Judaism are relentless. That relentlessness has to do with faith and transcends it as well, because primal loyalties, especially in times of crisis, trump liberal sensibilities. Rubenstein often pointed out an example of this sensibility in his own life. Ceasing to believe in a God of History does not for a moment break his tie with the Jewish world. Despite his arguments, despair, and even exile from the community, Rubenstein sees himself as part of the Jewish community. There is no other place for him to go.

Rubenstein's exile was as palpable as his Jewishness was self-evident. I wondered if Rubenstein's fate was singular or proscriptive. Sometimes I felt that he courted this exile. Other times I thought the Jewish community was responsible for it.

Certainly his understanding of the Holocaust as a defining event that bore no hope of renewal was part of the reason for his exile, yet it was also his conception of Judaism and Christianity as defined by their origins and inherent contradiction. In Rubenstein's mind, adherents to Judaism had to believe in the chosenness of the people Israel and that God's plan for the Jewish people was intact; hence there must have been a reason for the Holocaust. Being unable to affirm any aspect of God's will in the Holocaust, Rubenstein refused the Jewish God of History.

Still, he retained his loyalty to the Jewish people, from whom he came and through whom he must be understood. Christianity is impelled to oppose and deride Judaism and Jews; its birth and history determine its future. The superiority of Christianity over Judaism has to be affirmed by Christians. To Rubenstein, for Christians to distance themselves from that affirmation would mean detachment from Christian belief itself.

Listening to Rubenstein, I became curious as to what Christians did with that detachment if, in fact, they abjured anti-Semitism. Did they, like Rubenstein, continue with their primal community after their faith had waned? Could Christians, unlike Jews, simply drift into an increasingly secular society, shedding their identity completely? Perhaps there are too many Christians for this distancing to have any effect on this fundamental rivalry. Or perhaps many continue to call themselves Christian after the essentials of their faith have been jettisoned. Is liberal Christianity their equivalent to Jewish tribal loyalty?

Primal Paganism

Though Rubenstein believed that tribal loyalties define us, his definition of the primal was expansive. Hegel, the great German philosopher, was extremely important to him. During the 1970s, only one contemporary Christian, Paul Tillich, interested him at a deep level. Like Hegel, Tillich influenced Rubenstein's sensibility, yet he rarely mentioned Tillich's Christianity or even his early and sustained opposition to Hitler. As a German theologian and social commentator, Tillich could only be defined as a liberal. If you were drawn to this way of thinking, Tillich was extremely important, as he explored new ways of communicating the essentials of Christianity. Conservatives saw Tillich as almost reinventing Christianity—he might be understood as pioneering a postmodern Christian sensibility.

Rubenstein was a student of Tillich at Harvard, and he recounted numerous times Tillich's palpable involvement with Greek philosophy and myth. Rubenstein saw this aspect of Tillich—the only aspect that I recall him discussing—as a paganism Rubenstein was himself attracted to, especially its attachment to the earth and its sense of finality.

This primal paganism is also found in Judaism, at least among the ancient Israelites, and Rubenstein argued that the rabbis made a fundamental mistake in intellectualizing Judaism and distancing themselves from Judaism's primal roots. The state of Israel is foremost for the protection of Jews, yet for Rubenstein it also provided the opportunity for a return to the primal pagan roots of the Israelites. Though Rubenstein did not give credit easily, it was clear that Tillich's evocative understanding of the pagan ethos offered a way for Rubenstein to understand his Jewishness despite the Holocaust, the rabbis, and the very personal torment of exile he was undergoing.

Albert Camus was part of Rubenstein's pantheon, and, as with Tillich, it was Camus's orientation toward the earth that interested him. Here again the tragic beauty of life and death was evoked, as Camus loved life in the present without hope of God. The beauty of earth and love sustains the human, but the universe is indifferent. Our only obligation as humans is to recognize that we share this tragic situation. Within the limitations set by nature, we have our brief moment in the sun. Camus, and Rubenstein as well, felt it more mature to recognize the limitations of life than to conjure the myth of the sky god or a messiah. As with Tillich's love of the Greeks, for Camus, tragic beauty and the limitations of life—what he labels "the absurd"—are the watchwords.

The most primal of all for Rubenstein was clearly Sigmund Freud. Freud, the founder of psychoanalysis, was a Jew and a refugee from the Holocaust; while these were natural topics of interest for Rubenstein, it was Freud's psychoanalysis that intrigued him. To be more accurate, it was the combination of the three that Rubenstein explored.

It was his own experience with psychoanalysis that allowed Rubenstein to be free of illusions or at least to struggle for that freedom. As with the pagan, psychoanalysis is primal, penetrating beneath the veneer to the roots of consciousness and desire. Rubenstein clearly relished his discussion of these themes—the before of civilization, religion, and identity. Religion, like civilization, attempts to construct myths around the truth of the subconscious and, at the same time, to discipline the violence and desire found there. Rubenstein never tired of reminding us that the difficulty of civilization was delaying gratification of the most fundamental elements of our subconscious, for just beneath the surface of life is an anarchy we deeply desire. If unrestrained, this anarchy can only lead to doom.

Seen from this perspective, political revolution tends to express and unleash these tendencies as the repressed hatred of limitations is overturned and articulated. In revolutionary situations, everything is up for grabs, and the violence that often precedes and follows revolutions demonstrates the need for restraint. For Rubenstein, Jews especially should be wary of the unleashing of restraint, and, following that line of reasoning, the first and longest chapter of *After Auschwitz* is mainly an exploration of the death camps from a psychoanalytic perspective. The Nazis, fearing and expressing the primal qualities of their own community, wanted to turn Jews into excrement. Hence the living conditions of the camps were designed to force Jews to live precisely that debasement.

The desire for anarchy—where everything becomes possible—is defining and must be avoided. It is a primal temptation. While we want the freedom to express the primal and thus gratify ourselves at the deepest level—we, and society, cannot survive that expression. Thus consciousness of the primal and its restraint represents a mature way of coming to grips with our base self. No one else pointed the way in this direction as did Freud. It was the reading of Freud and then the experience of psychoanalysis that Rubenstein imparted to us as essential.

Rubenstein shared many aspects of Freud's thought with us, but the stories I remember well—stories he repeated in various contexts—had to do with Freud's Jewishness and his near obsession with Moses. I recall vividly Rubenstein's evocative story of Freud's visits to Michelangelo's *Moses* in Rome and how Freud would sit for hours in deep silence before this magnificent sculpture. The primal quality of such reverential visits was obvious, at least to Rubenstein. Freud saw himself as a contemporary Moses leading his people to new understandings, perhaps even to a new place of liberation.

The psychological conflict was clear to Rubenstein. In *Moses and Monotheism*, completed just before his death in 1939, Freud took on what he considered to be the ultimate mythic figure of Jewish history. It amazed Rubenstein that in the midst of the Holocaust, in exile in London, as he suffered his final illness, Freud sought to describe the origins of the faith from which he had ostensibly distanced himself. Freud's speculation as to who Moses was and the fate he suffered was, at least for most Jews, scandalous. Freud saw Moses as an Egyptian who led the Israelites to freedom, and then an ungrateful people, protesting his stern leadership, murdered him in the desert.

The subversive power of Freud's narrative fascinated Rubenstein. I, in turn, was fascinated by Freud's assertion and the power in Rubenstein's telling of the story. It was all in line with Freud's understanding of the beginning of religion, the gathering of the sons in rebellion against a tyrannical father, their murder of the father, and, with the ensuing sense of guilt for that murder, the projection of the murdered father into a deity to be feared and worshiped. For Freud, at least as told by Rubenstein, the story of Jesus, the murdered prophet, was a later projection of the same impulse to slay that which restrains us.

Rubenstein was especially drawn to Catholicism for its dramatic re-enactment of this primal murder and the "pagan" ritual of the Eucharist as a way of atoning for it. Clearly, the pre–Vatican II church, with the body and blood offered in the most basic and ritualistic ways, attracted Rubenstein in its essential primal elements.

Rubenstein was also drawn to Paul. In Rubenstein's writing, we find Paul as Rubenstein's brother as much as the apostle and founder of Christianity. While not totally neglecting history, Rubenstein placed Paul on the psychoanalytic couch. There Rubenstein finds a Jew who can no longer live within the Law. Paul's rebellion was preceded by his attempt to force upon others—and thus upon himself—what he ultimately could not abide, and then in a breakthrough he saw the impossibility of it all. The Law, though hardly evil or simply a code of repression, was a dead end for Paul. Indeed, the dead end elicited the very propensities and desires the Law sought to control, thus the lashing out at others who experienced the freedom Paul longed for. When the internal turmoil came to the boiling point, Paul experienced a conversion—through the acceptance of Jesus as Christ—that freed him.

As a Jew and a rabbi, whose practice of Judaism grew as he entered the rabbinate, Rubenstein experienced much of the turmoil that Paul writes about in his letters. He also experienced the same need to be free. As he realized that need, he redoubled his piety in order to beat down those feelings. Again like Paul, this projection outward failed and Rubenstein experienced a turmoil that threatened his mental and physical health. Unlike Paul, Rubenstein's release was accomplished without a salvific figure like Jesus. Instead, Rubenstein's burden was loosed through psychoanalysis that allowed him the freedom to explore who he was and to be at peace with this discovery.

Paul's embrace of Jesus was his happy ending, a type of resolution that eluded Rubenstein for the rest of his life. It was here that the brothers parted company. Still, I noticed the camaraderie that Rubenstein relished. Both he and Paul are Jews, both come to the end of the Law, both are courageous enough to admit the end and explore possibilities beyond the Law, both suffer for this exploration by the very community they were born within, and both find a peace and acceptance within themselves because of the choices they make.

3

Encountering a Prophetic Christianity

Political Realities and
Spiritual Questions

Like many young adults, I was drawn to the religious mysticism and eclectic affiliation of Martin Buber's *I and Thou*. His "I-It/I-Thou" paradigm captured my imagination. For Buber, the "It" world is necessary for survival, as objectification allows us to secure the material basis of existence. The material world offers little beyond that base and can become a trap if seen as the only reality. In contrast, the "Thou" world is extraordinary, a spiritualization of the material, or, in Buber's understanding, the Thou is the essence of the material.

Buber uses the example of the tree as having a material and spiritual reality. For Buber, it is the individual's perspective that determines which aspect of reality one dwells within, or rather whether the material or spiritual level predominates. Both exist. Our choice determines our perception. To be mired in the material or elevated to the spiritual world is a choice that determines who each of us is.

Buber's mysticism was a worldly one that emphasized choice and commitment. It was quite different to me than the ecstasy of Sufism or the fated quality of Hinduism I was learning about. This element of choice intrigued me. As a scholar of the Hebrew Bible, Buber emphasizes decision as a free choice, or rather an obligation chosen freely.

Buber's essays on the Hebrew Bible are enlightening. Instead of reading the Bible in the tried and often tired way, the reader should reencounter the Bible as a narrative that is strange to us, from another time, awkward in its rhythms and style. As we encounter this strange narrative, we realize it is also our own narrative. Thus we encounter the Bible as it, in turn, confronts us.

For Buber, the Bible is a series of calls to decision. Though historical in content, the Bible calls us to decision in the now. It does not call us to a decision on the external or factual truth of the narrative—did the burning bush really burn without being consumed?—but calls us to enter the inner meaning of the narrative beyond the factual. By entering that inner meaning and the responses of those called by God in the Bible, we are better able to discern our own meaning and calling. Buber saw the individual decision as always existing in the larger context of community and history.

The community too is under obligation to listen and respond, for it has a mission as well. In Buber's understanding, the individual and community complement each other, or should, though often they are at loggerheads. The individual hears and responds to the call, while the community is often lethargic or even hostile. Buber envisions a long line of the prophets, all in their own way failing, but always faithful to their calling. Again it seems part of his practical mysticism, as the prophets are real and connected in a chain of history beyond the concrete moment of their existence. Nonetheless, for Buber, these prophets are often hidden from view.

Buber distinguishes between the power to command and the power to decide. Like Rubenstein, though for very different reasons, Buber stood outside mainstream Judaism with its concentration on the Law. For Buber, the ability to command or the obligation to respond interferes with and makes superficial our response. Obligation without choice or performance of the obligation without intent nullifies the obligation itself. It renders superficial that which points to depth.

If Buber believed in a God of History, this God was quite different than the one Rubenstein could no longer affirm. They represented two separate lines of theological thinking, the hard logical pursuit that Rubenstein represents, and the softer, more poetic quest that Buber epitomizes. Rubenstein crosses boundaries through his understanding of the primal, while Buber epitomizes the more mystical side of spirituality. Yet Buber dealt with the primal as well. His Thou was the before of the It.

Unlike Rubenstein, Buber's primal is engaging rather than frightening. It is far from Freud's sons banded together to murder the father, or the rambunctious unconscious that undermines the facade of bourgeois respectability—Freudian themes that Rubenstein loved to emphasize. Rather, the primal is found in the origins of humanity, especially the people Israel, which dwells in an intimate connection with the natural world and the spirit. Buber's understanding of return is to the primal yes of Thou and community that has increasingly been lost over time.

In modernity, Thou is in danger of disappearing. If the object world triumphs, humanity is lost. Without humanity, Thou is lost, or at least adrift. The spiritual is found in relation, and no matter how disjointed that relation becomes, a return is always possible. For Buber, the spirit remains to be rediscovered, or better yet uncovered from the detritus of history.

"History is a mysterious approach to closeness," Buber wrote in the early part of the twentieth century. This observation certainly seems to contradict Rubenstein's understanding of the chasm in history that opened during the Holocaust. After his exile from Germany in 1938, Buber traveled to Jerusalem, and it was there, in 1942, that *The Prophetic Faith* was published. Soon after, he wrote *The Eclipse of God,* in which he argues that it is indeed difficult to find God after the Holocaust, especially if you objectify God and define God in advance. Being open to God, even and perhaps especially after the Holocaust, is our task. God is covered over, veiled, waiting to be rediscovered.

Witnessing Radical Christianity

Soon after leaving university life, I arrived in New York to live for a year in the Catholic Worker community. The idea of service to the poor in light of a religious commitment intrigued me. Once there, I realized that the Worker in its essence embraced the thought of Martin Buber.

Rubenstein rejected Buber's theology and politics as Pollyannaish. He saw Buber as a Diaspora Jew who did not understand the threat of the Nazis or the reality of evil in the world. How else could Buber return to Germany less than a decade after the Holocaust in a spirit of reconciliation and peace? Buber also argued that Jews and Arabs should live in fraternity in Palestine and controversially—in Rubenstein's mind, naively—opposed the creation of Israel as a Jewish state in 1948. Didn't Buber understand that only Jewish power would protect Jews? Rubenstein shuddered at the idealism that continued to permeate Buber's spirituality after the Holocaust and the contentious birth of the state of Israel.

My arrival at the Worker coincided with Rubenstein's time in Germany, where he delivered a lecture on Buber's life and spirituality. Though in the main the conference was a celebration of Buber's life, Rubenstein delivered

a scathing analysis of Buber's lack of political acumen, linking that defi-
ciency to an inherited spirituality that helped to doom the Jews of Europe.
It struck a decidedly discordant note at the conference, yet it was entirely
predictable and vintage Rubenstein. So it was with surprise that, reading
the lecture some years later, I came to his concluding thought, a provocative sentence completely out of character with the rest of the lecture: "We
needed him. Why, I do not know."

Rubenstein also acted out of character in 1970 in a debate with Elie
Wiesel about the meaning of the Holocaust. Wiesel responded to an earlier lecture in which Rubenstein denied that the victims of the Holocaust
were martyrs. Simply stated, Rubenstein believed that Jews killed in the
Holocaust did not die for their faith but simply because they were Jews. To
revere them as martyrs was to elevate the victims of the Holocaust to a status they did not deserve and, at the same time, to mobilize the dead of the
Holocaust for a post-Holocaust spirituality that Rubenstein thought naively
sentimental. Rubenstein further angered Wiesel when he claimed that
Israel's victory in the 1967 war should be seen exclusively in military rather
than theological terms. The dead of the Holocaust were victims, and the
1967 war was "no royal road back to the God of Israel." Wiesel was livid at
Rubenstein's lecture, tore up his prepared remarks, and responded directly
to him. Wiesel's remarks were personal, even suggesting that Rubenstein
was a self-hating Jew. Yet at the end of this personal attack, Rubenstein rose
and said, "I as a rabbi want to give you my blessing."

I wonder if this was Rubenstein's attempt to bridge the chasm in Jewish
life he had helped to introduce. It could be that Rubenstein was trying to
heal the division within himself, between the primal darkness and the light
of ordinary reality. For the rest of his life, Rubenstein engaged in an internal wrestling that would remain largely unspoken. Still, I felt Rubenstein's
appeal to Buber and to Wiesel to be a genuine plea. As the violence within
the Jewish world increased, Rubenstein's plea to Buber and Wiesel fell on
deaf ears. The divergence was too great. Never again would Rubenstein
reach out in such a way.

Whereas Rubenstein articulated the end of Judaism and Buber counseled always to search the end for another beginning, the Christians I traveled among articulated their commitment in overt and intact religious
imagery and ritual. At the Catholic Worker, vespers is said daily and the
Mass on Sunday is considered the focal point of the week. Many, including
Dorothy Day, the founder of the movement, attended Mass daily.

The Worker combined the spiritual and the intellectual. There was
much reading and discussion, and the intellectual probing was wide-ranging

and often avant-garde. The Worker is a committed community with such issues as nuclear armaments, civil rights, and ecology taking front stage. The Worker's always controversial pacifism demands rigorous analysis of a variety of issues from modern warfare to capitalism, and the Roman Catholic Church is split on many of these issues. The Worker opposes war in general and feels that even the just-war tradition of the church is obsolete within the context of modern warfare. Understandably, this latter position heightens the controversy. Because of its stand on war, the Catholic Worker opposed America's entry into World War II. Closer to my generation, it voiced early and ongoing opposition to the Vietnam War. Later it opposed America's invasion of Iraq.

Amid all of this controversy, the Catholic liturgy is celebrated at the Worker without discussion or fanfare. Questions about politics, war, and economy are vibrant, ongoing, engaged, while religious ritual is assumed, the Christian narrative of salvation unassailable. Perhaps this is stated too strongly. In many ways the Christian narrative fell to reinterpretation by the Worker, the challenge to Christian participation in war being among the most dramatic. Likewise, the Worker's call for Christians to embrace Jews and the Jewish people is representative of a revolutionary reversal in Christian history.

Still, the reinterpretation of Christian obligation does not interfere, from their perspective, with the continuity of Christian and Catholic traditions. Nor does it raise for them questions about God. The suffering throughout history, including the Jews but also the poor whom they serve, seem absorbed or addressed by the suffering of Jesus.

This suffering is commemorated in the Mass and projected into the present. The suffering of the world is at the heart of the suffering of Jesus, yet it is also here, especially in Jesus' resurrection, that suffering is ameliorated. The Worker community does not celebrate the resurrection of Jesus as the happy resolution of suffering without knowledge of the continuation of misery. They are surrounded by suffering before, in the middle of, and after the liturgy. Living among the poor, they celebrate their resurrection faith where they live.

Being an outsider in this context allowed me to think in ways that my own tradition discouraged. How do Christians assent to a faith that seems so contradicted by the reality of the world? How do they affirm a church that is so compromised by its own history? In my journeys among Christians, I have become aware of an internal debate within the Christian community. Christians at the Worker or in liberation struggles are drawn to a Christianity repentant of its past collaboration with injustice and active on behalf of justice in the world. With that confession and commitment, they are once more drawn to the Christian faith and participate in its rituals with little or no difficulty.

At the Worker and in my travels among the poor in Latin America and beyond, the consistency of Christian religiosity is apparent. Even the evident hypocrisy of Christianity itself, alternately conqueror and liberator, sometimes dissolves in the places where the poor are served and treated with dignity. Yet for me, the drama of the Passion is broken by Jesus' deification. Somehow I feel that the deification is a betrayal of Jesus. I am drawn to the life and death of Jesus the prophet, not his resurrection.

As I witnessed more and more Christian liturgies, I became curious as to why Rubenstein wrote about Paul rather than Jesus. Paul was, in Rubenstein's view, more his brother than Jesus, and it was Paul's choice between the Law or the resurrected Jesus with which he identified. For Rubenstein, Jesus exists only through Paul's interpretation. Buber also wrote about Christianity, but Paul figured little in that analysis. When Buber mentioned him, Paul was seen in large measure as a negative figure, the inventor of another religion, Christianity. For Buber, Christianity simply reproduced the negatives of all religions, including Judaism.

Yet again in opposition to Rubenstein, Buber wrote quite a bit about Jesus and in an astonishingly positive way. Jesus represented, perhaps even quintessentially so, what Buber saw as the essence of the Jewish way. Jesus combined the grace of God with the will to do what is necessary on earth, that is, to forge a true human community with the spiritual at the center. What happened to Jesus after his death, through Paul and the development of Christianity, was for Buber a tragedy. Jesus was a Jew without the Law, and Christianity, its protestations to the contrary notwithstanding, resurrected the Law, albeit in a different symbolic and ritual structure, in his name.

It is interesting, perhaps instructive, that Rubenstein and Buber seek to reclaim Jewish figures as essential options of the spiritual life. Though they disagree on which figures, their affirmation of either Jesus or Paul is dependent on the rejection of the religiosity that grew up after them. Rubenstein's Paul is less the founder and saint of Christianity than he is a Jew struggling to make sense of the limitations of the Law. Buber's Jesus is less the son of God, as later articulated in Christianity, and more the Jew who embraced, almost perfectly, the essence of the Jewish spirit.

Rubenstein and Buber embrace these Jews before they were "corrupted" in a later time by religion and Christianity. Though they interacted with the central figures of Christianity in the present, it was, at least in their perspective, from a tremendous distance. Or were they, in Rubenstein's Freudian framework, subconsciously subverting Christianity of its foundation? Was their boundary crossing a disguised attempt to revive Judaism or, in light of their sensibilities, provide more space for the continuity of Jewish identity after the Holocaust?

Though both lived and worked in an ecumenical world, their ecumenism can be judged one-sided, arguing from and within the Jewish perspective. Yet it is also true that Christians in the post-Holocaust era borrow freely from the old Israel that historical Christianity felt wanting and replaced. Now the old is part of the new, so that the boundaries between the testaments seem to disappear. Christians appropriate Jesus as a Jew and the Hebrew Bible as central to their contemporary faith.

Fusing the Spiritual and the Political

Rather than inclusion in community ending questions, it limits them. Boundaries are then set out that define loyalty to a community. Boundaries shift over time; each generation has them. At one time in Christian history, anti-Judaism, even anti-Semitism, was a tenet of community loyalty. Now in the Jewish community the commemoration of the Holocaust and the support of the state of Israel define the parameters of membership.

What is to be done with the realization that loyalty tests for community membership almost always conceal lies or at least fissures in thought and action? When the community is under duress, loyalty may be defining of an underlying commitment to the survival and flourishing of a narrative beyond its absolute truth. Clearly this is important to affirm, and, under duress, the suspension of critical thought and cross-boundary exploration may be necessary.

Yet inclusion and loyalty under circumstances of status and power necessitate questions and sometimes confrontation. Often the subversive thinking and doing when outside of power and affluence beget an allegiance to a community that seems binding even when the community becomes something quite unlike what it was before. Remaining with communities over time and in their various incarnations courts a danger of requiring an allegiance that was once voluntary, fixing as essential what once was fluid and developing.

In Latin America, Africa, and Asia, I have seen the effects of Christian efforts to implant their narratives in native peoples. I have also seen something quite different. The emphasis on justice for the poor provides shelter for an unprotected population and an impetus to oppose the violence against them. Since the force against them has been and, in some cases, continues to be Christianity, a counternarrative from another form of Christianity provides resources for that ongoing struggle. To transform a war against the poor into a civil war over justice and faith is a new phase of the struggle.

Distance from the "truth" of a religious narrative, or at least its articulated absolute, provides space to realize that the contexts of faith and community loyalty are important. Still, the haunting questions about the God of History remain.

Rubenstein raised this question of God in relation to Jewish history. Can the same question be raised in relation to the suffering poor of Latin America? The Christian assertion that God is among the poor in the form of Jesus Christ is often maintained and even boldly asserted. I find it difficult to assent to this, even if I transform the messianic language into God-talk. I also find it difficult to say that God was not among the Jews of Europe but is among the poverty-stricken Christians of Latin America.

It could be, as is often asserted by the Christians of Latin America, that the poor are in an Exodus situation, relying on God as did the ancient Israelites. For Jews at least, the God of the Exodus has been thrown into question by the Holocaust. Could this God of the Exodus be resurrected now among struggling peoples, a God who appeared, disappeared, and now reappears?

In 1981, when I stayed in a poor community outside Lima, Peru, a community cut off from the city, where only poverty and destitution are in evidence, I felt a sense of loss and despair. Within a few days even the God question disappeared. Only survival mattered, and survival was dependent on food, water, and medicine. All were scarce. The priests I stayed with could only dispense a hope beyond the despair, a place beyond the life people experienced there. For all practical purposes, though, even the liberationists were reduced to being with the people in their agony. The kingdom of God on earth that they wrote about so eloquently and argued so vociferously in church and academic circles made very little sense here, to the people and sometimes even to themselves.

One day as I was walking with a priest, a woman came up to me with a child suffering from malnutrition. She asked the priest to bless her child and then, thinking that I was a priest too, asked me for that same blessing. At first I recoiled, wanting to inform her that I was neither a priest nor a Christian. After a moment, I realized that such a discussion was impossible and irrelevant. Instead, I reached out my hand and placed it on the child's head.

Did my blessing, tentative at best, and coming from a Jew, help the malnourished child and his mother? Did God see my blessing and judge my religion as inadequate? My own sense was that Latin America—in its political, cultural, and religious configurations—was under judgment. What my blessing meant for the priest, the mother, and myself was beyond answering.

The poor had their world, and it was difficult for the liberationists, who either were from elite families or had left their poverty-stricken upbringing for the middle class world of the church, to enter their world. The poor were Christian, but they also combined indigenous sensibilities and rituals that were closed off and far removed from the more refined religion I had come to know as Christianity. Gustavo Gutiérrez, a native of Peru and the father of liberation theology, especially spoke of the need to enter the world of the poor, a world he himself had come from. Even for him, with his education and status, this was difficult, if not impossible.

Latin American Christians read the Bible by and for themselves. I was fascinated with their focus on the Hebrew Bible. They seemed to see the journey of the Israelites as their own, the Exodus story as well as the tribes with their various customs. They were drawn to the leaders in the Bible who had dreams and visions, who were spoken to directly by God, who rose and fell through justice and sin. They even resonated with the collective griping, divisions, and solidarity depicted among the Israelites.

The Promised Land was enticing, the wandering defining. One called out to God in need, and sometimes that need was answered—not always and not everywhere and certainly, for the most part, not now. In short, the Hebrew Bible appealed to a population that saw itself in a narrative that had significance beyond what is apparent. Systematic theology was absent.

This resonated in part with my own sense of Jewishness. To the people, I was from an outside world that was indistinguishable from the priests I traveled with. I came from the world of affluence, and the specific form of religion I identified with meant little.

Judaism, in its various manifestations over time and in its attempts to be seen as a world religion, has downplayed the indigenous qualities of the Bible, especially those of the ancient Israelites. The gods of the Israelites were not always the *one* God. The Tent of Meeting, so defining of the ancient Israelites, was shrouded in mystery, its ritual system so intricate and expansive that it can be seen, from our modern vantage point, as pagan and fetishistic.

Among the poor in Latin America, I read my own scriptures as an outsider, at least in comparison to the people around me. They were living within these stories in a way impossible for me. Yet I also realized that if the poor of Latin America became affluent and powerful, they would become outsiders to the Bible as well. The Bible seemed to work that way, promoting the empowerment of the poor and then critiquing that empowerment. The Bible purported to be the word of God. Was God like the Bible, consoling the poor while consigning the wealthy to the status of the outsider looking in?

4

Liberation and Loneliness

Searching for God
and Community
in North America

In the 1970s, I worked among poor Blacks at Hope House, a housing project near the affluent Garden District in New Orleans. After Hurricane Katrina, that project, along with so much of New Orleans, was destroyed. It had housed a vibrant and difficult community. New Orleans was beautiful. It was also desperately poor.

What many of us saw on television in the aftermath of Katrina, I knew well from my work there. Over time, some things change. Other things don't. New Orleans was split in two. What is left after Katrina in New Orleans is also split.

I taught Black history to African American women who lived in city projects and who were themselves products of the Jim Crow sharecropping era. During my time in New Orleans, as I looked at the faces of the women and saw the embodiment of their history before me, I was outside and they were within. They often related the biblical narrative and their African origins and slavery, or rather, in their own narration, the two were conflated and soon in the telling it was difficult to separate them. To their minds, the merging of the narratives made perfect sense.

Again the Hebrew Bible was paramount and the stories of liberation central. The women were thoroughly Christian. Yet they were Christian in a way very different from the European and general American Christian history I had been taught. Their language about Jesus put him in the context of Israelite history as if he were part of that history—not coming after as a completion of the Israelites' journey or being superimposed on it. The narrative was hardly linear, and elements of it were inaccessible, as it were, out of order. Moses was invoked, as were Solomon and David, with Jeremiah and Jesus, Isaiah and Ruth also at the ready. Did living within the biblical narrative grant these African American women a special license or, even better, a special insight that others do not have?

Toward a Black Theology of Liberation

While I was working in New Orleans, James Cone, then a young African American liberation theologian, came to speak at a local university. Before his talk, I was introduced to him as a young white radical, an introduction unlikely to endear me to him.

Cone was an angry person in a difficult position. He had been raised in the segregated South and was trying, against great odds, to initiate a theology of liberation for his own people. It was a time when the civil rights movement was in disarray—both Martin Luther King Jr. and Malcolm X had been assassinated. The Black Power movement was also fading into history. The white power political establishment was reasserting itself, and the white theological establishment—an establishment Cone found complimentary to the political one—was intact.

The white theological establishment found Cone wanting on a variety of levels. To them, Cone was dividing the universal Christian message, pitting Christian against Christian. Cone's tone was political while the Christian message is one of faith, they repeatedly informed him. Did he doubt the faith of white Christians, placing new political demands on the assent of dogma?

These were serious charges that could be substantiated with Cone's writings. He asserted, for instance, that if Christians were not for the liberation of African Americans—a liberation that Jesus, in light of the God of History found in the Hebrew Bible, demanded—they were not true Christians. Christians who fought the liberation of Blacks were, for the early Cone, apostates disguised in church gowns, in fact, the Antichrist. One can imagine the stir Cone caused in theological circles, especially in the academy where most white theologians saw themselves as liberal and working for the cause of justice. Cone's point, that in America the exclusive agent of liberation is the African American community, challenged their liberality. For Cone, this liberality spoken in the language of universality would not allow the Black community to be free. It made Blacks invisible and ultimately supported the racist status quo.

It was only through a radical reversal, such as the Israelites experienced in Egypt, that African Americans could become free. Fighting the particularity of their cause in the name of God was similar to the Egyptian religious claim to control the destiny of their empire. "Let my people go" was the refrain of the Israelite leaders. Blacks in America repeated this refrain in the political and religious spheres.

Cone also found himself under attack within the Black community. For some African American Christians, Cone's Christianity was too political and disturbed the African American church structure, asking for something it could not (and perhaps should not) deliver. The church was a place of refuge for an oppressed people, and release from that oppression was found in a Jesus linked to the struggle for freedom applied in the political realm outside of the church. Cone seemed to be bringing the Black Power movement, a movement that rejected Christianity, into the church. Was he, in effect, what he accused white Christians of being, a disguised Antichrist?

For those who rejected Christianity, Cone's Christianity was suspect because Christianity itself was seen as a white man's religion, a tool of control that whites used to keep Blacks in church and on their knees. Christianity had been forced on slaves as an attempt to get them to assent to their condition. Hadn't the apostle Paul, at least as interpreted by the slave masters and the clergy who served them, called upon the people to accept the condition they were in as divinely ordained? In the next life all would be well—perhaps the role of first and last would be reversed. The promised afterlife made the struggle here seem small and beside the point. Christianity served the master then—no matter the rhetoric, it served the master now.

The time I spent with Cone was short and the conversation subdued. Cone was clearly uncomfortable with whites, the legacy of the segregation of his youth. His mistrust was palpable. In our discussion, Cone was adamant about the division of white and Black, but I couldn't help but feel that he was attempting to bridge the white and African American communities.

When I met Cone, he was just discovering African American history and beginning to piece together a Black theological tradition. At that point he was arguing against white European Christianity from within, but for what? In one sense, as his critics within the Black Power movement often pointed out, his very acceptance of Christianity trapped him. Cone was drawn to the African within America, not the African within Africa. Neither Malcolm X's initial conversion to the Nation of Islam as a religion for people of color, nor his second conversion to a colorless international Islam, was compelling to Cone.

Years later, Cone and I sat together during a plane ride back from a conference in Montana. It was one of the few times he queried me about my life and work. He told me that he recognized from his own experience how difficult it was to start a new phase of theological discussion. He realized the strength of opposition and the personal toll it could take on someone. Then Cone shared a personal story: One night at a major university, after giving hundreds of lectures on Black theology, he stopped in the middle of his lecture and was unable to continue. At that moment, the audience thought he was ill and needed medical assistance. Cone quickly realized that he was fatigued in a deep and abiding way. The constant travel and pressure overcame him.

I heard in his story another dimension of the prophetic. Cone spoke the anger and vision deep within him, yet over the years he came to understand that it would not be realized, or that the vision might be achieved in a different way, through a number of other voices, including his own students. Actually, the vision itself was never to be realized, as these different students, with the benefit of his witness, would begin on their own journeys to actualize their respective visions. These would be similar to, yet distinctly different from, Cone. Each would, in his or her own way, fail.

In speaking the truth as he saw it, Rubenstein also had announced a vision of depth. Perhaps his announcement of God's retrenchment, so seemingly different from Cone's proclamation of God's presence among his own people, is really little different, or the flip side, the necessary complement, to the assertion of liberation with the power of God.

In Cone's early work, he mentions Rubenstein in passing and his struggle with God after Auschwitz. The reference is respectful—Cone understands this impasse. Yet Cone's assertion of God's presence in the struggle for liberation seems untouched by this understanding. It remains the same before and after his comment on Rubenstein. Recalling Cone, I wondered if this struggle with God was simply a Jewish question. For Cone it seemed to be so, at least in his published work, but it is difficult to see how once the question is affirmed in another community, it can be denied completely within one's own. It remains difficult for me to understand how the death of six million Jews raises the question of God's existence, while the death of millions of Africans and the enslavement of the survivors leave belief in God untouched.

Perhaps Cone's inability to continue that lecture represented also a realization that, though his theology was built around the God of liberation, God had not fulfilled this role. His heritage was one of slavery, and the liberation of his people, if and when it would come, would be more complex than his own articulations and be achieved through a struggle that could not count on God.

Community in the Midst of Loneliness

In my time with Dorothy Day, it seemed that her questioning of God was less important than the search for community and the solitude within that search. Her own autobiography, *The Long Loneliness*, written in the 1950s, is about that solitude as a place that is lived out even within community. The communal dimension is the search for family beyond biology, the place where one's commitment is lived out in care and compassion. Inclusion was central for her, especially the inclusion of those on the margins.

Day understood life as a pilgrimage, the title she gave to her monthly columns in the 1960s. The pilgrimage was with God in community and the communal aspect of life. Jesus was among the community, less in the struggle for liberation than in the struggle to be caring and compassionate. The systems within society were secondary to this endeavor or were there to assist the creation of community. For Day, particularity increased the diversity of community without having inherent value of its own.

There were two kinds of poverty for Day, spiritual and material. The former is chosen as a way toward the embrace of God and community; the latter, when forced, is a deprivation of the necessities of life, leading to isolation. The denial of justice to anyone was an affront to her vision of community, as it increased the solitude of the individual to a level at which they could become lost. This was her understanding of the difference between poverty and destitution. The way of liberation was the embrace of a material simplicity that led to a spiritual reliance on God and community. Liberation could not be accomplished on earth, if that meant an empowerment of particular communities in a society that then isolated others.

So for Day, a time beyond injustice could only be found in a community that witnessed to that possibility. Since violence always accompanied the attempt to bring the beyond into the present, as a pacifist she stood against violence even to bring about justice. For her, this was more than a theoretical understanding of the relation of means and ends, postulating that violent means would bring about a violent end even if the end could be seen as a good. This understanding had to do with a sense of the limitations of life and society and a sense that reaching beyond those limitations is destined to failure.

Surely failure would further break the bonds of community. Yet this break was also instructive, demonstrating the need to pursue individual and communal life in another way. That way was smaller and with fewer worldly ambitions, and, paradoxically, it was also more demanding. Staying within the limitations of the human demands a discipline and an embrace of restraints that we naturally seek to suppress.

If Rubenstein and Cone share the prophetic differently, Day seemed to counsel against the prophetic altogether. Yet, as with Buber, it is difficult to sustain this understanding. In Day's presence, one had the feeling that she was indeed a prophet. She spoke harshly to oppressive political systems, criticizing in equal measure state communism and capitalism. Still, her underlying vision was one of community against the isolating and debilitating forces of depersonalization. Her "no" to industrialized, aggregate societies was a prophetic call away from a violence that could subvert, and perhaps was subverting, the possibility of maintaining the human.

On a personal level, Day had much in common with Rubenstein and Cone. To begin with, she was a towering figure, one who produced adulation in her admirers and consternation in her opponents. Her call for community did not in any way endanger her own individuality, just the opposite. Day was an assertive, dedicated, and single-minded person. Though her style was somewhat different because she lived in an intentional community among the poor—she did not have academic and institutional titles and forums—her folksy demeanor was deceptive.

With friends of hers and with people in need, Day was solicitous and compassionate, at times chatty as if you were sitting with her in a coffeehouse. When it came to issues of peace, war and justice, Day could be angry and defiant. In this mode, she was as untouchable as Rubenstein and Cone. One felt a space between her and others that could not be bridged, as if her long loneliness and pilgrimage separated her from others.

I spoke to her infrequently. Day was already in her early seventies when I arrived at the Worker, and she valued her time alone. When she did appear in public, there were often visitors who claimed her attention. By this time Day was a living legend, and despite her attempts to downplay or even denigrate the adulation shown to her, that seemed almost impossible to achieve. This no doubt contributed to her isolation. When she appeared without a public audience, Day was likable and appealing. Sometimes she would simply offer me a greeting, while other times she would motion me to come sit by her.

These moments were special, and I recall them fondly. Day was often quiet, and to the casual observer, she could seem distant, even aloof. Then, without advance notice, an impish smile would cross her face. I felt that smile to be a window into the joy of her life, hard fought for and sustained.

It was like night and day: in different moments she could be stern and playful, two sides to a complex woman in her later years.

Like Cone, Day had a special feeling about Jews. While with Cone there was a sense that Jewishness might trump one's whiteness, placing you in a somewhat different political category, with Day, Jewishness was a religious category. In many ways, she and the Worker had been visionary in terms of where the Roman Catholic Church would move after the Second Vatican Council. Worker issues, such as war and peace, community and vocation, were highlighted in that council, as was the Worker's evolving understanding of Jews.

In her early years, before her conversion to Catholicism, Day had many radical Jewish friends. Though they were decidedly secular, even antireligious in their sentiments, she had fond memories of these friendships and rarely, if ever, judged them in her post-conversion life. It was this conversion that highlighted the importance of Jewish religiosity in her own life, first as the precursor to Christianity through Jesus, then later as a people who continued in God's way. Though she wrote little about this relationship before the 1960s, in her later years she contemplated the mystery of God's fidelity to the Jews and marveled at their survival through the trials and tribulations of history.

Upon meeting my mother, Day reminisced about her early friendship with Michael Gold and her life on the Lower East Side, then a haven for Jewish immigrants. She also recalled a meeting with Abraham Joshua Heschel, the great rabbi and theologian, at the end of which she solicited his rabbinic blessing. Day told this story slowly, as if savoring it. I could tell that his blessing was symbolic for her, representing a blessing of the Jewish people on her and her work.

As she told me the story, I couldn't help but think of Rubenstein's relationship with Heschel and Heschel's writing on the prophets that captivated her. Clearly Day had read much of Heschel's work and his interpretation of the prophets as inspired visionaries whose passionate connection with God consumed them. The *Catholic Worker* newspaper was full of images of these prophets, drawn by a Jewish convert to Quakerism, Fritz Eichenberg. Yet it was these very images that Rubenstein found difficult in our post-Holocaust age.

Day's stories intrigued me, and yet, as I listened to her, I couldn't help but hear Rubenstein as well. What would Cone say to these romanticized images, these stories of blessing and community? Through power Rubenstein sought to eliminate the solitude of the ghettos and death camps of Eastern Europe. For Cone it was revolution that would end the travails of his own people. Yet though the comparison in outlook was stark, I found in Day a healing presence, a bridge over turbulent waters.

Martin, Malcolm, and James

By the 1990s, Cone's writing had changed in tone, if not in scope. Now in his fifties, Cone began to look back over his life and work, seeking, if he could, to reconcile conflicts in his own theological work, perhaps trying to make peace with those around him.

I saw this in his discussions of the legacy of Martin Luther King Jr. and Malcolm X, his attempt to reconcile the seemingly antithetical visions of two great African Americans. Over the decades, the following of each man seemed to ebb and flow according to the mood of the African American community and the nation. King had been lionized with the national holiday in his honor. Malcolm X never reached that level of acclaim, and his image of playing against King, as the radical rival who drove whites to King's banner, has dissipated over time.

In his early writing, Cone used Malcolm X to drive King's message of liberation beyond integration and as a response to criticism regarding Cone's embrace of Christianity. Thus Cone focused on Malcolm's separatism rather than his later color-blind Islam. The Nation of Islam, Malcolm's original affiliation, was marginalized, but so too was King's understanding of Christianity. For Cone, the Nation of Islam and Christianity took a backseat to the driving force of the personalities and followings of Malcolm X and King. The engine of Cone's analysis was the force Malcolm X and King generated, while Cone supplied the radical Christianity that neither Malcolm X nor King articulated.

That was the 1960s and 1970s. As the 1990s approached, Cone's own Christianity, at least as it applied to African Americans and America, was changing. If earlier neither Malcolm X nor King were comfortable in America, and only a radical overturning of the American system would suffice, now Cone portrayed both as American icons. Since race was and is the dividing line in American history, Malcolm X and King were key to overcoming that division.

In Cone's *Martin and Malcolm and America: A Dream or a Nightmare*, the two figures, though quite divergent in their early years of public life, merge into one dynamic pattern in their later years and after their deaths. The pattern is one of justice, combining radical critique with the hope of reconciliation, the threat of separation as a plea for integration. The God of both Malcolm X and King is a God of justice and compassion, compassion only sparingly found in Cone's earlier writing.

So in the end the prophetic messages of Malcolm X and King, mediated through Cone, are tempered. Instead of a radical call for the end of white rule, the vision is now of a reconciled national community characterized by forgiveness. The particularity of the African American community and its struggle is viewed through the broader prism of America.

In Cone's early work, Blacks are the key to God's kingdom, and, at least in America, God is only present to and among this community. In this sense, Malcolm X and King are prophets in the Exodus and prophetic traditions, calling a particular people to freedom over against the ruling powers. African Americans are called out of this white European and American empire, and yet the "where" of their journey is never clear. Paying little heed to his Afrocentric critics, Cone glossed over the difficulty that there was nowhere for African Americans to go, no Promised Land destination.

This sense that African Americans are more American than African and that their future is here in America forced Cone to reevaluate the messages of Malcolm X and King. In these later years, Cone sees both as products of the Black experience in America, which is now less distinct and separate, perhaps becoming itself quintessentially American. What was distinct in history and witness is now the bridge that can bind the wounds of America and make it what it promised to be, a light unto the nations. Separatism was forced upon African Americans; the Promised Land is here in America. Malcolm X and King call forth that particular promise of the universal aspect of the Hebrew tradition that Christianity claims to embody.

Was Cone's sense of the particularity of his own people and their role in salvation history fated by the religion he refused to abandon? Did the claim of the universal in Christianity ultimately reduce Cone's insistence on the prophetic to a footnote in Christian history? Did he come to believe that his earlier insistence on the white community as the Antichrist was in error? The subtitle of his seminal book on America—*A Dream or a Nightmare*—focuses Cone's transition and, though posed as an interrogative, is answered differently in the two phases of his career. There is no question that earlier in his life and work America is a nightmare far removed from the possibility of redemption. Later America is the dream that can become a reality—perhaps is becoming that in actuality—if only it transforms the nightmare of racial exclusivity. This can be done—*is* being done—as the twenty-first century dawns.

Yet in surveying the theological landscape, I also feel that Cone's concentration on and affirmation of the dream of America are an attempt to ward off the internationalization of theology and spirituality. In one sense, Cone himself helped in the transformation of Christian theology by emphasizing theologies at the margins of the European and American experience.

By using the journey of his own people as paradigmatic, he subverted normative Christian theology and exposed it as a particular theology empowered through injustice.

This early breakthrough helped spawn other Christian theologies on the margins, most especially Black theology in South Africa. Here Cone became extremely important in galvanizing internal and international church resources for the fight against apartheid. At the same time, other theologies were emerging around the world—from Africa, Asia, and, of course, Latin America. It was also happening in America, with Latino, feminist, and North American theologies taking center stage.

Celebrated as a major figure in that movement, Cone was part and parcel of the explosions of theologies. Yet the arguments Cone had with those who articulated these theologies are legendary. Some felt that all these religious perspectives, coming from particular historical experiences and seeing justice as the core, were together in their outlook and prospects. It was only by joining a common front that any or even all could succeed.

Cone participated—at a distance. Was this again because of a conflict within him between the universal and particular message of Christianity? If the universal was oppressive to his people, why not have a joint movement of particular theologies as a new universal? This then could be Cone's bridge of the universal and particular, satisfying both ends of this spectrum within Christianity and himself.

Seemingly fighting the universal of the particulars in an international setting, much like the false universal he had encountered in white America, Cone demurred. Perhaps this is because he felt that, in this new universality, the experience of his own people would be lost, summed up and subsumed in the same way as before. Perhaps this is why Cone, as unlikely as it once seemed, ultimately chose America, not because America would fulfill his dream, but because African Americans were central to the American experience and therefore were more likely to preserve part of their special destiny here rather than as a mere component of an international movement.

Whatever the future holds, it is clear that the path Cone pioneered has fragmented and changed course. He is a memorable figure, and I count it a blessing to have witnessed Black theology come alive. Our initial meetings were at arm's length. As the years went by, when we met, Cone embraced me. Few words were exchanged. He told me the struggle would be long. Those words were enough.

5

Gustavo Gutiérrez and Liberation Theology

The Voice
of Faithful Struggle

James Cone was not alone in his dilemmas. One of his close friends and confidants has been Gustavo Gutiérrez, the Peruvian liberation theologian and a fellow person of color.

Cone and Gutiérrez emerged on somewhat different stages at the same time. The late 1960s and early 1970s saw both write their breakthrough books on liberation theology. They spent the decades after enlarging and defending their central insights. The geographical and cultural aspects of their respective communities were quite different in that Cone wrote for an exiled and now diaspora people, while Gutiérrez lived among a conquered but still vibrant indigenous people.

From the beginning, Gutiérrez's landscape was broader. Cone's community was African American; only later did he approach his own community within the more expansive American landscape. Gutiérrez wrote about the poor, rarely mentioning or differentiating among different communities. His landscape was continental Latin America and, later, international.

Because of the friction between Cone and other theologians, Gutiérrez could have been seen as a natural competitor. In theological circles, Gutiérrez became known as the founder of liberation theology. This slighted Cone's achievement, confirming his own sense that African Americans would be left on the margins. Gutiérrez, however, was a connector who openly affirmed other emerging theological movements. He mentioned Cone frequently and as an equal.

When *A Theology of Liberation* was translated into English in 1973, it circulated around the world. The theologians of Latin America read his book in Spanish, while in Africa and Asia the connecting language was English. Since Gutiérrez's book was about the poor and their struggle for justice and Cone's was more specific to African Americans and America, Gutiérrez's work was more accessible. It was more readily applicable in other contexts.

The wounds were still raw in 1988 when, in honor of Gutiérrez's sixtieth birthday, I hosted a conference at Maryknoll. It was an international celebration where theologians from around the world came to honor Gutiérrez and the movement that he had impacted significantly. I invited Cone as well, but it was clear from his tepid response—he did appear but only briefly—that he felt the emphasis on liberation theology outside of America slighted his role in the beginnings and evolution of liberation theology.

In retrospect, Cone was right. I had not thought out the ramifications of featuring Gutiérrez without Cone. One aspect of the celebration was the Catholic Bishops' Conference in Medellin, Columbia, in 1968, where the bishops of Latin America affirmed Gutiérrez's call for the Roman Catholic Church to make a "preferential option for the poor." It was a seminal event, one that resonated around the world and that other Bishop's conferences in Africa and Asia took as a signal event for their own work. The call of theologians for a new tack in theology and commitment is rarely taken as a challenge by official church bodies, so the Medellin conference was also worthy of celebration in that regard. Perhaps the voice of the few could become the voice of the many. The twentieth anniversary of Medellin was therefore worthy of celebration as well. Of course, my oversight of Cone was further compounded by my oversight that 1988 was also the twentieth anniversary year of the publication of Cone's first essay on Black theology and Black Power.

The Preferential Option

Gutiérrez's work was perhaps the most important Christian theological breakthrough since the Reformation. Through his work, the Roman Catholic Church—and other Christians as well—were being called to a radical commitment to uplift the poor as the central act of Christian faith.

For Gutiérrez, this call to justice is found in Jesus' mission and his journey among the poor and his call for their release from the bondage of material poverty. Instead of a spiritual poverty that often disguises wealth and injustice, Gutiérrez felt that Christians should read the Gospels in a material way. For Gutiérrez, this is central to Jesus' understanding of the kingdom of God. In short, the kingdom of God, though always incomplete, has a material basis here and now, and only through solidarity with the poor can that kingdom be claimed. In some ways—and this is central to the controversy surrounding liberation theology—Jesus' announcement of the kingdom is for the poor because the poor are God's chosen, his preferred, and their liberation is central to the mission of Christianity wherever Christians live.

Jesus' understanding is crucial to the definition of what it means to be Christian. This is obvious, and yet beyond this obvious statement is a complexity and a battleground. Who was Jesus historically, and who is Jesus today? The answer to these two questions defines what it means to be Christian. Cone and Gutiérrez ask these questions in a radical way. In their minds they are simply reclaiming the Jesus of history before the churches appropriated and reinterpreted his message. To reclaim means to recover, and therefore the prelude to Jesus, the Exodus story and the Prophets, are crucial.

Christianity claims Jesus and, at the same time, freezes him into a pattern of religious stability and authority. The prophetic is left behind. For Cone and Gutiérrez, it is this very prophetic that defines Jesus and the people's rejoicing in his appearance. Jesus lived and acted within a colonial and impoverished situation, his people suffering under the Romans and their own elite religious establishment too often in collaboration with those powers. This is the same position of the poor of today, ruled by internal and external colonial powers, the military, global capitalism, and the churches.

For Cone and Gutiérrez, the prophetic Jesus needs to be freed from his captivity. Here the Exodus story becomes as central to Christians as it is to Jews. The God of History is a God of liberation, and that God is Jesus' God. Jesus understands his mission as coming to be with and for God's chosen, here transformed from the Israelites to the poor. The poor and oppressed are always God's chosen, which is why Israel was chosen in the first place, not because they were Israel, but because God is on the side of those on the outside and on the margins. As a Jew, Jesus chooses to be with the outcast as a continuation of the prophetic line that criticized the people Israel because of the way Israel had marginalized its own poor. In recreating the type of society that the Israelites were led out of by God, the prophets warn that God's choice of Israel is endangered. At one important level, Jesus, in the line of these prophets, simply reiterates God's preferential option for the poor. Gutiérrez evinced many similarities to Cone's analysis. They shared the understanding of Jesus in the line of the prophets and the central question of what it meant to identify as a Christian, in sum the following of that prophetic call. As with Cone's early work, Gutiérrez's *A Theology of Liberation* sought to elucidate the meaning of Jesus and the Christian vocation.

Yet there are also differences. Operating from a Protestant sensibility, Cone deals little with the history of Christianity and even less with church structures and authority. The Catholic Gutiérrez spends many chapters on the role of the Roman Catholic Church in interpreting and structuring the meaning of Jesus' life. In a sense, Cone has to break through the ossification of the Reformation—he is calling for another radical reformation—and Gutiérrez has to deal with a church that denies any need, historical or contemporary, for reformation. Cone is free to break with any church, while Gutiérrez is trying to explore a rupture within his Catholic communion.

Gutiérrez, like Cone, does not raise the question of God. Both assumed God in the life of Jesus. As the incarnation of God, albeit now in the dress of the prophets, the call is for Christians to follow this witness. Questions are present, but they are directed to society and Christianity. The building of the kingdom of God is challenge enough.

Yet the struggle for liberation had taken its toll on Gutiérrez as well. The commitment he helped galvanize changed the face of the Latin American church and the face of theology in different parts of the world. Within a short time, there was a backlash in church circles, led by the Vatican. The political and economic situation of Latin America, including his native Peru, was deteriorating. If God was among the poor, that God seemed unable or unwilling to liberate them—at least this was the situation in material terms.

When I first met Gutiérrez in the 1980s, I heard him speak in passionate terms of the deepening impoverishment of his people. People were dying from poverty. Those who served the poor—many of them influenced by liberation theology and Gutiérrez himself—were being killed by repressive governments. For the first time in hundreds of years, priests and sisters in the liberation line were being murdered for their commitment to the poor. Liberation theology said that Christians must choose sides, and many were doing so. The results were mixed at best and tragic at worst. Meanwhile, the church showed every sign of abandoning not only liberation theology, but the poor as well.

A Latin American Voice for Liberation

As I began planning the summer conference, I met with Gutiérrez on a regular basis. Our meetings were often unplanned and unannounced. Responding to a knock on my office door, I would find Gutiérrez waiting to see me. It was humbling, as one of the most important and best-known theologians in the world hoped that I would be able to meet with him.

Gutiérrez early on realized that I had little idea of the difficulties ahead of me in preparation for the conference. Nor did I have any understanding of the controversy that would surround the coming summer. In the 1980s, the Vatican initiated its crackdown on liberation theology, and one after another liberation theologians were called to Rome. The call itself was an admonition, and the ongoing investigation of the orthodoxy of liberation theology was an arduous process to endure. The possibility of being censored, which could include, among other things, a retraction of theological writings and a time of silence, haunted the background. Then the question of commitment—to the church as it was represented by the hierarchy or to the people, especially the poor—became paramount. It was a question of power and strategy. The Vatican had liberation theologians on the run.

This was the heyday of Pope John Paul II, the energetic and charismatic pope. He was at once traditional and attuned to modern communication, and I knew him through the liberation theologians he admonished and censored. He was immensely popular and feared, and thus his presence was a mixed blessing. Beneath the pomp and ceremony of masses that attracted the multitudes, John Paul II conducted a war against liberation theologians. I had a front-row seat to the pope's dichotomous presence.

Maryknoll itself was under scrutiny. Maryknoll had several priests involved in the revolutionary Nicaraguan government, for years under assault by the Vatican and by American foreign policy. In 1980, four churchwomen, including two Maryknoll Sisters, were brutally murdered in El Salvador, and other Maryknollers were seen to be on the side of liberation theology. Yet I was ignorant of the possibility that Gutiérrez might be called to Rome. As it turns out, it was precisely at the time that I sought to honor him that Gutiérrez's orthodoxy was being questioned. My naiveté was soon to be tried in a Vatican court.

I found it difficult to understand where Gutiérrez might have erred, if indeed he had. In his work, Gutiérrez demonstrated his respect for the Roman Catholic Church and its tradition by devoting many chapters to its history and philosophy. He engaged the very heart of his tradition in detail and deliberated in a way that a church theologian might. Of course,

Gutiérrez is a church theologian, albeit without title. A diocesan priest in Peru, he was far from the rarified atmosphere of Rome.

In some ways he was like Dorothy Day, a person within the church but on the periphery. Both were attempting to live the lives they wrote about. In Day's case, she wrote mostly about her life, so the radical dimension of her Christianity was masked or so personalized that it was difficult for the church to call her to account. With Gutiérrez, his writing was philosophical and theological, a visible confrontation with the powers that be. Still another difference was that Day lived in a small community, an alternative community not unlike the origins of communities that, with official status achieved over the years, religious sisters now lived within. Gutiérrez was a priest and an activist one at that, advising bishops and organizing with other clergy to propose a new tactic for the church at large.

Gutiérrez essentially saw his work as a natural extension of Vatican II, the reforming council of the 1960s that opened the Roman Catholic Church to the modern world. Vatican II was a call for renewal, for Christians and the church at large to respond to the "signs of the times"—to take the essence of the Gospels and apply them to contemporary reality.

His writing operated on many levels and appealed to many people in varying situations. At its center was a grappling with Vatican II in the Latin American context. It was an attempt to work toward a Christian commitment in a situation in which the majority of people were poor.

It was also an attempt to present a convincing argument for Christianity in a situation where the church was either seen as on the side of the oppressors or irrelevant. In my time spent around Gutiérrez, I saw this consistently, people who were on the verge of leaving Christianity for a more relevant social engagement, now returning to faith and the church because Gutiérrez had convinced them that to be a Christian was to take sides on behalf of justice.

Though I only dimly understood it at the time, I was learning that religious authorities persecute those who reach out effectively to the alienated members of their broader community. And that the persecution continues unabated, indeed increases as the evidence of their testimony is acknowledged as important and considered valid. Also, the boundaries of this persecution are almost unlimited. Distortion is the common theme, often through purposeful misreading and misinterpretation. In the end, what is said about a person misrepresents him to the point of a violent distortion. It is very nearly an out-of-body experience for the individual so charged, and when meeting that maligned person, one understands the description to be fraudulent.

As I entered the controversies surrounding liberation theology, I found these aspects to be writ large. The Maryknoll Sisters who had been brutally murdered in El Salvador were characterized as "gun runners," hiding "guerrilla fighters" and more. The Maryknoll priests who worked with the poor in Central America were "communists" and "atheists." Gutiérrez himself was often described as such. But in my office, with this man who stood less than five feet tall, who inquired about my life, accepted me as a Jew, and traveled the world without economic, political, or ecclesiastical power, I found it difficult to associate him with these categories. In fact, nothing could be further from the truth.

During the fifteen years since his book had been translated into English, Gutiérrez had become known in theological circles, and it would have been easy for him to use his celebrity to gather disciples or even a community of followers. Indeed, he did have these, without encouraging or cultivating them. They were drawn to his witness because he articulated something deep within them. Not only did he not use his name to enhance his ego; he refused to remain quiescent in a spiritual sense. Gutiérrez continued to search beyond his own theology, and as he did, his spirituality deepened. Gutiérrez is a spiritual person who cannot be circumscribed, neither by supporters nor by detractors, even as all seek to define him.

Job and the Defense of the Poor

When I met Gutiérrez, I was reading his new book about Job. The subject matter and subtitle, *God-Talk and the Suffering of the Innocent*, suggested a shift in his understandings. Clearly, Job could not be used for political mobilization and the social critique of liberation theology. Gutiérrez's much criticized and misunderstood "Marxist analysis" would find little room in the discussion of such a figure. Job had often been analyzed in relation to his suffering, the suffering inherent in life and the reconciling of that suffering with belief in God.

Rubenstein had explored similar themes. When the subject of Job was raised, Rubenstein reminded the questioner that Job's "happy" ending—the beginning of a new life with children and wealth—was a later textual addition. For Rubenstein, Job is a tragic figure, with losses incommensurate with his failings and with an ultimate belief in a God that cannot rationally be argued. Though Rubenstein admires Job's intensity and tenacity, it is not his way. What God could demand assent to this kind of test, and if this was indeed the God of History, could one believe in him and retain one's dignity?

Though liberation theology was a Christian project, its effect was political in the sense that it demanded that the poor be seen as citizens with human rights and dignity. It was a two-front strategy, church and state, that had converged. If the church is involved with the poor, it becomes the protector of the poor in the political realm. In many areas of Latin America, the church is the only agent to further the human rights of the poor. Thus turning against liberation theology is in a sense abandoning the poor, and though the church is weak, often failing to protect the poor against the power of the state, it is their only advocate.

Questions proliferated. Can an internal struggle over orthodoxy blind the church to its greater responsibility? Is denigrating liberation theologians a way of denigrating the poor? Can standing with the poor, even to the point of being persecuted with them, transform the church's history of complicity with colonial powers? And how can one actually stand with the poor if the economic and political structures that oppress them are left unaddressed? Can a Christian spirituality be embraced as a lived reality if it shields itself from the complexities of the world?

All of this was controversial, contemporary, and embodied in Gutiérrez himself. *On Job* is less a political manifesto than a questioning of the liberation project itself.

The poor are defenseless, in need of protection. Though flawed like all human beings, the poor, like Job, are innocent. They are in need of God's protection and deserve an explanation for their suffering. After all, Job knew and liberation theology teaches that God is a God of History, active in the world for justice. In this sense Job comes to represent the poor and the innocent of our day, and they, like Job, cry out for justice. Again like Job, they enter God's court because they have been reduced to paupers and abandoned by the systems of the world. The poor are innocent, and God has promised to protect them. Have they also been abandoned by God?

Like Cone, Gutiérrez recognized the Jewish difficulty with God after the Holocaust. He also recognized the complicity of Christians in that suffering, a difficult admission. Though he confronts Christian complicity, Gutiérrez, like Cone, also moves on from the question of God. Or rather, he questions God in relation to the suffering of the innocent, then advises us that suffering continues in the present. The Holocaust is a recent memory that needs continuous probing—the actual suffering is over though the meaning of the event is not yet finished—but that probing cannot let the matter rest as if the suffering of the world has ceased. The murder of the innocent continues, Gutiérrez cries out, so memory is not enough. God must be questioned because justice continues to be denied.

This is the situation of Latin America, which means that Gutiérrez and others have a responsibility, like Jews have in another context. With Cone, Gutiérrez cites Rubenstein, but then pursues it no further. Perhaps communities have their own wrestling with God that should not be interfered with. No doubt this is a sign of respect. Could it also be avoidance? It is clear that Rubenstein's answer to the question of suffering and God, while not adopted, is seen as a viable possibility. It could be that Job and the poor of today are abandoned by God. Still the cry to God continues. It may be less a rational conclusion that is searched for than it is an ear turned to the perpetual cry of the human heart. The search for faith may come up empty when confronted with the suffering of the innocent.

As a believer, Gutiérrez makes certain assumptions of belief. This is clear in his liberation theology, in which commitment to justice is central. Job is also approached from an engaged faith perspective. Yet from the outset, the challenge of Job is also seen from the perspective of commitment to justice. Now questions of faith are added as well. The challenge of commitment and belief are seen as intertwined.

There is no sense in Gutiérrez that the continuation of injustice provides the option of abandoning the commitment to justice or to God. Rather, the seeming disjunction of injustice and God force a deeper grappling with the questions. Though Gutiérrez is silent on the option of abandoning the pursuit of justice and faith—the option Rubenstein ultimately embraces—it is clear that he feels this to be the easy way out. The more demanding path is maintaining the tension of the reality of the world and the difficulty of faith.

Here Gutiérrez moves beyond the answers of religion, even beyond his own Roman Catholic beliefs. These beliefs remain valid, as Gutiérrez never directly challenges Catholic doctrine. Rather, they are seen as signposts that point in a certain direction. Perhaps this is why Gutiérrez chose Job rather than Jesus or Paul for his exploration, because Job, neither Jew nor Christian, is relatively free of dogmatic content and importance in Roman Catholic theology. In many ways Job is an anomalous figure in the canons of Judaism and Christianity, compelling yet almost always ignored in the definition of faith.

Job, like the poor, is a stumbling block to doctrines and definitions of belief. In consideration of God, both may be too difficult. Perhaps this is another reason Gutiérrez may have chosen him. To the accusation that liberation theology is simplistic, Gutiérrez may have chosen Job precisely because this Job demonstrates the simplicity of those with a doctrinal faith. They flee from Job in the same way that they turn from the poor.

For Gutiérrez, Job is both the pursued and the pursuer. Job is innocent, as are the poor, which, of course, does not imply individual purity. Job is innocent because he does not deserve what happens to him; his tragic condition raises the question of justice and a just God. Like Job, the poor cry out for a justice that is denied them. Yet it is not just the poor. Those who see their condition and seek to ameliorate it also have questions.

These questions are multilayered. Society as we know it is a problem, hence the need for social analysis and political action. Clearly injustice is caused by human beings and the social order they create. Yet the seeming impossibility of moving society toward inclusion and justice—the stubborn persistence of oppression—forces further inquiries into the power behind the universe. Injustice continues to triumph, and the suffering of the poor and those in solidarity with them endures. Job asks what this tells us about the primary force in the universe.

I realized after meeting and spending time with Gutiérrez that Job's uncertainty was his own. At sixty years of age, Gutiérrez saw clearly that the forces of evil were triumphing. The early energy of liberation theology and the forces it unleashed were dissipating.

At one level, this loss had to do with global economic, political, and military forces and internal elites who benefited from them. At another level, and one that was even more significant to Gutiérrez, those who claimed God were also increasingly aligned against the poor. Did they in fact represent God? Had Gutiérrez been wrong in his belief that God was on the side of the poor and oppressed? And if God was on their side, was God exerting the requisite power to triumph but being thwarted by another, stronger power? Perhaps God was uninterested, too weak, or involved in other matters.

Much is at stake, human lives to begin with, but also God's reputation, the sanctity of God's name on earth. With many others, Gutiérrez staked his life on God as a deliverer, being for those on the outside. Had Gutiérrez, in effect and unbeknownst to himself, lied to the poor and the world? It would be tragic beyond words if Gutiérrez had given the suffering false hope. Had he fooled himself as well, believing that God was just and impatient with the purveyors of injustice? No less than the very testimony of the Bible, the biblical witness that had guided believers for thousands of years, was on the line.

Is the Roman Catholic Church correct in persecuting Gutiérrez and his fellow theologians? It is one thing to battle the church and its definitions of orthodoxy as the church is flawed, along with the human beings who exist within it. In that struggle with religious authority, Gutiérrez can hold his own, intellectually and theologically. Yet the power is uneven, and in a worldly sense his defeat is inevitable. His appeal has to be to the higher power as a way of justifying a course whose victory can be assured only over a longer haul and in relation to a reality that is, at this moment, unverifiable. The unknown has to be at work to reverse what is so easily seen. In a larger sense, the book of Job is less about justice itself and more about the fidelity that ensures the possibility of justice. This fidelity has two sides, God and humanity, and thus assumes a covenantal relationship between both. There is a relationship between God and humanity and mutual responsibilities. God is more powerful and free. Nonetheless, God is bound and responsible.

Though God's authority is supreme, God's actions can be examined and questioned. It may be that a person's fidelity to God is without doubt. Does this mean that the failure of that person places God's fidelity in question? It may be that God's fidelity is assured but that the time frame, method, and circumstance are unknown, indeed beyond our ability to comprehend.

Yet perhaps human beings, even more so, need to be assured that this is the case so that our very fidelity and the proclamation of God's name are not in vain. There can be no greater blasphemy than proclaiming to the weakest that the most powerful is with them, or any greater failure of discernment than dedicating one's life to an illusory God whose very words are only contradictions and false leads.

These are Gutiérrez's concerns. Job is the biblical figure who focuses his own questions and allows space for their exploration. Who in the church hierarchy can challenge such self-reflection? Is there any reason to fear a biblical text analyzed to shed light on the present? In some ways, Gutiérrez hid his motives, as he did in a far less serious way when he apparently casually dropped by my office to check on the progress of the summer program in his honor. I have heard from others that Gutiérrez is a master strategist in navigating the church labyrinth, surviving yet at the same time maintaining his own convictions and voice. I also came to know this from my experience with him.

Gutiérrez accepts the story of Job as an innocent man who, after questioning God, accepts God's power, righteousness, and plan for the world, even though, on appearance, it seems contradictory. Job is unable to decipher this plan, and God convinces him that this inability to discern is a human limitation, not God's. God remains free, without limitation, and neither theologian, nor church, nor society can know God completely. From the human side, belief in God is a wager, a commitment that can be lived but one that is beyond complete comprehension.

For Job this does not mean an acceptance of fate, as if the suffering of the innocent is preordained. For the most part, Job is humble and respectful of God, so much so that despite suffering, his questions are spoken without anger or desire for retribution. Nonetheless, he is persistent, rejects the judgment of others, and refuses to accept the dogmatic answers of his so-called friends. Job declines the easy answers that box in and narrow God, even if to do so would help Job endure his trials and tribulations. When Job does bow before the mystery of God's creation and power, he does so without asserting to any human expression of God's word organized by religion and guided—one might say dominated—by religious authority. Job is under God and free.

It is here that Gutiérrez finds his own voice. Gutiérrez has come to an end where the world is too powerful and the church authorities are calling upon that power to defeat him. This defeat may occur, indeed it certainly seems the way of the world, but Gutiérrez is interested only in the fidelity that may one day become the norm. This fidelity is of the person and God—and with them, perhaps, the community—to live justly in peace with a compassion that moves beyond judgment.

In the end, only God can confirm this fidelity and possibility, the day when the odds are reversed and the just society, against the historical record of the day, comes into view. Gutiérrez does not know the time and place of this reversal, and until that day, like Job, even under God's power and perhaps precisely because of this, Gutiérrez refuses to restrain his tongue. Nor will he back off from his quest for justice. He remains in the tension, and will remain, until the end.

It is this tension that makes Job so compelling. Here is the man on the dung heap speaking, arguing, pleading, and accepting God, a being beyond his understanding yet nonetheless truly God. Like Job, Gutiérrez finds his voice within a commitment that is his own, one that is challenged by the political and religious forces of his time.

In Job, I heard Gutiérrez. In Gutiérrez, I heard Job. An ancient and a contemporary voice of commitment and dissent. Marveling at Gutiérrez's journey, I thought, I might one day find my own voice in the ancient text.

6

Among the Palestinian People

Discovering a Jewish
Theology of Liberation

During the summer of 1988, liberation theologians from around the world came to Maryknoll to honor Gustavo Gutiérrez. While some refused or were "too busy" to honor Gutiérrez—several months before the event, the Vatican questioned the leader of Maryknoll about the session—a number of bishops sent notes honoring his contribution to the church and the world.

The response from the public was overwhelming. Soon after our first announcements about the session were distributed, I was inundated with requests to attend. Our venue was too small to accommodate even a fraction of those who wished to come. While liberation theology was under assault within the church hierarchy, to many lay Catholics it was part of the future they desperately wanted to embrace. Of course, the appeal of liberation theology went beyond Roman Catholics alone. It crossed over into other Christian groups and even across faith lines into Judaism, Islam, and Buddhism. As I read the many requests to attend the session, the diversity of those who were influenced by liberation theology astounded me.

Most of the applicants related how their faith had been strengthened and how liberation theology helped them bring together God and the world in their own lives. For many, liberation theology articulated a spirituality they felt deep inside themselves but had been unable to articulate. Their own church leaders had done little in this regard, failing to offer a spirituality they could embrace, and many were becoming alienated from their baptismal church. Liberation theology, and Gutiérrez especially, drew people of faith searching for a committed life and a spirituality grounded in faith.

It might have been preferable to have a low-profile strategy. In the long history of the Roman Catholic Church, patience is sometimes a virtue, and waiting out certain personalities and trends can work in one's favor. Yet there was also a sense of urgency. If liberation themes did not become the center of Christianity, they would hardly remain credible in the eyes of those committed to justice. At the same time, the reactionary elements of the churches were gaining ascendancy. As in the Jewish community, a civil war was brewing within Christianity about its past and future. Much was at stake. It was hard to be patient.

Then there was suffering and the war against the poor. Would this be joined by the churches? With which side might it ultimately align? History had shown a culpability of the church and Christianity in general. Those who came to Maryknoll to celebrate liberation theology wanted a new history in which Christianity became the defender of the poor and the oppressed.

All of this was in the air as the summer began. Our venue was small and, in a worldly sense, powerless. Surely a meeting of liberation theologians with a little more than one hundred participants could mean little to the powerful or even the poor. The plight of the poor would remain. The powerful would remain also.

Confronting the Uprising

With all this excitement, I was very engaged with the conference. The months of planning had paid off, and now I could enjoy my time with those who had come from around the world. I was there, but I was also somewhere else.

The Palestinian uprising against the continuing Israeli occupation of the West Bank and Gaza began in December 1987. By the summer, the uprising was in full force as was the Israeli repression of this struggle for freedom. Voices were speaking out on behalf of the Palestinians. Few of these voices were Jewish ones. At times mine seemed like a single and solitary voice.

In 1986, just a year before I had the idea for the Gutiérrez event, I completed my first book on Jewish identity and theology. The title, *Toward a Jewish Theology of Liberation*, was influenced by my contact with the

Christian theology of liberation. Though the inspiration for the title is obvious—my travels around the world with Christian liberation theologians and among the poor and the oppressed had impressed me deeply—the root issues of identity and history I grappled with were profoundly different. Or so I thought.

The question for me was my Jewishness and the challenge facing Jews like me in the contemporary world. All around me the fundamental issues of our day were being challenged and contested by Christians, especially in the arena of faith. They were asking the question of what it means to be Christian today and exploring the challenges that they face in integrating faith and justice concerns. The literature on these subjects for Jews was scant. Almost all related to the past, the Holocaust, and as far as I knew, little addressed the new challenge: Israel and the Palestinians.

Liberation theologies faced these questions squarely. I admired this even as I remained distant from aspects of their approach to God. Liberation thought and action seemed to be always associated with ritual, especially the eucharistic celebration of Jesus' life, death, and resurrection. Even the liturgies held for the slain sisters in El Salvador were traditional, a consecration where death was transcended by life.

My book was published in the spring of 1987, just months before the Palestinian uprising began. Ostensibly the book was about the Israeli-Palestinian situation and its evolution into a crossroads for Jewish and Palestinian life, yet the book was hardly a political treatise. It moved through the terrain of reflections on the Holocaust, from people like Elie Wiesel, Emil Fackenheim, Rabbi Irving Greenberg, and, of course, Richard Rubenstein.

I saw them as a group and named them "Holocaust theologians." They emphasized the debate about God after the Holocaust and the ramifications of that debate for a Jewish identity that revolves around the Holocaust and Israel as the response to the Holocaust. While Rubenstein saw the end of Judaism and Jewish identity and embraced Israel as a place of protection for those Jews who remain, others embraced Israel as the continuation of Judaism and the center of Jewish identity. For Wiesel, Fackenheim, and Greenberg, Israel is a shining light, the dream after the nightmare, a coming home after a long and dark detour through a violent Christian Europe. All believe that a break with Israel, public or private, is a denial of the demands of contemporary Jewish life. To break with Israel is to commit an act of cowardice or self-hate.

In the aftermath of the 1967 war, the twinning of the Holocaust and Israel became the norm, and Rubenstein entered that discussion as a dissident. The argument from others was a moral one. Jews had suffered in

the Holocaust; Israel was compensation for that suffering; Arabs opposed
Israel because of their anti-Semitism; the world needed to acknowledge the
Holocaust and the moral rightness of Israel. Rubenstein saw the need for
an empowered Jewish state without any need to justify it on moral grounds.
Once powerless, we now assume power. Let them try who would seek to
take it away. Jews must defend the state unto death and punish those who
seek to disempower us.

For Rubenstein, there is almost no ethical cost to empowerment that
is not worth the creation and maintenance of a Jewish state. Since after
the Holocaust he was not committed to the continuation of the moral and
ethical tradition of Judaism, the use of Jewish power carried no risk to that
tradition. Other Holocaust theologians were in a more difficult situation
since they were arguing Israel as reestablishing the continuity of the Jewish
ethical tradition after the Holocaust. Thus where Rubenstein saw a power
equation in politics and the need for Jews to exert an equal or greater power
than our foes, for the most part Wiesel, Fackenheim, and Greenberg denied
that force was being exerted by Israel.

Since Israel is necessary and innocent, Israel's wars are only defensive
responses against enemies sworn to its destruction. Rubenstein understood
the Palestinian and Arab desire to destroy Israel, as Israel was created on
their land and through their displacement. The other theologians, though,
were unable to understand that desire, except as a new and virulent form of
anti-Semitism, precisely because they could never acknowledge that Israel,
like most states, was born through dislocating and cleansing an indigenous
peoples.

War in the Holy Land

Israel's invasion of Lebanon in 1982 threw into doubt Israel's presumed
innocence, as did the seeming impermanence of the Israeli occupation of
the West Bank and Gaza. The territories in the West Bank and Gaza had
been conquered by Israel in the 1967 war, and Israel's occupation of those
territories continued with the creation of large settlement blocs. There was
a permanence to this situation, a reality of force and misuse of power that
was becoming evident but was in thought and media ignored. In short, it
was increasingly difficult to sustain the Jewish self-image of suffering, innocence, and justice.

The real lesson of the Holocaust is not only the six million Jews killed—
a number so difficult to comprehend as to become almost an abstraction—
but the shameful degradation and annihilation of an entire people. These

lessons have hardly been heeded by the world. After the Holocaust there have been other events of mass suffering, including Cambodia's killing fields in the 1970s. Later, in the 1990s, the Rwandan massacres reinforced this point. In the 1980s, it was becoming clear that Israel was involved in actions that were, if not on the scale of Cambodia and Rwanda, morally reprehensible. I wondered why Jews seemed to be turning a blind eye to the very lessons we were teaching the world. I doubted that these lessons could be for others and not for us.

In 1973, I visited Israel for a month during my junior year abroad in London. My stay was interrupted by the October War, which began on Yom Kippur of that year. When the sirens first sounded, I was traveling in the Galilee, walking through an apartment complex. Since there was no smoke, I thought it must be a fire drill. That is, until people waved for me to join them in a basement that was, in fact, a large bomb shelter. At the same time I saw synagogues full of worshipers. Yom Kippur is the holiest and most somber day in the Jewish calendar. People moved in and out of the synagogues, listening by radio to the progress of the war and attempting to find news about their military units.

Through it all I was calm, surrounded by confident Israelis. Though there was a steadiness around me, there was also a sense that everything was at stake. After the first few days, it was clear that this war was unlike the one in 1967. In a surprise attack, Egypt had struck across the Suez Canal and was moving forward. Syria was also on the move. Israel was caught unaware, suffering significant casualties. For several days the outcome hung in the balance.

Before the war, I spent a month traveling through Israel, spending time in Acco, a port city, and in Haifa, outside of Tel Aviv, and of course in Jerusalem. I could sense that the still-developing Israeli culture—in 1973 Israel had only been in existence for twenty-five years—was both dominant and foreign to the land. Though Jews had lived in the land for thousands of years and thus Jews and Judaism could make their claim to be indigenous, this newest incarnation of Jewish culture was European and transplanted. As one Israeli said to me, "The Arabs live in the land; we Jews live on top of it."

Encountering it for the first time, I found Arab culture unnerving. There were, of course, the Palestinians I had read about. I could see immediately that their culture was supplanted and, in the language of the American experience, their civil rights were being violated. In short, they were second-class citizens in Israel proper, and in the Occupied Territories they were denied even nominal citizenship. In the West Bank and Gaza, they lived under military rule. Israeli solders governed their lives and so in many ways determined their destiny.

As an American Jew, I found it strange seeing Jews in military uniforms patrolling large areas of Jerusalem. It was even stranger seeing Jews without uniforms with rifles walking the streets. In America, Jews were distant from the military, with the war in Vietnam only reinforcing this distance. Like many men of his age, my father served in the military during World War II. Still, in my home, neither the military nor my father's service was glorified. That struggle was fought with the hope that wars might come to an end. Jews were about other things.

Friendship and Martyrdom

As I returned to my studies, my focus was on the Holocaust, not on Israel. Only some years later, after my experience at the Catholic Worker house and my enrollment as a doctoral student at a university in the Midwest, did the Middle East issue surface for me again.

During an argument with a fellow graduate student about racial inequality, a woman farther down the table spoke up on my behalf. From her appearance, I thought she was Jewish. When I asked, she replied that she was Palestinian. I had never formally met a Palestinian nor talked with one. Jerusalem, she added pointedly, had been her family home for generations.

Her name was Naela Ayaed. Naela was strong—she had no trouble narrating the Palestinian story—yet she was never polemical. Though the Palestinian question was always in the background, her life was filled with many interests. Much like Jews, Naela was secular in a distinctive way. Her identity was defining and open, and she was able to travel far and wide without losing her essence.

We kept in touch sporadically. I last saw Naela in 1998, in Palestine. As we revived our friendship over three days, I was able to visit her home in Jerusalem and meet her family. Naela spoke nervously and defiantly about the continuing occupation of her land. She acted like a person with her back against the wall. When I left, she handed me a traditional Palestinian embroidered cloth that had been in her home for years. Then, as I walked outside, she called me back and embraced me. I remember thinking that this too was very unlike Naela, who regularly defied convention. I left and didn't give it any further thought. It was the last time we would see each other.

In many ways Naela was the beginning of the "after" for me. Naela's face was now before me when I heard the word "Palestinian" and also when I heard the word "Israel." It was something that had happened after the

Holocaust to us as Jews, something that pointed beyond Holocaust theology. Her story became part of a larger story that includes her people, but also my own.

After the Holocaust, Rubenstein cited the need for power, a power for survival without ethical constraints. His fellow Holocaust theologians, with the broad support of the Jewish community, sanctioned that same power dressed in moral and ethical concerns. The Palestinians challenge both understandings simply through their own experience of that power. Is it necessary for Jewish survival to displace another people in the creation of a Jewish state and to continue that displacement over the years in war and occupation? Can we continue to think of ourselves as just and good—as innocent—by simply ignoring the Palestinians as if they do not exist or as if their fate is determined solely by their "opposition" to Jewish survival?

The "after" I began to see—an "after" already present in *Toward a Jewish Theology of Liberation*—is that we as Jews come after the Holocaust *and* Israel. Grappling with the second "after" is as essential as grappling with the first. After I met Naela, the face of the "other" was clearly visible. It could not be absorbed solely under the need for Jewish survival, nor would it vanish as if her face did not exist, *could* not exist, because it implicates us as a people. There has to be something beyond survival, oppression, and a pretense to innocence. But what can that "after" be? Where can it be found and named? And what will become of those who, once understanding this "after," cannot return to a previous consciousness?

Almost a year later, in the spring of 1999, I returned to Jerusalem to lecture and visit friends. My visit with Naela was still fresh in my mind, and I inquired of my Palestinian hosts where she might be. The response was muted. One friend who knew Naela responded that she did not know whether she was in town or not. I found the response a bit strange, as it carried a tone of avoidance and secrecy. It emerged that several months earlier, in January 1999, Naela had been murdered. I was stunned and asked her if indeed we were talking about the same person. We were. To the question of how and why, she knew little. As it turns out, only the "why" is a mystery.

I immediately traveled to Naela's home in Jerusalem. Right outside the Old City, from Naela's front yard, you could see the Dome of the Rock and the ancient walls surrounding Jerusalem. As I approached her home, Naela's sister Nadwa greeted me and led me inside. Her mother was there, and Nadwa reminded her that we had met just months earlier. She was deep in mourning, alternately in tears and offering fruits and tea. Other family members were present. It was remarked that though Naela had friends in both the Israeli and Palestinian communities and, as a health worker, worked with people and institutions from both communities, I was the first Jew to come to pay his condolences.

What happened to Naela? The facts are sparse. As a nurse, she was attempting to secure medical files and medicine for a Palestinian in need, and to do this she had to travel in a Palestinian-operated taxi to West Jerusalem, the Jewish part of the city. Though the city was declared unified after the 1967 war when Israel annexed it, in practice the city remains divided. Naela could not find an Israeli taxi to bring her back across the line that separated the communities. As she began walking back home, she was assaulted, a knife stabbed in her heart.

It was just a single stab wound, indicating to some, especially to her family, that her death was a murder done by a professional. But by whom and for what reason? Had Naela, a health professional, become politicized and joined a Palestinian faction, thereby dying in the internal struggle among Palestinians? If she was indeed with a certain political faction, was her murder ordered by the Israeli secret police? And if so, for what reason?

Naela's family home, the one I visited, was located in Silwan, a neighborhood that Jewish settlers were trying through legal and monetary ways to pry loose from the Palestinian owners. This was a tactic used by Jewish settlers to claim land in and around Jerusalem, which then would be Jewish forever. Often settlers would simply occupy land or a home; other times they would offer outrageous sums of money to the family. Naela's family had been approached directly to sell their land and had refused. Was this the reason she was murdered, as a sign that "no" was unacceptable?

Naela's family took me to her grave. It was on the Mount of Olives right outside the walls of the Old City. The burial grounds are so ancient that graves are piled one upon the other. To accomplish this, each casket could be opened, allowing others to be buried in layers, one upon the other. Naela's casket was sealed, a special honor reserved only for martyrs. Though the reason she died remains unsolved, she had been declared a martyr. This was the final and highest tribute the people she served could give to her.

Journeying among Palestinian Refugees

My second visit to Israel in 1984 was occasioned by an invitation from Tantur, an ecumenical center outside of Jerusalem. Tantur was born in the hope and ecumenism of Vatican II as a Roman Catholic interfaith center in the Holy Land. Here Jews, Christians, and Muslims could come together to work on a common agenda for peace and reconciliation and encourage the work of reconciliation around the world.

I was asked to speak on the prophetic, a subject I had written about, though as yet I had not addressed the context of Israel and the Palestinians. When I received the invitation, I was anxious to go back to Israel. I was also determined to meet Palestinians on the ground. Naela had spurred this desire in our meetings in the United States; now I wanted to travel among Palestinians where they lived. I made a deal with Tantur that in exchange for my lecture they would provide accommodation for me over a two-week period.

At Tantur, I made a few contacts that led to others and then to the Mennonite Central Committee, a Christian group that worked among Palestinians in the West Bank. This was my first contact with Christian groups in the Holy Land, though later I would come into contact with others. The work of the Mennonites fascinated me. In general they operated in the area of agricultural and economic development. They had a worldwide outreach, and as a historic peace church, they saw their work as a path of non-violent social change. Here they were among Palestinians, an interesting twist for me since I was increasingly involved in the ecumenical dialogue between Jews and Christians in the United States.

This ecumenical dialogue was about being Jewish and Christian after the Holocaust, and one crucial element of this dialogue was support of Israel. That support was filtered through a sometimes unconscious and at times explicit silencing of the Palestinian voice. Now it is common for Christian groups to speak for Palestinians. Then it was uncommon and controversial. Among the Mennonites I found a Canadian, Kathy Bergen, who worked as a coordinator of several programs with the Palestinian population on the West Bank.

Since 1967, Israel had occupied the West Bank. When discussed at all in America or within the Jewish community, it was known as a benign occupation, but in reality it was like any occupation—arbitrary, militarized, brutal. The settlements, another topic rarely discussed and when mentioned misunderstood, were continuing to be built. By the 1980s, they had become small cities that intruded into and dominated the Palestinian landscape.

The only Jews encountered by West Bank Palestinians were soldiers. Most Palestinians have never known a Jew they can trust, admire, or befriend. For them, Jews are brutal occupiers who have taken their homeland and now occupy what is left of it. Palestinians want the end of occupation. They want to return home.

So the first issue to deal with was trust. Why did I want to meet and travel among Palestinians? It was an unusual request for a Jew. What were my motives? How could Palestinians trust that the knowledge I gained would not be used against them? Was I simply a person who wanted to know more or an agent who sought to further their oppression?

These questions were real, and Bergen communicated them to me. She was not hostile toward me or toward Jews, far from it, yet her situation could be easily compromised. The Palestinians themselves would also be taking risks by being seen with a Jew. A Palestinian seen with a Jew could always be seen as a collaborator.

I was completely unprepared for these sentiments. I had only heard derogatory comments about Jews through the lens of history, by enemies of the Jewish people. These comments and the actions that followed were defined as anti-Semitic, condemned now by the entire world. The questioning of my integrity because I was Jewish startled me. It also hurt me. Jews are for justice. Didn't everyone recognize this, indeed assume it unless proven otherwise?

Here the assumption was reversed, and as the interrogation continued—not too strong a word for how I perceived the questioning—I began to realize that things had gone very far. There was an entire history here where Jews had acted in a way that encouraged mistrust and even hatred. Furthermore, this was not a spinning of theories about the Jews, like the anti-Semitic canards that permeated medieval Christianity. Rather, this came from the experience of an entire people, beginning in the 1940s and continuing today. It was like a time warp for me as a Jew, looking for a certain understanding of my people's history and landing in another people's experience of Jewish history. I glimpsed a fault line within my sense of Jewish history and my identity as a Jew. It was only a matter of time before the clash between these worlds would become a clash within me.

Soon the trial ended. The trust that Bergen and the Mennonites had built up with Palestinians was sufficient to allow me to venture among them. So I began my travels to the larger cities in the West Bank—Ramallah, Bethlehem, Nablus—and to smaller towns and villages.

I initially traveled with Bergen, then was handed off to Palestinians. At project sites and in Palestinian homes, my hosts were sometimes told I was Jewish. Other times I was just American.

The settlements and the refugee camps were the most difficult for me. Though I had heard of both, the physical reality and the disparity between them made me physically ill. The settlements were for Jews, massive building projects, small cities, built around Jerusalem and the West Bank. For Palestinians they represented in bold strokes their continuing dislocation.

These settlement cities are permanent and dominate the landscape. They represent the height of modernity and development and are in stark contrast to the forced underdevelopment and occupation of the Palestinian areas. Israeli troops protect these settlements and the settlers who live there, guarding them against the Palestinians, who naturally resent this permanent intrusion into their lives. At the same time, the soldiers enforce restrictions against Palestinian development. They also carry out orders of land confiscation and house demolitions. It is the opposite of a mutual and cooperative venture of joint development. The Palestinians are being supplanted on their very own land.

The refugee camps, inhabited by Palestinians who had been driven out of their land in 1948, were eye-opening. The camps originated during and after the creation of Israel, and now, almost four decades later, their inhabitants still expected to return to their homes. Initially their return was thought to be imminent. With the sealing of the borders, their return was delayed. It was difficult for them to admit that they would never return.

These camps were makeshift, housing people and creating patterns of life for decades yet refusing, even in the architecture, to claim permanence. The only thing I could think to compare it with was a shantytown, improvised, poor, with inadequate housing, open sewers, and an economy that operated at subsistence level.

An American could only experience these refugee camps as filthy and in need of destruction. A Jew could only experience them as a blatant contradiction to Jewish history. I had both feelings inside of me just from their outward appearance.

The story I heard from the refugees themselves made matters worse. Most had been expelled from their homes in the creation of Israel. They called it al-Nakba, "the catastrophe" in Arabic, and spoke of it as a formative event in which their homeland was lost. For the most part, the refugees worked the land without owning it, farmers, craftsmen, and owners of small businesses. The more affluent and educated were also driven out, often landing in better circumstances, some living well in the West Bank, others fleeing and finding citizenship in other countries. Refugee camps were not restricted to the West Bank. Gaza had them as well, with many also existing in the surrounding Arab countries, especially Syria, Lebanon, and Jordan. Refugees outside of the West Bank and Gaza were also waiting to return to their homes.

The number of refugees was staggering, as I learned from others who worked among the Palestinians. In the creation of Israel as a Jewish state, between 700,000 and 900,000 Palestinians had been driven off the land. Some had fled the violence, others had suffered massacre at the hands of Jewish forces, still others had surrendered, hoping to stay in their villages and towns, and had been forcibly expelled. In the aftermath of the 1967 war, thousands more Palestinians were driven off their land. The expulsions were continuing, and the land that was now recognized as Palestine—only about 22 percent of the original Palestine—was being occupied and settled by Israelis.

The Palestinians were trying to resist a further displacement, another catastrophe. Lacking the possibility of military victory, they employed various forms of resistance. Stubbornness—remaining on the land—was their chief form. Yet there was also increasing disquiet concerning the tactic of the older generation. Among the young other strategies were in the making. These included negotiating and sometimes confronting the Israeli occupation, or courting Arab governments to move from rhetorical to vigorous support of the Palestinian cause. At the same time, these young Palestinians were beginning to organize creatively active resistance on the ground.

Experiences of Occupation

The refugees' stubbornness went beyond ideology and nationalism. I found them traditional in their outlook and their ways, with an attachment to the land that was visceral. The history of their expulsion had not been taught to us in Hebrew school nor in our public education. The Palestinians had been hidden from our view. There was no voice for them. In contrast, the story of the creation of Israel and its victory in the 1967 war was trumpeted as a heroic saga of an oppressed people. Claiming its rightful place in history by establishing a state and transforming its historic homeland from a landscape of barren desert and swamp, Israel, and Jews in general, were heralded around the world.

The sole exception was the Arab world. In Europe and America, this reluctance was seen as a form of defiance, a kind of delinquency from the norm. Even more, this defiance became an active resistance to Israel that must, according to this sensibility, be anti-Semitic. The Palestinians and Arabs in general were seen as the new Nazis, seeking to reverse Jewish empowerment and even destroy Israel and annihilate the Jews who lived there.

After listening to Palestinians speak their story, I had no question about their desire to eliminate Israel. Few used the word "Israel" and almost all referred to the land that comprised Israel as Palestine. At the same time, when I or others referred to the Holocaust, the term itself was often disparaged. It was seen as an exaggeration of Jewish suffering, if not made up entirely.

The Holocaust was being used, at least in their mind, to drive them out of their land and to force the world to sit by in apathy or even to help Israel in its project. Couldn't the world see through this use of the Holocaust? The refugees I met with recognized the plight of the Palestinians for what it was, systematic injustice carried out against an innocent people. They also questioned why, if the Jews did suffer in Europe, the Palestinians had to give up their land as a compensation for Jewish suffering. Why didn't Europe either invite Jews back to Europe or create a homeland for Jews within their own territory?

Being a Jew was a source of tension during my time in the West Bank. A Palestinian I met in a refugee camp showed me a scar on his back from "torture by the Jews." He ended his comments by saying the Holocaust, if it happened at all, paled in significance to Palestinian suffering. The suffering here was "worse than Auschwitz," he said. Then he turned from me and spit on the ground in disgust.

During my visit there were many such experiences. Once, when introduced to an elderly Palestinian as a Jew—but as someone who could be trusted, implying that Jews as such could not be—he simply said that he couldn't trust Jews, that Jews had driven him from his home and were continuing to oppress him. Could I really be different? I was simply the decent face of "the" Jews, a trickster trying to lull him and other Palestinians into accepting what had been done to them.

The concept of "the" Jews, of course, brought forth dark implications. Even when Palestinians used the word "Zionist" instead of "Jew," the group attribution of Jews in a negative light was difficult to hear. Could "Jews" or "Zionists" do these things as a group? A differentiation seemed necessary, a sorting out of the good from the bad. And were these policies that negatively impacted Palestinians only the fault of my own people, or was there a shared blame to apportion? I thought that Palestinians also had to take responsibility for their own plight.

In the refugee camps, I also visited with families that had lost children in the struggle against Israel's occupation. Their lost children were, for the most part, young men who had joined the armed resistance against the Israeli occupation or were caught in the crossfire between the two sides. They were known as martyrs, and their pictures were prominently displayed in the family homes, and often throughout the refugee camp itself. They were young, usually only in their teens, and their portraits were framed with the colors of the Palestinian flag.

For some of these families, my presence represented a hope, but what hope was this, and where could it be carried? The bereaved families were almost always poor, their homes filled with children and little else. There was a heartbreaking sense of dignity in the home, their child having given his life for their nation. There was also a sense of desperation, as if the sacrifice might be in vain. When I was introduced as a Jew, the value of my visit intensified. I became the representative of my people and therefore the possible carrier of a message to those in power. As a Jew, it was assumed that I had instant entrée into the corridors of Jewish power. It was also assumed that if I as a Jew could see their plight, all Jews would.

The term "martyr" provoked ambivalence within me, as it seemed to have multiplied in usage over the years, its core meaning perhaps diminished. I had always understood the martyr as a sign of fidelity to Jewish history. This was now becoming a sign of contradiction, claimed by a people in the face of Jewish power. In a way, these martyrs and their families were an unfolding of the catastrophe that had befallen the Palestinian people in 1948. They suffered then and suffer today.

I was experiencing the duality of beauty and injustice as I had on my first trip to Israel in 1973. Then I had seen this only from a distance. Now I was seeing close up the faces of those who were suffering. I also was beginning to confront an even more difficult task of putting into words what I had seen. The overwhelming narrative of Jews—one that I had internalized—is one of goodness and innocence. The portraits of the martyrs suggested another narrative. As the Jewish narrative was changing within me, I was beginning to recognize the narrative of another people, that of the Palestinians.

After visiting the West Bank, I traveled to Gaza, where the situation was even more difficult. Compared to Gaza, the West Bank was developed and thriving. Gaza was and still is incredibly poor and cut off from the world. Its sole experience of the outside world was as a cheap labor supply to Israel. Gaza could only be described as a large ghetto with over a million people, mostly without jobs or decent housing and with little sense of a future. Sewage flowed openly in the streets, and the children seemed condemned to lives of poverty and destitution.

In Gaza, the distinction between destitution and poverty was bold. Poverty, at least from the perspective of the affluent, is a lack of material goods. Often the poor live a life of comparative simplicity, but with their culture intact. Culture gives the poor their dignity and also resources to survive and even challenge injustice. In the American movement for civil rights, for instance, we witnessed the struggle of a materially poor community rich in culture. Gaza seemed poised between poverty and destitution. Like those Palestinians on the West Bank, many are refugees. Unlike those on the West Bank who had experienced Jordanian rule between 1948 and 1967, an occupation with some progress and institutional development, Gaza had been ruled by Egypt, whose interest lay in the containment of Palestinian life rather than its development.

Unlike the West Bank, Gaza was not integrated into the life of Israel. It was cut off from the limited trends of integration that, to some extent, helped balance the negative consequences of occupation. Besides, Israel had no intention of keeping Gaza, as the Israeli withdrawal from Gaza in 2006 demonstrated. The Egyptians too seem to be part of this plan, as they now, with the Israelis, man the barriers and borders to Gaza. Palestinians are sandwiched between two diffident yet controlling powers. This in-between status paints a surreal veneer on the reality in Gaza. There one experienced a culture of concentrated density, stuck between powers, with a sense that there was no room to move. In Gaza, the only Jewish presence was Israeli soldiers. The closed-in quality of Gaza was ghetto-like, a ghetto that alternated between collapse and insurrection.

During my first visit there, I felt Gaza was on the verge of both. The economic situation was impossible. Jobs were scarce, families were large, and education was too difficult to come by or sustain. There was a sense of being trapped, closed in by power and the sea, with nothing to lose but life itself. The actual loss of life during skirmishes and insurrections contributed to this sense of ennui and hopelessness. Little could be done to rescue the dead from a meaningless loss. Even Palestinian resistance could not move Israel out. Israel was staying in Gaza primarily as a political act to discipline the Palestinian desire for freedom. It had no plans to remain, only to wreak further destruction. The situation was diabolical in its intent and cynicism.

The political leaders I met in Gaza were well educated, often in business or the medical field, and were accorded respect. Most of them simply wanted the occupation to end and a Palestinian state to be declared in the West Bank and Gaza with East Jerusalem as its capital. Though most were refugees, few spoke about the possibility of returning to their homes in what now was Israel. In the midst of a crumbling infrastructure—demonstrated in the condition of hospitals and schools—they spoke in practical and political rather than ideological terms.

Some of these leaders were Christian, the majority Muslim. I had the sense that most were secular in their politics and that religion was for them part of their historical and cultural identity. They feared—they spoke of this explicitly—that if the occupation did not end soon, a fundamentalist Islam would rise and make their pragmatic politics seem weak and collaborationist. They were surprised that Israel, who ostensibly had an interest in moderate Palestinian politics, seemed bent on driving the moderates out of community leadership.

The policies Israel pursued were thus undermining moderate political authority. Israeli authorities spoke often about Palestinian terrorism as justification for the need to control the Palestinian territories, yet Israel's policies encouraged these ideological positions, undermining the very people who saw the disaster that would come upon Palestinians if these views became a political platform. Perhaps Israel was not really interested in a two-state solution but instead encouraged the fundamentalists because it would reinforce Israel's political propaganda that Palestinians were not committed to living side by side in peace with Israel. It was a self-fulfilling policy: tighten the screws on the moderates and criticize the fundamentalists Israel helped bring to power.

At this point, no politician in Israel had officially recognized the Palestinians as a political force. Few spoke publicly about the possibility of a Palestinian state. This was true about American politicians as well. The Palestine Liberation Organization had not yet officially recognized Israel and thus had not taken a stand on a Palestinian state side by side with Israel. It seemed that everyone was trying to avoid the obvious, inevitable destination of the political process. Yet beneath and around this avoidance was the constant chatter of the arrival of a Palestinian state. It was like being in on a secret that everyone knew was going to happen yet no one wanted to announce to the general public. Perhaps there was a fear of announcing the inevitable. But why the fear if everyone knew the destination?

Years later, the much-vilified Hamas would come to power through the democratic elective process. Through the eyes of the moderate leaders I was visiting then, I saw Hamas and other Islamic religious movements in their infancy. They predicted the future as if they had a crystal ball. Israel seemed to relish this future. Was this because it didn't want a peace settlement with the Palestinians?

This led to another disconnect, with Hamas vilified in a way that distorts its political and religious agenda. When Hamas came to power decades later, it was treated as a pariah. Yet, when through intermediaries I came into contact with a leading Hamas politician, I was impressed by his understanding of the situation on the ground and his expressed wish to meet more Jews and understand Jewish history at a greater depth. This man was frequently mentioned in newspaper articles about the Hamas government, and I wondered if he was fated to become a martyr. After all, Israel had declared open season on the Hamas political leadership, targeting many for assassination and imprisoning others.

Justice and the Other

When I left Gaza, Kathy Bergen had a party in her home to introduce me to some of her Israeli friends. They were diverse, some from European backgrounds and Americans who had come to settle in Israel. Still others came from North African backgrounds. All who attended were interested in peace with Palestinians. What was surprising to me was their uniform assertion that there could be no peace without justice.

Justice was difficult to define for Israelis, and also for Palestinians. Is justice a two-state solution, Israel alongside Palestine, or a secular democratic state for all who live within the borders of Israel/Palestine? Can there be justice if a Jewish state continues to exist? After all, Israel was created at the expense of Palestine. Can there be justice if Palestinians are not allowed to return to their homes?

If Palestinians did return, there would be no Jewish state. Do Jews deserve their own state, and thus, because of their history in Europe, are they to be excused for the injustice they have caused to Palestinians? Is it correct to say, as some Israelis do, that there are two rights involved, the right of Jews to a homeland and the right of Palestinians to a homeland as well? In this sensibility both Jews and Palestinians have been wronged. The righting of both wrongs can be achieved when there are states for two peoples.

These were some of the discussions I listened to that evening. The interchange was heightened because Palestinians were present as well. I noticed that the political interaction of Israelis and Palestinians was complemented by a distinct tenor, for clearly some of them were friends. They had first met in mutual projects, sometimes through human rights work, other times in joint demonstrations. Their involvement created bonds of trust, and soon their intellectual discussions moved beyond the desire for peace. Some of the Israelis used language I associated with Palestinians, and for some the border between the two communities seemed thin, if it existed at all. Others interacted in a friendly manner but were clearly on different sides of the question.

Israel has its own culture and intellectual life, and dissent in Israel, though limited and on the margins, was far beyond anything I experienced in America. The Palestinians present were also on the cutting edge of Palestinian society. Simply interacting with Jews on the political and social level was dangerous. It could arouse suspicions that they were collaborating with Israel.

The danger for both Jews and Palestinians was that they were both getting to know the "other," and, at least in some ways, their mutual otherness was disappearing. To become known to each other also exposed the vulnerabilities of each individual and through them their communities. Could either side afford this vulnerability? The political leaders of both sides thought not. Obviously the people I was listening to thought differently. Perhaps if they showed their vulnerability, the cycle of violence could be halted. Could they simply bond together as individuals and through that bonding demonstrate that there was another way?

A few days later, I was at Hebrew University, speaking on a panel discussing views on the Middle East. I was to give an American perspective, but after my travel among Israelis and Palestinians, my categories had changed. In the end, I said very little. Still, the discussion was enlightening.

Most of the panelists—and the audience—were liberal Jews. They knew something was wrong, yet their perspective was almost completely Jewish in tone. For them, Zionism is the liberation movement of the Jewish people, and though there are occasionally rough patches, the enterprise is intact. The problem is extremism, and on the Jewish side the extremists were identified as Jewish religious zealots and Jews from North African background. They referred to these Jews as Arab, and, at least from their perspective, they had taken on some of the worst values of Arab culture, intolerance being one. As these Arab Jews were becoming more prominent politically, especially through the recent victories of the Likud party, Israel's European flavor and democratic traditions were being undermined.

Was this what was wrong with Israel? The "Arab" Jews I had met at the party told a different story of being forced through a European cultural assimilation to become the "right" kind of Jews. They spoke of their arrival in Israel in the 1950s as a culture shock. Everything about them was questioned, including their Jewishness. Their entire culture was suspect and in need of change. They needed to be introduced to European civilization and leave behind their "backward" ways.

The point in our conversations at the party was completely missed at the university, as Jews from North Africa had more in common with non-Jewish Arabs than with their European co-religionists. Perhaps they could be a bridge to Palestinians and thus also to the Arab world. This led my conversation partners to a question that I had never heard broached before. Did Israelis want to be a part of the Middle East, or did they see themselves, for the near future or perhaps permanently, as Westerners, a European enclave in the Middle Eastern Arab world?

At the university, I felt that we were in Europe or North America rather than in the Middle East. Israeli culture itself is heavily Western in orientation, and this is clearly part of the reason for its success. Huge sums of money come from abroad, from Europe, Germany (especially in reparations for the Holocaust), and also from America, both from Jewish donors and from the United States government. At Hebrew University it was taken for granted that Israel was Europe's, and more specifically America's, friend in the often hostile, oil-rich Middle East. It was believed that Israel could be a catalyst for changing Arab culture within and outside of Israel, if only Arab hostility to Israel's existence could be transformed.

At Hebrew University I wondered how Israel could help elevate Arab culture if it debased its own. Surely Arab culture had flaws and needs galore. My travel to Israel, however, convinced me that the need was mutual. Could both cultures need each other?

7

Speaking Truth

Israel and Palestine
in the American Jewish
Understanding

In my own experience, the American and Jewish love affair with Israel
has little to do with Israel. In fact, many Americans know little about
the Middle East, and Jews, who assert they understand the situation perfectly, know even less. For most Jews in America, Israel is a response to
the Holocaust and a safe haven for them should a new persecution of Jews
begin. The reality of Israel, its diverse society of creativity, identity politics,
and corruption, is beyond the comprehension of most American Jews.

This lack of knowledge would be excusable if Israel wasn't such a contentious issue and the subject of so much public debate. Advocates for Israel
often mistake their passion for knowledge. When knowledge contradicts
their views, their passion reaches higher decibel levels, and, as with most
issues of public import, angry and threatening language usually means that
something is wrong with one's argument.

In the 1980s, Israel seemed trapped in a cycle of defense and expansion
that many felt powerless to stop. Israel seemed fated to perpetual war with
the Palestinians. Additionally, there was an increasing war within Israel
on a variety of fronts, between secular and religious Jews, between those
who sought a withdrawal from the territories conquered in 1967—generally

referred to as the "peace camp"—and those who sought to build the greater land of Israel—broadly gathered in the settler movement.

The Lebanon war, which reached its apex in 1982 (though the occupation of parts of Lebanon would continue into the late 1990s), was sobering for Israelis and for some American Jews. Israel's innocence was thrown into question, along with the justification for the war. The massacres at the Sabra and Shatilla refugee camps in Lebanon, where Christian forces under the direction of Israel massacred hundreds of Palestinians, as well as Israel's relentless bombing of Beirut, brought these questions to the fore.

Some Jews in America also felt a new struggle in their support of Israel. The question was whether the Lebanon war was an aberration or signaled a more fundamental, perhaps foundational, problem with the Jewish state. The Israeli peace camp that came into being as a protest against the war saw it as an aberration calling for immediate correction, but what to make of the occupation and the settlement movement that enjoyed financial, military, and ideological support from the government? Was this too an aberration or a fundamental characteristic of the Israeli state? Nevertheless, American Jewish identity, and thus the community's rationale for supporting Israel, revolved around the Holocaust. From this vantage point, details on the ground in Israel were less significant.

If Israel was a difficult topic among American Jews, discussion of Palestinians was even more so. When mentioned at all, Palestinians were seen in a negative light. They were defined as terrorists and anti-Semites, uncivilized, with poor leadership. Rarely were they seen as moral agents or as a people rooted in the land. Palestinians existed as enemies who sought to thwart the Jewish return to the land. Most Jews had no sense that Palestinian complaints might be legitimate and that if Jews were in the same position, they might also feel and act in the same way.

Since Israel was seen through the lens of the Holocaust, Palestinians could only be seen through that same lens. It mattered little that Palestinians were not actors in the Holocaust until they were added onto the narrative as latecomers. In the Holocaust narrative, Palestinians seek to bring Jews back to those horrible years, and for that reason they are included as the last act of the Holocaust trauma.

Palestinians, for their part, perceived themselves as the last victims of the Holocaust. The creation of Israel occurred because of the Holocaust, and since Palestinians were victims of that creation, the logic of their perspective was clear. Jews, on the other hand, saw themselves as victims then and now, with Palestinians being the new Nazis.

This is true even today. To speak of the Palestinians in a positive light—mentioning their grievances, hopes, and aspirations—is to be accused of speaking for the new anti-Semites who threaten Israel's existence. The combination means that you as a Jew are attempting to bring your own community back to the days of the Holocaust and forward to a new Holocaust. Why would Jews speak in a positive way about such a vile people if they respect themselves as Jews and want the best for the Jewish community?

Speaking about Palestinians in a positive light means that there is something wrong with one's Jewish identity. Only someone who hates himself and his own identity would speak of Palestinians in such a way. It is breaking a solidarity that all Jews have with one another. The consequences of such speech are seen as tremendous, perhaps leading, intentionally or unintentionally, to the final destruction of the Jewish world.

The stakes are high, so high that a reasoned discussion seems almost impossible. Could it be that Jews, so known for intellectual work and argumentation, have lost this ability with the establishment of Israel? In other intellectual areas of life, Jews continue to excel. The professions are full of Jews, and while many of the leading intellectuals in America are Jewish, developed thought on Israel is rare.

Even during the 1980s, the question remained, if unspoken by the majority of Jews and Jewish leadership. How could we discuss Israel in a mature way if we didn't also discuss the Palestinians in the same manner? There were Palestinians within the 1967 borders of Israel, part of the remnant that had not been driven out in the creation of the state. Their population had grown from 150,000 in 1948 to almost a million, and they were citizens of Israel though in a second- or even third-class way. By the 1980s, they had formed their own civil rights movement and were struggling for a full equality within Israel. This growing minority even had representatives in the Israeli parliament. The 1990s saw a strengthening of the Palestinian Israeli community. Still, they were absent from the Jewish discussion of Israel. In the post-9/11 world, the difficulty has become exaggerated. Again Palestinians are seen as terrorists but now in league with al-Qaeda and the Islamic groups that seek to destroy Israel and America. The diversity of their grievances and separation of struggles are conveniently deflated.

In fact, Israelis were not only Jewish; there were also Palestinian Israelis. Many were fluent in Hebrew and quite aware of Jewish history and culture. After all, they were educated in the Israeli school system with a certain percentage even attending university within Israel. I met some of these Israeli Arabs, as they were then known, and was quite embarrassed when I had trouble understanding their situation. How many Jews knew of this population or, if they knew, cared about their plight?

In some ways the Palestinians within Israel are in a situation quite similar to that of African Americans in the 1950s. Palestinians, while citizens of Israel, live in a segregated society. Often commented upon by Jews within Israel, Palestinians rarely are allowed to articulate their own case for human and civil rights. Israeli society was created for and favors Jews. Unbeknownst to most American Jews, Israel's laws of land ownership and community development are highly discriminatory. Israeli Arabs are tolerated but often seen as a possible fifth column. Could their loyalties be anywhere else than with their Arab brethren?

During my travels to Israel, I have heard Jewish Israeli professors speak of Israeli Arabs as "our unwanted minority." In Europe, we had been the unwanted minority. The dilemma, however, is clear, especially to Jewish Israelis. If the unwanted minority becomes a wanted minority, ultimately fully integrated into Israeli society, the Jewish state disappears. Israel might continue—without prioritizing its Jewishness. The other possibility, the one that most Israelis favor, is to deny equality, thereby preserving the Jewish state. Some even argue for the transfer of this minority population out of the state of Israel completely. In their mind, Israel is for Jews only.

But what does such a Jewishness mean? It means, first of all, that we as Jews have conquered another people and relegated its remnant to "unwanted" status. It means that any Palestinian Israeli community is to be continually denied its rights, rights we struggled to win for ourselves. Israeli laws remain discriminatory at their core. Many of the benefits of Israeli democracy are restricted to Jews.

Without an open discussion, it is difficult for most Jews to understand the grievances that Israeli Arabs and Palestinians have or even to understand how the Palestinians of the West Bank and Gaza arrived where they are. In Jewish discussions, the Palestinians seemed to have arrived where they are out of thin air. The idea of indigenous Palestinian life existing before the establishment of Israel, a life interrupted and destroyed in the creation of the state, seems outrageous. Jews would not do such things to others; therefore, it was not done. Palestinian grievances have no ground to stand on, certainly not their claim to the land they call Palestine.

Holocaust, Memory, and the Neoconservative Agenda

Attempting to speak effectively within the North American context, I explored the newfound reality of Jewish empowerment. I began my reflections on Israel with the Holocaust and asked whether or not the present course of Israeli policies toward the Palestinians was bringing us closer to the freedom and liberation we sought as a people. From the perspective of the Holocaust, Israel could be seen as a necessity or at least as a logical desire for a place of our own. But another people, the Palestinians, were being wronged. The occupation of the Palestinian territories is the problem.

One important consequence of our empowerment was the increasing neoconservatism of American Jews. If Jews in America supported Israel in its policies against the Palestinians and Israel was dependent on American aid and military protection, the neoconservative's logic went, then American Jews had to favor a politics at home that guaranteed that support. As Israel became more and more controversial in the world, especially because of its continuing occupation, settlement building, and the 2006 Lebanon war, its alliance with the United States became increasingly more important. In fact, because of its policies, Israel was becoming almost completely isolated in the world. The United Nations passed resolution after resolution calling for a two-state settlement of the Israeli-Palestinian dispute. It was only the veto power of the United States that kept the Security Council from demanding action against Israel.

With neoconservatives, as with other ideologues, politics is an interest-oriented business. If the Jewish community wants this kind of support for Israel, it has to police its own dissidents who desire a more internationally responsive foreign policy for the have-nots of the world. Often countries and revolutionary movements that seek justice for their people see the Palestinian cause as representative of their own.

If Palestinians are identified as a Third World people, Israeli policies and alliances can be seen as a form of colonialism. Moreover, Israel itself has supported efforts in the Third World to delay or push back movements for justice. In different parts of the world, Central America and South Africa, for example, Israel supplied weapons, counterinsurgency forces, training, and equipment to support repressive governments.

By the 1980s, Jewish leadership was identifying with the global reach of the United States and Israel's policies to counter insurgencies in the Third World as a way of combating anti-Semitism and those who sought to destroy Israel. The United Nations was seen in this light, especially in relation to the 1975 resolution equating Zionism with racism.

Jewish leadership began analyzing what they called the "new" anti-Semitism, an anti-Semitism that moves beyond individual prejudice against Jews and focuses on negative views of Israel. These views were not seen within the political arena as differences of opinion coming from different historical and geographic locations and struggles. Rather, they were seen as a continuation of Jew-hatred, the European virus spread to the Third World. The lesson being that progressive forces in the world are against

Israel, so Jews have to be against these forces. The salvation of Israel comes from Jews in America and American support for Israel. From this logic, a Jew who supports Third World movements supports movements that seek to destroy Israel.

I argue against this perspective. I understood that anti-Semitism existed historically and in the present. Israel was becoming isolated in the world, but that isolation did not always or even primarily come from anti-Semitism. To admit that Israel can indeed do wrong and that Jews are not always innocent does not intensify the demonization of our people. We need to take responsibility for our own actions, regardless of how others interpret it. Therefore, Jewish dissenters are essential to providing an alternative reading of the contemporary Jewish situation and, possibly, righting the course.

In my view, Jewish dissenters, far from leading Jews to another Holocaust, explore an empowered and ethical way for Jews to be in the world. Ethics is central to the Jewish tradition. Can we survive injustice and hold on to the ethical only to become powerful and lose the center of our being? If it is true that powerlessness is, after the Holocaust, unethical for Jews, it can also be said that power without ethics is a kind of moral suicide. The isolation Jews were beginning to experience was not fated and became, over the long run, quite dangerous. We need to navigate a way forward. This takes maturity. It also means that we have to admit to ourselves and to the world that we are no longer innocent.

Through an attempt to publish an article with these perspectives, I met Rosalinda Ramirez, who served on the staff of a Christian liberation theology group called Theology in the Americas. Ramirez is a Catholic sister and an unusual one. Hailing from Puerto Rico, she wants to liberate her island from its colonial status.

Ramirez was interested in my work since it fit the perspective of a newly developed organization, the Ecumenical Association of Third World Theologians. Known as EATWOT, this association is dedicated to developing liberation theologies around the world. It represented a first attempt for theologians of the Third World—from Latin America, Africa, and Asia—to gather together and come into dialogue with one another. They hoped to develop a series of theologies responsive to the needs of their people, especially the poor of the Third World, rather than be beholden to theologies and theological methods coming from Europe and America.

If the Third World, with a globally structured poverty and marginalization, needed theologies of liberation, didn't North America, with an economy and politics that provide influence for its populations at the expense of the Third World, need one as well? The idea was that only through a mutual sense of liberation, from the side of the poor and the side of the wealthy, could true liberation occur. But it was also true that the liberation struggles in North America would have to be led by those suffering within the First World—African Americans, Latinos, women, and beyond. There was a place for those who came from the white affluent community but only if their political and theological commitments were liberationist in perspective.

Ramirez and others involved were interested in my work as a critical voice within the affluent sectors of America. They saw Jews as empowered and situated at the levers of powers within the American and global capitalist system. Their agreement to publish my article was controversial. Some resented Jewish insistence on narrating the Jewish story. Some feared that the Jewish establishment might retaliate against their fledgling organization. This debate troubled me.

The neoconservatives said that there was no room for Jews on the Left, either because they would sell Jewish interests and the community down the river or because, at the end of the day, other communities would jettison Jews as belonging somewhere else. Many Jews on the Left fled from their particularity, and other Jews who warned against the Left used their own particularity as a blunt instrument against others. All of this placed Jews like me in a difficult, if not impossible, situation.

A Different Path

I was not prepared for the role I was assuming. For all practical purposes, Jewish Studies began in earnest as I was receiving my doctorate, and I had no interest in rabbinic studies. At the same time, Rubenstein pushed me to explore the fields of sociology and political science. I did not even see myself as primarily an academic as the term is often understood. Rather, I was interested in the question of commitment to justice, peace, and community in our time. I studied and followed teachers who embodied this quest for me. It led, somewhat by chance, to a doctorate and then, again somewhat by chance, to a teaching position at Maryknoll.

Maryknoll stumbled onto liberation theology in the Third World in the 1960s and was transformed by it. As a seminary and then a school of theology, Maryknoll was hardly academic in the classical sense of that term. Though fully accredited with a major theological library and resources for study around the world, the school at Maryknoll was formed around the question of commitment rather than technical expertise.

It was there that I came in touch with liberation theology in its contemporary form. The setting itself in which I taught seemed to raise questions of my own commitment to Judaism and the Jewish people. At least this was true after I began writing and speaking about Israel and the Palestinians. Who is this Jew to speak? He is neither a rabbi nor affiliated with a Jewish organization. He teaches at a Catholic missionary school. Is his liberation theology really Jewish? What are his real intentions?

Maryknoll was often on the front pages of newspapers around the world for its commitment to the poor. Maryknollers had been murdered by soldiers from repressive governments for their work in Central America, and its support of liberation theology through its publishing arm, Orbis Books, was an important vehicle of liberation themes around the world. The grassroots support that Maryknoll had among its following in the United States—its monthly magazine had over a million subscribers—was significant. Maryknoll's status as a mainstream Roman Catholic institution lent it credibility for its emerging stances regarding the global economy and politics.

Maryknoll was connected in the global context but isolated on the Jewish front. I was isolated as well or fairly so, until I met a local rabbi in Croton-on-Hudson near Maryknoll. Rabbi Michael Robinson, now deceased, a Reform rabbi, then in his fifties, had presided over his synagogue for decades. Over the years, he had been involved in many social justice issues, the civil rights movement in the 1950s and 1960s and the movement to abolish nuclear weapons in the 1980s and 1990s. He had been a frequent protestor against the Vietnam War and was clearly against the policies of Israel regarding the Palestinians.

Rabbi Robinson was a pacifist, hence his lifelong involvement in the Fellowship of Reconciliation, and his views on Israel can be described as non-Zionist. Though he certainly was not against the existence of Israel as a Jewish state, he was against the militarism that he found in Israel and among many of its supporters in America. I could see that this was a constant struggle in his own congregation, the balancing of his concern for Jews wherever they lived and for the concerns of his congregation even when he disagreed with them. Still, he spoke clearly on matters of violence and war. For Robinson, Israel was not exempt.

Rabbi Robinson was the first rabbi I met who combined a deep spirituality and the active quest for social justice. I began attending services at his synagogue, and I met with him on a regular basis. He was quite interested in liberation theology and the work I was doing. For my birthday, he gave me a prayer book for the home. This too was a first for me. Using this prayer book, I began to fashion a prayer life that was meaningful to me, beginning with Shabbat and later extending to morning and evening prayers. With that and my attendance at synagogue, I embarked, for the first time in my life, on a more formal journey of religiosity.

Rabbi Robinson spoke the truth as he saw it. He also never succeeded in the rabbinic establishment. He was consigned his entire career to a small-ish synagogue without influence in the larger Jewish world. His stands on social issues, including Israel, had limited his career as a rabbi.

Rabbi Robinson advised me that speaking publicly on these matters involved risk. Opponents urged me to be silent, and some expressed an implicit, sometimes explicit, threat of my being silenced. Personal intimidation, organizational pressure, and character attacks seek to diminish one's ability to speak. Even those who were favorable to my thought wanted a presentation that they were comfortable with, an admittedly more nuanced, but nonetheless real, pressure to conform to their own understandings. But Rabbi Robinson modeled spirituality in action. He encouraged me to speak the truth as I saw it. As he had done and would continue to do. Even as the certainty of God faded from his life.

Some years before we met, Rabbi Robinson lost his only son in an automobile accident. This loss affected him deeply as a father and also as a rabbi. On a few occasions, over lunch or on long mountain walks he loved to take, we talked about this loss and how it changed his relationship with God. It was heartbreaking for me to listen to this sensitive soul speaking about what no parent should ever experience. Once, God had been for him a rock, a being who had the destiny of the world figured out in some detail. It was a matter of our doing God's will. After his son's death, Rabbi Robinson was not so sure. The rock had disappeared; Rabbi Robinson's view of God changed. Now Rabbi Robinson could only do what he thought had to be done. He had ceased to believe in a God from whom he could discern a destiny.

8

Struggling for Fidelity

Encountering
Post-Holocaust
Theologians

I knew the work of the Holocaust theologians through my study with
Richard Rubenstein. In the mid-1980s, in light of my growing interest in
Jewish fidelity after both the Holocaust and the reality of Jewish empowerment in Israel, I needed to update myself and read other materials they had
produced since the 1970s.

Elie Wiesel was the easiest read, as his simple yet powerful narratives
were already in place by the mid-1970s. They also were deep inside of me.
At least this was true for his Holocaust narratives. I was aware of Wiesel's
commentary on the Israeli-Palestinian situation, and I found that Wiesel
had actually written little on the situation. For him, Israel was a dream.
The details were for others to discuss. Yet even so, Wiesel's commentary was
more than the limitations he vowed to keep—that is, he felt only a Jew in
Israel could comment on the situation—yet he demanded that no one else
speak about Israel either, at least if that speech was critical. Praise for Israel
was, of course, allowed.

Emil Fackenheim was more complicated. With Rubenstein, I had
read Fackenheim's lectures at New York University—gathered into a book
titled *God's Presence in History*—in which he described his own shift in
understanding the demands of Jewish history. Fackenheim described the

Holocaust as the root experience in Jewish history, comparable to the Exodus/Sinai event.

For Fackenheim, the Holocaust challenges the Exodus/Sinai event and overwhelms it, at least as far as we can see today. In fact, the Commanding Voice of Sinai that emerged from the Exodus is now stilled or at least compromised by the Commanding Voice of Auschwitz that emanates from the Holocaust. Jews today hear the latter voice and the commandment that issues from it, a new 614th commandment, which cautions Jews to pay attention to Jewish survival lest the haunting voice of Hitler win in history. For Fackenheim, this is exactly the commandment that Jews heard when they fought and won the 1967 Arab-Israeli war.

The Holocaust as a formative event was clear to Rubenstein, Wiesel, and Fackenheim. Still, reading these thinkers only through the lens of the Holocaust obscures some implications of their thought. For Holocaust theologians, the defining practice of Judaism and Jewishness after the Holocaust is not religiosity as we usually think of it. The defining concern is support for the survival of the Jewish people. That support is demonstrated in support for Israel. In fact, for Fackenheim especially, only that support counts. Indeed, it counts for everything.

Narrative and Counternarrative

On the practice of being Jewish, Fackenheim was adamant. The past primary identification with causes other than our own was over. The universal call of the Jewish witness could not be sustained after the Holocaust, and this could be proven even now by the contemporary and gathering assault on Israel. The Jewish condition was singled out at Sinai, in the Holocaust, and now in Israel. It is this singled-out condition that bothers others about Jews. Sometimes it even bothers Jews. Nonetheless, it is this very condition that Jews are called upon to embrace, even without God. Without God or the support of humanity, Fackenheim argues, Jews are commanded to carry on.

When I first read Fackenheim, I felt a sense of pride about the stubbornness of Jews and Jewish history. As he points out, there were and are so many reasons for Jews to opt out of Jewish history. This is what Fackenheim indirectly accused Rubenstein of doing by his refusal to imagine a Jewish future. Fackenheim's anger was such that he would not address Rubenstein directly in print or in person.

There was more than stubbornness here. Fackenheim's defiance harbored a deep anger. This anger was justified, as the Holocaust was simply a continuation, albeit on a massive scale, of a long history of anti-Semitism. Yet I felt this anger led to violence against others, the Palestinians, for example, and against fellow Jews who said or heard something different from the Commanding Voice of Auschwitz. Anger compounded lashed out at others. Could the Commanding Voice of Auschwitz multiply anger until it had no limits?

Anger has its place. There are many reasons to be angry about life. Jews in particular have grievances with the world and with God. The first time I encountered this anger was when I studied with Rubenstein. It is difficult to encounter an angrier person than Rubenstein was. He often tried to disguise that anger by speaking about the logic of the Nazi system or the logic of Christianity with regard to Jews. As to the question of God, he simply dismissed the possibility of belief after the Holocaust. It could not make sense unless you accepted God's culpability in the mass death of millions. But here too beneath the outright dismissal was a simmering anger about the God who had promised to be with the Jewish people.

In contrast to Rubenstein's and Fackenheim's anger, Wiesel was a suffering saint in public. He spoke movingly and often within the context of Hasidic stories about loss of faith, disappointment with the world, and hope among the ruins of life.

When challenged on Israel, however, the stories disappeared and the accusations of anti-Semitism and betrayal came to the fore. It was almost as if the narrative of Jewish suffering could be articulated only by Jews. This was true for hope as well. If the narrative is woven only by us—and in the way we want to hear it; otherwise even Jews are counted as enemies—we can speak and write it forever. When interrupted by a counternarrative, accusations of anti-Semitism are issued—hope turns to anger in a heartbeat.

Fackenheim and Wiesel, especially, refused to understand that narratives always produce counternarratives. They lacked an understanding that the world is bigger than ourselves, even bigger than our own suffering, and that Israel's joining the world of nation-states would increase the contested quality of our narrative and actions. Did these Holocaust thinkers believe that the story of such a small people, insignificant in the percentage of the world's population, could assume and maintain center stage? Did they think that others did not believe their own histories to be as significant or even more so? Is it legitimate to criticize others for doing the same thing we are doing?

The most interesting Holocaust thinker I read was Irving Greenberg, an Orthodox rabbi, who was largely unknown to the general public. He was certainly unknown to me when I first came upon his writing, and I only learned later that he was quite significant in Jewish life. This was especially true within the Jewish establishment. Greenberg operated almost as their resident theologian. His charge was to educate the affluent movers and shakers of Jewish and American life who embraced Jewish identity but were largely ignorant of Jewish religiosity and symbol structures. Essentially, Greenberg helped make these powerful men and women more literate in things Jewish so their identity quest was more informed than simple emotion or pride.

For the most part, Greenberg did not concentrate on publishing books or articles in academic journals. Most of his writing was published by the organization he founded, the National Jewish Leadership Center, and even then only in pamphlet form and circulated mostly among the members of his center. I came across one of these pamphlets almost by happenstance, and I found it so interesting that I searched for his other publications. I found a major speech that had been published from a conference on the Holocaust held in New York City in the 1970s and then a series of pamphlets that addressed more or less the same themes as the one I had stumbled upon. In general, Greenberg tried to gather the main trends of Holocaust theology, synthesize them, and place them in motion through his own particular perspective.

By the 1980s, Greenberg had seen the growth of Holocaust reflection and agreed with aspects of most of the work that had been done. What he added was his particular perspective on the covenant and the role of Jewish activism that was needed today in relation to Israel. He also addressed relations between Jews and Christians after the Holocaust. Greenberg structured his discussion within the framework of eras in Jewish history. He identified three eras, naming the first two, the Biblical and Rabbinic, and leaving our era, the third, unnamed. Each era has a historical context and guiding principle.

The Biblical Era features the formation of Israel, the promise and entry into the land, as well as the consolidation of Israel in the land. The Biblical Era also features the prophets who call the now-established people of Israel to the justice it had struggled to achieve in the Exodus. To the Israelites, God was present, a powerful force that was self-evident and omnipresent. This certainty about God's existence in the Biblical Era allows a continual dialogue between God and the people. This dialogue is two-way, allowing God to interact and interrogate individuals and the people and in turn to be challenged by them.

The Rabbinic Era began with the fall of Jerusalem and the destruction of the temple in 70 and 132 c.e. With this destruction, God fell silent, and the rabbis are called upon to interpret God's word in the biblical text in light of reason and the immediate needs of the people. While the Israelites had responsibilities in the Biblical Era, they were dependent on God, who took the lead. In the Rabbinic Era, Jews are called to assume equal partnership with God, if not more. They can rely on God's word as a guide, but since God has fallen silent, the word of the rabbis and the community is as important.

In the Biblical Era, there was a back and forth with God about the situation of the Israelites. It was not always obvious that the Israelites were headed for liberation, and struggles and violence occurred that did not comport with God's promise of peace and justice in the land. The Rabbinic Era also confronts tragedy, the destruction of Jerusalem and the temple first and foremost, and then the subsequent and seemingly endless dispersal of the Jews from the land. This Diaspora means distance from the biblical promise and a minority status among the nations that make Jews vulnerable to discrimination and violence. While in the previous era the Israelites called out to God and expected a response, in the Rabbinic Era the reasons for the suffering of Jews have to be considered and thought through by the people. Their cries to God bring forth no answer other than their own.

The Third Era begins with the Holocaust and continues today. For Greenberg, this era differs from the first two in significant ways. God's silence has now become a hiddenness. Whereas in the Rabbinic Era the scriptures, representing God's voice in the Biblical Era, could be searched for clues as to God's will, after the Holocaust even this once-removed voice is further silenced. If in the Rabbinic Era Jews were called to an increasing responsibility, in the Third Era the responsibility is greater still. Those who have survived the Holocaust must decide for themselves and on their own what they are to make of Jewish life, or even if they are to continue on with Jewish life at all.

The decision to continue means assuming consequences for difficult choices. The decision to continue on with Jewish life means, first and foremost, establishing the material conditions for that survival. For Greenberg, the most important material condition is political empowerment in Israel and America. Without that tangible basis, Jews remain vulnerable to the nations, an unacceptable consequence in light of the Holocaust. Greenberg believes that Rubenstein was right in saying that this vulnerability can never again be an option for Jews. In closing off this possibility of victimization, Jews can achieve their goal of continuing to be Jewish in a secure and viable way.

Empowerment must be struggled for, achieved, and maintained in a world that is hostile to Jewish interests, and that means, for Greenberg, a complete mobilization of Jewish energies for that one goal. Like Fackenheim,

Greenberg believes that the universal thrust of Judaism, while good in and of itself, deflects from the need to focus on this particular goal. Thus the Jewish impulse to move out to others must be disciplined in the Third Era, lest the community become confused and embroiled in internal questions at the expense of empowerment.

For Greenberg, it follows logically that the prophetic itself must be disciplined. In many ways, the prophetic has appeared in all three eras of Jewish history as a disturbing reminder of the essential mission of Israel and the Jewish people. Yet that impulse, so defining of the Jewish journey, always needs refinement and boundaries. The reasons for this are clear, at least for Greenberg, as the prophetic, loosed from its context and listened to only for itself, overwhelms the needs of the community for survival. In other words, the prophetic is too strong to sustain ordinary Jewish life. Yet it is also true that without the prophetic, Jewish life may lose its moorings. In every era, the prophetic and ordinary Jewish life are involved in a dialectical relationship, attempting to balance both demands for a community that often lives in dangerous times.

In the Third Era, Greenberg believes that the prophetic is especially dangerous. In the Biblical Era, Israel's sovereignty allowed, even demanded, the prophet's words. The Rabbinic Era needed the prophetic in scripture to reassure Jews that injustice was condemned and oppression would someday come to an end. The prophetic also encouraged Jews in the nineteenth and the early part of the twentieth century to criticize unjust political and economic systems. Though loosed from religious tradition, these Jews carried the prophetic to the secular world and in the process, though unbeknownst to them, maintained ties to their own tradition.

In fact, Jewish powerlessness encouraged the prophetic. Jews had little or nothing to lose, and unjust power was an important and convenient target. Now the tide has changed. Although the prophetic has contributed boldly to Jewish history and the world, especially in its questioning of power, Greenberg believes that the post-Holocaust need for Jewish power demands a reassessment.

Especially on the internal front, the use of the prophetic continues even as the situation of Jews has changed. Therefore, some Jews use the prophetic against Jewish empowerment itself. For Greenberg, the power of that critique may overwhelm the needs of the community for a place of refuge and security. Thus those who employ the prophetic vis-à-vis Israel and even the United States, as the prime guarantor of Israel's survival, have not understood the demands of the Third Era, which is to prioritize survival over the prophetic.

At the outset, one might think that these priorities could be brought together or that they represent somewhat different perspectives that complement each other. For Greenberg, however, the prophetic endangers Jewish survival itself. The critique of Israel, for example, can undermine its rationale as a haven for Jewish refugees and as a state that rebuilds Jewish life.

Criticizing Israel can also undermine its material support in the world and in America. Israel is already short of allies and existing in hostile surroundings; criticism can foment a breach in its security. In days Israel could be overrun, and then there would be no turning back. The consequences for the Jews of Israel are clear to Greenberg—massacre, Holocaust, the end of Jewish history.

It was hard to read Greenberg, indeed Rubenstein, Fackenheim, and Wiesel, without feeling my life in their analysis. It was complicated. On the one hand, I felt drawn to their anger and to their commitment. As Jews, we had barely survived the onslaught against us. The survival of Judaism and Jewishness was extremely important to me. On the other hand, I felt each of them criticizing—even demonizing—what I experienced as central to Jewish history and to my own life—the prophetic. Time and time again, and against great odds, Jews had chosen survival and the prophetic as if both were crucial to the lived life of Jews. Did we have to choose one or the other? Could we choose—and remain Jewish?

Reading these Holocaust theologians, I felt emboldened and judged, torn at the roots of my Jewish identity. I thought that there must be a way to mend that tearing. The only way to do this was to live a life that embodied this mending.

A Flourishing Jewish Dissent

Despite Greenberg's admonitions, the prophetic was flourishing. While reading Greenberg, I was contacted by New Jewish Agenda, a dissenting group founded as a response to the first Lebanon war. I also came across two interesting books, one titled *The Jewish People: Torn between Jewish Ethics and Israeli Power* by Roberta Strauss Feuerlicht, the other, *Jews without Mercy: A Lament* by Earl Shorris. Then in short order, *Tikkun*, a progressive Jewish journal, was founded. The Jewish community was alive with dissent.

The debate about how to address the mainstream Jewish community often influences and deflates the positions of those opposed to Israeli settlement and occupation policies. Some groups, like New Jewish Agenda, adopted an explicitly moderate stance by advocating for a two-state solution,

Israel living side by side with Palestine in peace and harmony. They attempted to negotiate with the Jewish mainstream and keep their platform within limits so they would be seen as insiders rather than as outsiders. Still, the fact that they were organized and sought to speak in public made them subject to attack. In effect, their strategy was doomed to failure.

Progressive Jews were split on these issues. How far could they go in public and be responsible as Jews? Would the general public use their critique to further attack Jews and Israel? Was Israel as strong as some said or as vulnerable as others thought? Should groups like Agenda and Tikkun discuss the Holocaust or leave it to others? If the United States abandoned Israel and Israel lost a war with the Arab nations, would there be another Holocaust? Is the Holocaust central to Jewish identity? Is Israel?

Feuerlicht and Shorris took a different tack. They claimed the Jewish mainstream instead of negotiating with it. Though Feuerlicht was more secular and Shorris more religious, they wrote from a similar sensibility, urging tolerance, suffering, siding with others who suffered, and a rational way of rejecting or accepting God. They described a Jewish world of the past characterized by agnosticism, justice, and mercy. This past was similar to Elie Wiesel's understanding of the covenant and God after the Holocaust, a reality that we can affirm as once having existed. Wiesel laments a lost age and innocence. On the details of the present, he is silent. But for Feuerlicht and Shorris, our community has taken a turn toward empowerment that must be taken seriously as a departure that threatens the Jewish future.

Shorris articulates the loss of innocence by invoking a clash between the past and the present. The Orthodox community of his childhood was less sure of itself, and it delighted in the variety of life, even when it contradicted elements of Orthodox belief. Judaism was practiced because it was part of Jewish life, an important part, but not the whole of it. Since Jews were on the margin of American life, humility was built into religious practice.

What Shorris describes is a Jewishness before it was militarized, a Jewishness characterized by the late nineteenth- and early twentieth-century immigration from Eastern Europe. Shorris argues against the centrality of Israel because of its potential to override other Jewish sensibilities that make being Jewish worthwhile and enjoyable. Working for the communal and common good is one thing; parading Jewish pride and power is another. For Shorris, his background exemplifies a Jewishness that prizes mercy. Today, Jews in Israel and the defenders of Israel in America show no mercy. Morris asks whether to be Jewish without mercy is essentially adopting another religion.

Feuerlicht provides an interesting balance to Shorris. Although an orientation toward justice is found in the Jewish community, this position struggled to be established. Her overview of Jewish history discusses injustices within it from the Biblical Era on. She cites biblical events, including the entry into the land, that, to moderns, can only be judged reprehensible. The Jewish rabbinic establishment is criticized for its authoritarian control during certain periods of Jewish history. For the modern period, Feuerlicht documents Jewish involvement with slavery to dispute the view that Jews were unanimously at the forefront of the civil rights movement. Jews benefited from a segregated America like other affluent whites. To say we as Jews are better on race is, for Feuerlicht, to cloud the issue.

Feuerlicht is also challenging on the question of Israel. The exigencies of the Holocaust were real. However, she reminds readers that the desire for settlement in Palestine preceded the Holocaust. The settlement occurred without taking into account the indigenous Palestinian population. The creation of the state of Israel, like Jewish history, is not innocent. If Jewish history is not innocent, neither are Jews. Thoughts to the contrary are myths that Jews need to jettison.

Toward Neoconservatism

For both Shorris and Feuerlicht, the struggle for ethics is a common theme throughout Jewish history, the Jewish gift to the world. But Jews are not innocent. The militarism of the community has now reached a new level. Perhaps this is only because for centuries in the Diaspora it was impossible to assume such a stance. Still, for Jews, there has been and perhaps one day will again be the possibility of being just and merciful in the world. The failings of the Jewish world are not fated.

A different, neoconservative perspective is latent in the Holocaust theologians. They see themselves as liberals, progressive on social and political issues, often opposing commentators who are overtly conservative. When, for instance, the chips were down and Israel was at stake, Rubenstein associated with and supported those right of center in the American political spectrum. This support for Israel was the beginning of Rubenstein's return to the favor of the Jewish establishment.

Greenberg was different—and not so different. His sole interest was training Jewish leaders to chart the future of Jewish life. Unlike Rubenstein, Greenberg was at the center of that future in a conscious and positive way. He was among the movers and shakers of Jewish life. Many of these leaders were also among the elite of American society. Yet his self-identification as progressive on social, religious, and political issues was more mixed than he understood. I found that his self-presentation was out of sync with his evolving post-Holocaust thought. A careful reading of his writing revealed that his sense of the Third Era of Jewish life was pulling him, almost relentlessly, toward neoconservatism.

In many ways, he was following the dynamic of the famous Protestant theologian Reinhold Niebuhr. Niebuhr posited the person as caught between the complexities of personal morality and the tendency of social and political life toward immorality. Simply stated, there is a tragic impasse between what we hope for as persons and communities and what we are liable to achieve. Life is mixed, and as we move toward society, perfection is much harder, perhaps impossible, to achieve.

The complexity of life is no reason to accept failings and injustice, either on the personal or on the corporate level. It is, however, important to note a dialectical sense of possibility and reality so as not to expect too much from others or the social and political realms. In this sense, liberals often ask the right questions and want the right outcomes, but they also expect too much. Conservatives ask too little and settle for less than they should. For Niebuhr, the reality is somewhere in between.

Greenberg's theology is highly and explicitly political. Jews need to form political action groups and support those already in existence. AIPAC, the American Israel Political Action Committee, is one of those groups that Greenberg affirms. AIPAC is one of the most conservative and highly pro-Israel lobby groups in Washington. In the 1980s, Greenberg supported specific acts of American interventionist policies, including the American-backed Contra movement in Nicaragua. He also favored the new arms buildup introduced by Ronald Reagan, including the introduction of American missiles in Europe.

Greenberg's logic followed this route: America needs Jewish support in its efforts to combat and contain communism; the Soviet Union is a supporter of the Arab governments that threaten Israel. To deny the Soviet Union advantage anywhere is thus important. As he wrote in his criticism of Reagan's 1985 visit to the Bitburg cemetery where German SS soldiers were buried, Reagan's support for Israel outweighs this egregious error. At this point, Israel trumped the Holocaust.

Even liberal alliances with the World and National Council of Churches need reappraisal. Though many Jews agree with their ecumenical efforts, including their recognition of the continuing validity of the Jewish covenant, their recent statements about Israel and the Palestinians demanded serious thought and reflection. Greenberg thought that the logic of their positions would distance them more and more from mainstream Jewish interest. On the other side, evangelical groups who feel that Jews have to undergo conversion to be saved, a position that most Jews reject as anti-

Semitic, are quite favorable toward Israel. Perhaps they are the new partners for Jews, not permanently and not because we are in agreement with them on all things, because we are not, but because our interests in a strong and secure Israel coincide.

As we now know, on politics and religion Greenberg was clearly ahead of his time. No doubt even he is surprised by his clairvoyance. Almost the entire Jewish establishment is now neoconservative. Evangelical Christians are among the last and most fervent supporters of Israel. Though the Soviet Union and communism have faded into the pages of history, challenges in the post-9/11 world have taken their place. The fight against terrorism, with the invasion of Afghanistan and Iraq, has drawn the support of the Holocaust theologians. As has the strong American stance against Iran.

These could be Greenberg's views on the issues, but he could not maintain them as liberal positions. In fact, his own writing, given as advice for Jewish leadership, showed Greenberg to be little different than Rubenstein except in tone. There was no agonizing or equivocation in Rubenstein, as he reveled in stating boldly what other Jewish leaders came to reluctantly. For Greenberg it was more difficult, and my re-presentation of his thought in analytical terms distressed him. The mirror told a story he tried to deny. His words, however, betrayed him.

9

Surveying the Jewish-Christian Landscape

Reflections
on the Political and
Ecumenical "Deal"

When my initial writing on Irving Greenberg found its way to him, he was not pleased. He voiced this displeasure in a long personal letter, which I received as my book was being placed in galley form. The letter began on a note of gratitude, as no Jewish scholar had ever taken his writing seriously enough to write at length about him. He felt, however, that I had distorted his thinking.

Greenberg was especially concerned that I labeled his thought "neo-conservative." He was, at least in his own mind, a liberal, though one chastened by the Holocaust and the slippage of liberal support for Israel. Still, he did not appreciate being grouped with conservatives. He wanted to be known as someone struggling to maintain his liberal alliances.

I met Greenberg almost a year later, after the book had been published. The venue was a conference on the Holocaust that bore an interesting and provocative title, Remembering for the Future. Robert Maxwell, the newspaper tycoon, funded and headed the conference planning. The conference convened at Oxford University. The keynote speaker was Elie Wiesel.

Halakhah and Culpability

As I prepared to leave for the conference, it seemed that the time for questioning and healing was upon us. Just a few months earlier, in December 1987, the Palestinian uprising had broken out. Some killings in Gaza by Israeli soldiers had sparked a general uprising. It spread to the West Bank, and soon the entire Palestinian community was mobilized.

The struggle was, for the most part, nonviolent and indigenous. The Palestine Liberation Organization had been exiled for many years in Lebanon and then Tunis, and many Palestinians felt that the leadership was out of touch with the situation on the ground. Those within the Occupied Territories took responsibility and were demonstrating their desire to confront the occupation and establish a Palestinian state in the West Bank and Gaza, with the capital in East Jerusalem.

Disturbances in the territories occurred periodically through the years and had been dispersed by the Israeli military. For the most part, these disturbances were easily handled and in a few days life returned to normal, at least the normality defined by occupation. But soon after the initial demonstrations, it became clear that this was different. For one thing, the demonstrations were massive and widespread. At the same time, they were coordinated with a leadership that was diverse and from bottom up in structure. Therefore, the leadership was hard to track down and confine. The participation went far beyond activists, and soon boycotts of Israeli goods were being organized. In support, Palestinian businesses closed. On certain days general strikes were called and, in the main, observed. The Old City of Jerusalem, a major tourist draw for the Israeli economy, was closed down. Attempts by the Israeli authorities to force the Palestinians to end their general strikes failed.

Faced with this militancy, Israel struck back and hard. Under the leadership of Yitzhak Rabin, then minister of defense, Israeli soldiers were ordered to stop the uprising through "force, might, and beatings." This policy was thoroughly implemented and, at least for the first month or so, shown on national and international television. The Israeli press, of course, was full of stories of the uprising and the methods, sometimes brutal, of suppressing it. These included breaking bones, imprisonment, torture, and shooting "rubber" bullets to disperse Palestinian demonstrations.

The term "rubber" to define the bullets is a misnomer, as the bullets, real bullets merely coated with rubber, proceed like any bullet when it enters the body. The causalities mounted daily. In the end, hundreds of Palestinians died and tens of thousands were injured, many of them for life. Everyone in the Palestinian community was involved and affected by the uprising. Almost every family suffered loss of a loved one through death or injury. Almost every family had someone imprisoned and often more than one.

Just months earlier, while there to deliver a lecture at Jerusalem's Shalom Hartman Institute, I met David Hartman. He, like Greenberg, is an Orthodox rabbi from America. Known as a liberal, Hartman and his institute are dedicated to modernizing Orthodox belief and practice, thereby influencing contemporary Jewish religious life. He is also like Greenberg in that he feels that the Jewish covenant has to be reinvigorated, or at least our understanding of it has to be revised, to take into account the new realities that face Jews, including the Holocaust, modernity, and the state of Israel.

Hartman asks important questions. What does it mean to be Jewish within an empowered Jewish state? How does Orthodox Judaism, formed in the loss of nationality, adapt its ways to a Jewish state? "Next year in Jerusalem," the plaintive cry of Jews over the millennia, has come to fruition. Now in Jerusalem, what is to be done?

Orthodox *halakhah*, the Jewish law, was, for the most part, formed outside of the land of Israel, anticipating a return at some future date. The temple rituals were suspended following its destruction. Some Jewish law could only be observed in the land of Israel. Thus the creation of the Jewish state raised questions about what part of halakhah needed to be observed and where, what could be reinstituted or discarded, and whether elements of Orthodoxy, formed in another time, were archaic. The religious sensibilities of the return of the Jews to Israel had already caused ruptures within the Orthodox community, some of them leading to violence. They also threatened to deepen the divide in Israel between secular and religious Jews.

These religious issues are also political ones within Israel and the Diaspora. The Orthodox definition of what it means to be Jewish has ramifications for those Jews who seek immigration to Israel. Automatic citizenship is provided for those who are Jews by birth. Those who convert to Judaism are only accepted if an Orthodox rabbi supervises their conversion. This affects few individuals, but the very definition itself sends shock waves through the Jewish community. Secular Jews within Israel resent the power of the Orthodox establishment. Who are they to define who is or isn't a Jew? Most Diaspora Jews are not Orthodox. Are they to be defined as outside of authentic Judaism?

The politics of definition plays out in many areas of contemporary Jewish life, including among Holocaust theologians. Hartman's liberal sensibilities represent only one aspect of the Orthodox establishment. Though, for instance, the Orthodox were not alone in spearheading the growth of the settler movement, they were the most vocal ideological adherents of what became a movement for an expanded Israel. Among those Orthodox, any attempt, even by the government of Israel, to reverse the taking of land is to be fought. There is a higher jurisdiction than the state, for the Orthodox are busy doing God's will.

Hartman fought these understandings. He believes that Judaism, while rooted in the past, must also be attentive to the present. The nation-state, especially the Jewish state of Israel, exists in a world beyond its own particular vision of itself. Within Israel there are religious and secular Jews, all of whom are citizens within a political structure of nationality. Even the religious are divided into groupings with diverse understandings of religious practice, so religious coercion should not be used in any form. Rather, religiosity should be lived in a way that attracts a broad cross-section of Jews to practice it. For Hartman, this will not occur if Judaism is seen as an anachronistic, ritualized throwback to an ancient age.

Hartman's analysis is especially attractive to liberal Christians from Europe and America. Since the general Orthodox sensibility in Israel is too extreme on the religious and political fronts for liberal Christians, Hartman's moderation appeals to them. He is distinctly Jewish yet is open to a new dialogue with Christianity. Since he supports a two-state solution and is against aspects of the Israeli occupation of the Palestinians, Hartman represents what most post-Holocaust Christians hope for, a renewed and secure Jewish community living in peace with them and the Palestinians.

Liberal Christians' interest in Hartman, though, betrays their own agenda. If Jews are secure and open to them, the confession of Christian complicity in anti-Semitism, proclaimed often and loudly, reconciles them with Jews and with themselves. The recognition of anti-Semitism is about the way Christianity interacted with the world; it is also about the possibility of making Christianity credible again. Who in their right mind can affirm Christianity after the Holocaust if it has not cleansed itself of the taint of anti-Semitism? And who better to affirm that possibility than an American Jewish rabbi who emigrated to Israel and now presents a face of Judaism to Christians they can understand and identify with?

Years later I encountered Hartman's influence on liberal Christians at Harvard Divinity School. Hartman cultivated the faculty on this issue by inviting them to seminars at his institute. There they were treated with the elite status they were accustomed to, all the while with the unstated intention of garnering their support for Israel. It amazed me that such an intellectually and theologically sophisticated group could be courted so easily. Hartman's effectiveness troubled me. It was also clear that this provided the

Harvard faculty with a clear conscience on Israel. After all, Hartman was a liberal, supported Israel, but could hardly want ill for the Palestinians.

My experience of Hartman was different. In Jerusalem, Hartman's reaction to my lecture on a Jewish theology of liberation was much like Greenberg's. While he understood it to have a legitimate place in Jewish discourse, it was too strong and provocative. Like Greenberg, Hartman believes that a Jewish state is necessary and beyond discussion. All Jewish discourse must begin with that affirmation. Though I did not speak of Israel's founding in my lecture, I did speak of the injustices done to the Palestinians in the founding of Israel, injustices that continued in the present. I spoke about the need for Jews to confess our complicity in those crimes and to stop them immediately. The framework I proposed was the moderate two-state settlement with East Jerusalem as the capital of Palestine.

Though Hartman could agree in principle, at least with the two-state solution, his embrace of Jerusalem does not extend to sharing that city with Palestinians, not, at least, an empowered political sharing. Hartman's problem with my vision of the future was that though it set apart Jews and Palestinians into separate states, it left open the possibility of a shared future across the border between them. My call for reparations to the Palestinians also disturbed him and much of the audience. I saw this call as natural. If Germans owed us compensation for the Holocaust, as did Christians for their tradition of anti-Semitism, how could we be exempt from culpability for the suffering we were causing?

The very possibility of Jewish culpability is tremendously disturbing to people like Hartman and those affiliated with him. It opens a Pandora's box; the admission of culpability leads to further questions. If Jews admit that a wrong has been done, is it far down the road where the very legitimacy of the Jewish state is called into question? Palestinians are concrete embodiments of this question. Their very presence demands that these questions be raised. This is why Hartman demands a depoliticized toleration of Palestinians within the state of Israel and a clear separation from them in the two-state solution.

But there was also something more troubling about Hartman than a disagreement on politics. In his tone and side comments, I detected a racism toward Palestinians. It was a racism I encountered often in discussions with Jewish academics and institutional leaders.

The Uprising's "Burning Children"

I returned to Israel and the Occupied Territories in 1988 and witnessed the brutality of Rabin's policies of might and beatings in the hospitals I visited in Gaza and the West Bank. The children I found in these hospitals— and children they were, as most of the victims of these policies were under twenty-one and many in their early teens—were to die or be maimed for life. Many were on respirators with irreversible brain damage. Others were amputees. There were few Jews traveling in these areas, and to be one of the few was heartbreaking. I felt that I was a witness to a historical event unparalleled in Palestinian history. It was also unparalleled in Jewish history.

Though few, there were other Jews, including Israelis, working across the invisible borders to help with medical care and other needs for this community under siege. It was a strange situation. Israeli soldiers were literally trying to beat Palestinians into submission. Other Israelis were siding with the Palestinians in their struggle for freedom. Sometimes, because of the small population and universal military service in Israel, the soldiers and the humanitarian workers were found in one and the same person. Those who felt the occupation immoral were also being called by the military to serve in areas where the resistance was fiercest.

The clash of these two populations, so close in proximity in such a small geographical area, was almost unmanageable. However, there was another closeness, an interior struggle within at least some Israelis. Could they be ordered to suppress an uprising they essentially understood and empathized with? Did they have to obey orders? Their participation in the military made it difficult for the Palestinians to respect their authenticity when they said they desired peace and justice. As telling was the question with the Israelis. Could they affirm their own integrity when their actions belied their principles?

Though close in geographical terms, Hartman was quite distant from what I saw in the hospitals. Greenberg was as well. Of course they could travel as I did—the territories were open for them as they were for me—but, as was true for other Holocaust theologians and Jewish leaders, they did not avail themselves of the opportunity.

The hospital setting cut through the slogans of ethnicity and nationality. To see the children and their parents attending them, to see the under-equipped hospitals and overworked staffs receiving still more injured children, may have humbled even their most prized pretensions. Hartman's cry for a Jewish Jerusalem, one I had read and then heard in person, felt empty when I came close to the beds of the Palestinian children and saw their fathers' and mothers' faces etched in grief.

Were these my children as well? It was a sobering poetic sense that I could not erase from my memory. When I saw the faces of the children, I thought of Greenberg's most telling and moving writing when he evoked the children of the Holocaust as "burning." When I first read this, I was moved beyond words. I often quoted it, including it in my book and my lecture at Hartman's institute: "After the Holocaust, no statement, theological or otherwise, can be made that is not credible in the presence of the burning children." Were these Palestinian children also the burning children of Greenberg's epigram?

I knew this assertion to be another point of anger for Hartman and Greenberg, the seeming comparison of the Holocaust and Palestinian suffering. For them, as for most Jews, comparisons to the Holocaust are never to be made. It is akin to blasphemy to suggest another event as parallel to the Holocaust. Though this was not my intention—the events were so different in place and scope—the very mention of the two in the same sentence made a connection for them that was impossibly evil.

I could not let it go. The burning children of Palestine were no longer theoretical. They were victims of violence by Jews for their simple struggle to establish a Palestinian state. Of course more and less was involved than a state. Palestinians were struggling for dignity in their own eyes and in the eyes of the world. We Jews, through military power and political and theological narratives, were denying them that dignity.

When I saw Greenberg at Oxford, the children I visited in the hospitals were deep inside of me. It was clear that we as Jews had a responsibility toward them. The Holocaust, an event that was so central to Greenberg, was also central to me. My experiences brought these Palestinian children into the Holocaust event, not because the suffering is the same, but because they reminded me of the suffering we had endured.

Clearly Greenberg wanted nothing to do with my experience. At least that was his outward demeanor. When I sought him out, he responded coldly. The entire conference was happening during the middle of the uprising. Except for mine, there was no comment on the event. I felt that we were in a time warp, discussing the past as a way of avoiding the present. We were supposed to be "remembering for the future." What better way to do this than to address our responsibilities in the present? Few, however, took notice of the irony of the situation. Our future was defined within the context of the Holocaust. Palestinians were present only as representatives of a threatening past come back to life.

Toward a Jewish-Christian "Understanding"

Jewish-Christian dialogue has a long, colorful, and often tragic history. The post-Holocaust dialogue is quite different from past Jewish-Christian discussions both in presuppositions and in outlook. No longer do most Christians debate Jews about the authenticity of Judaism or even broach the need for conversion. The questions and positions have been transformed, and often in these dialogues Christians affirm Judaism and question their own tradition's authenticity. With such horrors behind them, Christians can hardly claim a faith of justice and reconciliation. Their authenticity is at stake, and Jews are often asked to help them redefine their Christian identity.

At Oxford, the Christian dialogue partners were looking to Jews for help. They knew their beliefs were, at least historically speaking, covered with blood. The hope they have is that we will forgive them and that ultimately they will be able to forgive themselves. This is only possible, however, with the change in Christian attitudes toward Jews. Christians have to affirm their own Jewish background in the Hebrew Bible and also in the Jewishness of Jesus. Instead of being independent of Jews, they are dependent on us. Instead of two separate and distinct covenants over and against one another, thereby raising the question whether both can be true, many Christians now posit one covenant, first given to Jews and then to the Gentiles as an expansion to the other peoples of the world.

The continuing validity of the one covenant means that the Jewish people, loved by God and suffering under a misguided persecution by Christians, need a place of refuge. For many of these Christians, Israel is under siege. Thus Christians, because of their history of anti-Semitism, support Israel almost without qualification. When Christians feel like qualifying that support by critiquing certain policies of Israel, they censor themselves. If they broach that self-censorship, the Jewish community demands silence.

Yet the uprising was forcing Christians to speak. In private they heard some Jews dissenting. That dissent seemed to them reasonable and respectful, but when they broached it to Jews they thought might be sympathetic in the dialogue, the response was negative.

At Oxford, I proposed that the ecumenical dialogue had become a "deal," in which Jews were allowed to speak about Christians in a critical manner but Christians had to silence their criticism of Israeli policy. The deal is clear and negative in so many ways. A mature dialogue allows people to speak the truth in a respectful manner. When one side is silenced the other side is also limited. How can truths be explored, even the complexities that are part of truth, if the issue every one knows should be at the center of the discussion is outlawed?

The deal has consequences beyond the Jewish-Christian dialogue. Historically, Christians committed crimes against the Jewish people. Jews were the innocent victims in those crimes. Today another crime is being committed against another people, with the complicity of Jews and the silence of Christians.

Richard Rubenstein also participated in the conference and wanted little to do with this dialogue or the "deal" as I framed it. For Rubenstein, Judaism and Christianity have been rivals from their respective births as religions in the fourth century of the Common Era. At that time and, according to him, forever after, they are destined to compete with one another. The issue is who is the real Israel. Which is "chosen"? Both claim that designation. It is a serious claim to make, one that can never be erased through the desire to live in harmony and peace. Adopting Freudian categories as Rubenstein often did, he found this rivalry manageable at times, always simmering, sometimes explosive. There are ways to speak to one another about it for a time and live in peaceful coexistence. In the end, however, it would never be resolved. This is why Jews need power. Complaining is useless and demeaning.

The empowerment of Christianity in Europe in the fourth century and beyond had decided which community was "chosen." From that moment on, the Jews of Europe were fated. In the twentieth century that fate became the Holocaust. As for the role of the Roman Catholic Church during the Holocaust, Rubenstein was again stark and unremitting. The pope had obligations to his own flock. These obligations were his primary responsibility, and since he could only see the relationship of the church and the Jews in terms of the old and new Israel, the expectation that he would reach out to the Jews was unrealistic. The idea that the pope would sacrifice his own community's wealth, status, and prestige for this competitive and archaic people was, for Rubenstein, fanciful.

To what end, therefore, did we engage in this dialogue? Christian humility is misplaced and self-defeating, and Jews, in the end, should not trust it. Jews demean themselves by asking Christians to accept them as equals and, to be honest, do not accept Christians as equal to Jews. For Rubenstein, the entire dialogue is a thinly disguised attempt to convince each other of something that neither religious community accepts: the diminution of the claims that make the members of each community who they are.

Caught between Rubenstein's stark essentialism—Judaism and Christianity were born in opposition and will always battle each other—and my assertion that Jews are, as it were, commanded to speak honestly about the contemporary misuse of power, Christian voices remained mute. Christians were caught between their sincere intention to reconcile and honor Judaism and Jews and their sense that a forward movement was necessary, which included the critique of all misuse of power, including that wielded by Jews.

Here we were, hundreds of us, in the elite setting of Oxford University, with funding that ran into the millions, lamenting the suffering of the Jews as a way of approaching the future. We were defining that future as if Jewish suffering would continue, or at least the history of that suffering would be to the exclusion of any consideration of human suffering beyond the Holocaust. The Palestinians were absent.

Rubenstein and Greenberg were honest in their own disparate sensibilities. Yet I knew that neither presented a way forward. Like David Hartman, both men were dominating presences, charismatic in their own way. They were also alike in that they were holding to positions that were slipping away. The Palestinian uprising was upending their entire enterprise. The Holocaust could not ultimately be used to support injustice or silence those who speak for justice. Nor could the plight of a people in distress be covered over with the religious rhetoric of the Jewish return to the land.

An experience I had during one of our tea breaks was telling. Knowing that I was writing essays on the uprising, an audience member asked me if I had any written materials to hand out. I had just written such an essay and had brought copies, so I gave him one. As I did this, I was suddenly surrounded by others asking for the essay. As Rubenstein was sitting right next to me, I was shy about the attention and tried to dissuade others from approaching me.

At that moment, Rubenstein turned to me and asked if he could also have the essay. Embarrassed that he would ask for my writing, a sudden reversal in our teacher-student relationship, I told him that it was just some scribbling that he need not pay attention to. He insisted, though, and in the end I handed him a copy. At this august Holocaust conference, the title itself was provocative: "The Palestinian Uprising and the Future of the Jewish People."

As the conference came to a close, Robert Maxwell, the conference sponsor, took the platform to introduce Elie Wiesel. In his comments, Maxwell recalled his difficult journey from Eastern Europe during the Holocaust. After much tribulation, Maxwell arrived in the United Kingdom, and it was here that he made his fortune. A large man, short in stature but obese, Maxwell was clearly overcome with emotion and cried as he recalled his story.

Maxwell was famous; soon he became infamous. When he arrived in the United Kingdom as a refugee from World War II, he converted to Christianity. In the ensuing years he built a business empire that collapsed shortly after the conference. During the collapse, criminal charges were filed against him, and in 1991 he was found drowned off the western coast of Africa. The question remains whether the drowning was accidental, suicide, or murder. The difficulty in ascertaining the cause of death also added to the mystery. To avoid an autopsy, Maxwell's body was flown to Israel for immediate burial. This act further compounded the intrigue. Was Maxwell a spy for Israel? Did he have information regarding Israel that he could or would use to defuse his economic problems?

Listening to Maxwell, I spotted Irving Greenberg standing nearby. He looked uncomfortable, and I wondered what he was thinking as Maxwell spoke of his conversion and wealth. The whole performance startled me. I doubted that Greenberg, a serious man and a rabbi, could be pleased. The public spotlight is difficult, and this spotlight on Maxwell and the millions being spent on the conference to highlight the Holocaust had to make Greenberg uneasy. Years later Greenberg would have his own difficulties in the public scene when, after being elevated to the chair of the United States Holocaust Memorial Council, he was forced to resign after counseling President Bill Clinton to pardon the crimes of financier Marc Rich. Again, suffering, wealth, and power intersected. Was the Holocaust becoming a status object for the wealthy and the powerful, casting its net so wide as to trivialize the event itself?

After Maxwell's introduction, Wiesel rose to speak. I was surprised that he was of such small stature. His presentation, while brief, was as poetic as his writing. Yet his words seemed forced. Responding to Maxwell's introduction, Wiesel spoke of the enormity of the Holocaust and how the event was in danger of being forgotten or placed along other events of atrocity as if there was no distinction. The Holocaust was being trivialized, a refrain—like the speech itself—I would hear him repeat almost verbatim ten years later.

10

Shattered Hopes

Loss and Solidarity
in the Jewish and
Palestinian Diaspora

The two conferences—the one in Oxford and the one I hosted at Maryknoll
to honor Gustavo Gutiérrez, happening simultaneously—formed a stark
contrast. At Oxford, the history of anti-Semitism in Europe was discussed
in relation to the Holocaust. At Maryknoll, the history of colonialism and
imperialism was invoked in relation to the Third World. Jews, or at least
Jewish leadership, are now safely and happily ensconced in the First World.
The Jewish community too often chooses to identify with former oppressors
for its own benefit.

Some in Jewish leadership think liberation theology is anti-Semitic.
One concern is how liberation theologians typically support Palestinians
in their liberation struggle against Israeli occupation. The liberationist concentration on the Exodus event as a catalyst for Christian reflection—as a
prophetic call to revolution—is also problematic. Perhaps most troubling to
Jewish leadership is the focus on Jesus as prophetic leader struggling against
both Roman occupation and its collaborators. For them, to portray Jewish
leaders as rejecting Jesus and collaborating with the Romans seemed to raise
the anti-Semitic canards of the past.

In the mind of Jewish commentators, liberation theologians, writing after
the Holocaust, were reinvigorating Christian theological understandings

that often led to violence against Jews. The Christianity proposed by liberation theologians was too bold and certain of itself. Jews in the ecumenical
movement wanted liberation theologians to recognize the dangers of such a
revolutionary Christianity, especially in relation to Jews.

One of the primary Jewish critics of liberation theology was Leon
Kleniki, an Argentine Jew and a rabbi, then director of the Anti-Defamation
League's Department of Interfaith Affairs in the 1980s and 1990s. Kleniki
demanded that Christians proactively admonish liberation theologians—
Christian and Jewish—and keep them from participation in the ecumeni-
cal dialogue. Kleniki called for a common front against new Christian and
Jewish theologies.

My involvement with the liberation theology movement prompted
Kleniki to call me at home to caution me about my efforts. At issue for him
were the claimed anti-Semitic aspects of liberation theology and the movement of that theology into the issue of capitalism and the Palestinians. With
that caution in mind, he also offered me a way out. If I tempered my thinking and writing, and balanced my Maryknoll program with pro-capitalist
and pro-Israeli speakers, the Jewish community would embrace me. He was
sure that many "doors" would open for me in the Jewish world.

I remember the phone call well. It was unusual to receive a business call
at home—and it was on Thanksgiving Day. It took me a moment to understand the import of the call. Upon reflection I realized it was an advanced
warning of some kind as well as an offer to help me out of the difficult
situation I was entering. Those same words had been spoken to me a few
months earlier by a professor from Seton Hall, Asher Finkel. An Orthodox
Jew, Finkel taught part-time at Maryknoll for many years. His specialty is
postbiblical Judaism and early Christianity, and he teaches courses revolv-
ing around the Jewishness of these texts, with a special emphasis on Jesus as
a Jew. Finkel was part of the ecumenical dialogue and Maryknoll's involvement in the post–Vatican II church.

For Christian seminarians, whose explicit call in life is to preach Jesus
and his message, to learn from a Jew is, from the perspective of Jewish-
Christian history, revolutionary. The representative from the people who
have often been condemned by a certain reading of the New Testament was
now teaching it. Who could argue with this progress? Both Maryknoll and
Finkel deserved credit.

Yet the agendas at work in this arrangement were obvious. Christianity
and the missionary enterprise lost credibility in the Holocaust and in relation to modernity itself. Christianity's attachment to European colonial
and imperial powers, beginning in 1492, also was deeply problematic.

It is within this context that the ecumenical dialogue attempts to address Christian arrogance toward Jews. By focusing on the historical relationship, Vatican II pointed Christians to their special and enduring relationship with Jews and Judaism. The council asserted that while Judaism and Christianity may seem at theological odds, both communities are actually traveling together. Their exact relationship will become clear in the future.

By equipping Christians to accept Jesus as living his own Jewishness, professors like Finkel are an important element of securing, once and for all, Jewish life within a majority Christian culture. The acceptance of Jews as theological partners with Christians provides security for Jews in the political arena as well. Political discrimination against Jews will henceforth also be seen as theological discrimination, theologically speaking a sin, placing the sinner's righteousness into question.

Yet there is a deal here as well. Jews are now affirmed as a covenanted people. The targeting of Jews for conversion is unnecessary and even contrary to the teachings of the church. However, non-Jews, billions of people including Muslims, Hindus, and Buddhists, remain in need of Christian conversion. People of indigenous traditions are also liable to the missionary thrust of Christianity. Finkel affirmed this need, and when he traveled to Africa to visit the Maryknoll missions there, he returned with glowing reports. In a sense, Finkel, as a Jew, identified Africans and others as incomplete without the God shared by Jews and Christians. As it turns out, Christian liberation theologians—with their critique of global economic systems of which the missionary enterprise is a part—were much more critical of missionary work than the ecumenical dialogue allowed.

Finkel also provided a warning. Since he was part-time at Maryknoll, our paths rarely crossed. When they did, he turned away from me, avoiding eye contact. Then one day he appeared at my office wanting to talk. It was perfunctory, with the same warning the Kleniki communicated. If I toed the line, I was in. If not, the consequences were clear. Then he left.

Contrary to the presumptions of Leon Kleniki, Jews are rarely discussed and Israel rarely mentioned in the writings of liberation theologians. When Jews are discussed by liberation theologians, it is most often in the context of biblical Israel, the Hebrew prophets, and the Jewishness of Jesus. Contemporary Jews are discussed, but most often as contributors to civilization and radical thought. Karl Marx and Sigmund Freud are cited with some regularity; the Frankfurt School of radical Jewish thinkers is mentioned, as is the work of Martin Buber. If there is any fault to find with them, it is that they see the Holocaust as part of a pattern generated by dominant European Christians who remain alive today rather than a unique event abstracted from historical trends over time. In relation to oppression, liberation theologians mostly speak about institutionalized, unjust relationships between labor and capital, the First and Third Worlds, white people and people of color.

When I asked Pablo Richard, a Roman Catholic priest and a Chilean who lives in exile in Costa Rica, about Jews in history and today, he explained anti-Semitism as the original sin of Christianity. It was this sin that led to all others including the persecution of Christian subgroups themselves by the dominant Christian understanding (that is, Constantinian Christianity). It was in Christendom that Jews were first persecuted by Christians, and certain groups of Christians were as well. For Richard, Jews and Christians were bonded in the refusal of Christendom and the suffering under its reign. Contemporary Christians should be united in presenting a common alternative to it as well.

The Failure of Oslo

In 1993, the Oslo Accords were signed. All of America and much of the world held their breath as President Clinton, flanked on either side by Prime Minister Rabin and Chairman Arafat, strode onto the White House lawn. Hundreds of invited guests awaited their arrival. After speeches by Rabin, in English, and Arafat, in Arabic, the climactic moment arrived. Boldly and without script, Arafat extended his hand to Rabin. Rabin looked pained and then, with a gentle nudge from Clinton, accepted Arafat's gesture.

The Israeli-Palestinian conflict is played out on a stage vastly out of proportion to the size of the geography of the land or the resources up for grabs. What is being fought over is the Holy Land, home to the three monotheistic religions, and Jerusalem, a city that has been prized by many over the centuries and is a central location for the holiest sites of Judaism, Christianity, and Islam.

For the two peoples, Jews and Palestinians, the stakes cannot be higher. By 1945, the destruction of Europe's Jewish communities was complete. For Jews in Palestine after World War II, there was no turning back. It was unlikely that the fighting between Jews and Arabs would stop without one community or the other being vanquished. For Jews this was not an option. While the Jewish drama is known the world over, the Palestinians at that time had yet to be born as a people in the international consciousness.

Jews and Christians in the West do not see Palestinians as rooted in the Holy Land. That some Palestinians are in fact Christians is too exotic for most Western Christians to acknowledge. Those who do acknowledge

Christianity as existing in the Holy Land identify with the foreign churches and personnel there. The Palestinians have their own sense of place and significance, and they, like the Jews, have nowhere to go. They are tied to their land in a way Western commentators seem unable to comprehend.

Loss of land and possibility is the result of defeat in war. If it was ever in doubt, by 1993 it was clear that the Palestinians had lost the war with Israel and that, rhetoric aside, there was no friend that could or would save them. If the Oslo Accords ultimately produced a two-state solution, Palestinians would be restricted to about 22 percent of historic Palestine. Palestinians retained their claims only to the Occupied Territories of the West Bank, Gaza, and the eastern part of Jerusalem. For the first time, Palestinians officially recognized Israel as a permanent part of the Middle East.

The Oslo process was born out of Israel's brutal repression of that first Palestinian uprising. Thus the Oslo process involved a mutual recognition that the endless conflict was yielding a cycle of violence that was draining both peoples. On one side, Oslo confirmed Israel's victory and attempted to limit its extension. On the other side, it confirmed the defeat of the Palestinians and sought, likewise, to limit the effects of that defeat.

The two-state solution was seen as the end game in the Oslo process. Unfortunately, that was not to be. Over the next years, the facts on the ground showed a different story. In the end, the failure of Oslo also confirmed that a two-state solution to the conflict had already gone by the wayside. Israel, while willing to grant limited autonomy to a Palestinian national presence in parts of the Occupied Territories, was uninterested in a real Palestinian state existing on its pre-1967 borders. While recognizing defeat, Palestinians thought that the initial map of Oslo—a map that divided the West Bank into three zones varying from full Palestinian autonomy, mixtures of Israeli and Palestinian control, and full and final Israeli control—would, over time, give way to a full Israeli withdrawal from the territories.

In the end, power triumphed. In that triumph many parts of Jewish and Palestinian life were permanently lost, perhaps foremost among them the possibility of reconciliation between both peoples and their histories.

A day after the signing, Rabin appeared before a group of institutionally affiliated Jews to explain Israel's position with regard to the future of the Middle East conflict. His remarks were cautious. He argued that Oslo represented a chance for Israelis to have a peaceful future, one his grandchildren might experience.

Though portrayed in the American press as a dove, Rabin was hardly that. In the 1948 war, Rabin commanded forces that cleansed Arabs from their villages and towns. In this he was hardly alone. Over the years he had developed a reputation for hard-nosed politics and was a fierce opponent of Palestinian statehood. In the late 1980s and early 1990s, Rabin was Israel's minister of defense. As such, he was responsible for ordering the extreme force used against the Palestinian uprising. Palestinians I met in the West Bank viewed him as a fascist.

I had met Rabin years earlier, when I was a graduate student. Our conversation lasted less than a minute when I almost bumped into him at a reception following his lecture. I was taken by surprise when I was suddenly face-to-face with him. Identifying myself as a Jew, I innocently asked if there was any truth to a report I had read about Israel's alliance with South Africa's apartheid regime. I half expected him to say that it was false. I remember him turning toward me as he answered my question. In a grandfatherly tone, he said simply that Israel was a small country and had to relate to all sorts of countries in order to survive. Then someone else began to speak to him and he slowly turned away.

As I recalled this encounter, I noticed that the post-Oslo meeting I was watching on television was turning angry. Someone from an American-Israel lobby group in Washington was challenging Rabin for negotiating with the Palestinians. As Rabin responded, another person interrupted him, again challenging his naiveté on the Palestinian issue. With that Rabin had enough and began yelling at both men that he, an Israeli who had fought in all of Israel's wars, would not be lectured to by American Jews who spend their lives lobbying the United States Congress for aid to Israel. The confrontation escalated from there.

The Jewish community was split over Oslo. Most Jews in America supported the signing, if only to improve the image of Israel and Jews in America. Progressive Jewish dissenters on the question of Israeli policies toward the Palestinians were also split. Some were adamant about the need to support Oslo, even to the point of accusing those with reservations about Oslo as secretly wanting the destruction of Israel. Others felt that the entire process was flawed and could only lead to a permanent Israeli occupation, especially in the West Bank. The original map of Oslo backed the latter group, as Israel looked as though it would retain significant portions of the territory, dividing Palestinian population centers off from one another and surrounding them with Israeli settlements and troops.

Within a year after the signing of the Oslo Accords, the struggle among those who held these differing perspectives exploded in violence. In 1994, an Orthodox religious Jew from America, Baruch Goldstein, entered the Cave of the Patriarchs in Hebron with his assault rifle drawn to massacre twenty-nine Palestinian Muslims at prayer.

Hebron has for centuries had a strong Palestinian population. After the 1967 war, Jewish settlers came there hoping to reestablish a Jewish presence. The shrine contains the tombs of Abraham and Sarah, venerated by both Muslims and Jews, and a synagogue and a mosque. Outnumbered by Palestinians, the Jewish settlers are protected by a heavy Israeli military presence. While enjoying protection by the army, the settlers have maintained a steady campaign of intimidation and terror against the local Palestinian community. Palestinians could hardly mistake the settlers' desire to remake Hebron into a Jewish city. The injustices mounted, both large and small. Hebron was a powder keg waiting to explode.

I had visited Hebron and the shrine a number of times before this terrible slaughter. The settlers there were disgusting—there is no other word for it. They harassed the Palestinians, sometimes destroying merchandise in their stores, other times spitting at Palestinian youth on their way to school. I had never seen Jews act like that before. The Israeli army protected the settlers, even the ruffians, but many of them were also thoroughly disgusted. A new kind of Jew had arisen, one I could in no way identify with.

When the explosion came, it was heard around the world. Either this terrible event would prompt a final decision to end the cycle of violence, or it would be a catalyst for its escalation. In the Israeli parliament, Rabin condemned Goldstein in harsh language. It was not lost on Rabin that Goldstein was a religious zealot and an American. Rabin was a convinced secularist, and the increasing religious fervor of parts of the settler movement profoundly disturbed him. Instead of a fringe group, these settlers were now wielding power in political parties and on the ground. They were making any kind of compromises, even those that could secure peace, almost impossible. Attempting to distance himself and Zionism from this hideous act, Rabin referred to Goldstein as born in a swamp, an errant weed.

Was the distinction correct? The founding of Israel was replete with atrocities and massacres. Since the establishment of the state, disregard for Palestinian human and political rights has been part of governmental policy. Wasn't Goldstein acting within a continuity Rabin helped to create and define? At different times in history, both used force to accomplish or further the goal of a Jewish state free of a Palestinian presence. Without a confession of the historic wrongs against Palestinians, Rabin's condemnation was unconvincing.

Within a year, Rabin was dead, felled by an assassin's bullets. Yigal Amir was also a religious Jew, one who held Baruch Goldstein in a special place of honor. Amir's deed took the world by surprise. The idea that a Jew would take the life of another Jew was unthinkable. If the prime minister had been assassinated by a Palestinian, it simply would have confirmed Jewish prejudices. That the assassin was a Jew prompted different questions.

The assassination of Rabin confirmed the widening gulf between Jews within and outside of Israel. The political rhetoric that preceded the assassination was filled with invective. Instead of engaging in a debate over government policy, Rabin was often labeled a traitor. He was "giving away" the historic land of Israel and had "fallen in love" with the Palestinians. He was negotiating with a "murderer of Jews."

The day before Rabin's funeral, it was announced that Arafat would be flown by the Israeli military to Leah Rabin's home. There they would mourn together the passing of her husband and his former enemy, who became a partner in the search for peace.

This was a historic moment, ripe with significance. For the political leader of the Palestinians to pay homage to his former enemy, and for the wife of the slain prime minister of Israel to welcome him into her home at this time of mourning, could not help but place the politics of the moment onto a larger canvas.

The fact that Leah Rabin rebuffed Rabin's archopponent, Benjamin Netanyahu, later to succeed Rabin as prime minister, in his attempt to pay a condolence visit, was also telling. In a later comment, she said that she held Netanyahu and others of his political ilk responsible for creating the climate that led to her husband's murder. She also commented that if the recent trends in Israel continued, it was unlikely that her grandchildren would live in Israel. At least in her mind, her husband's attempt at reconciliation with the Palestinian people was essential for the physical and moral survival of Israel. This was now in doubt. The future of her grandchildren was at stake.

A Dust-up at the Carter Presidential Center

As the suffering of Palestinians increased and the uprising and then Oslo confronted the world with a choice, interest in the conflict intensified. Yet even as all of this happened, the reality on the ground was becoming dire. More people wanted to hear the other side of the story of the conflict that for years had been largely censored in the American press. Though this was often seen as the Palestinian side—and to a large extent it was—the other side also included Jews who differed from mainstream Jewish opinion. There were also those outside the Jewish and Palestinian communities who were part of this "other" side.

Even as the conversation opened, the intensity of this issue made it different than most others. The claim of representing the majority or the tradition was made repeatedly by all involved. Often the other side was declared destructive and demonic. A simple disagreement seemed impossible. It was all or nothing.

In early 1988, I was invited to give a luncheon address for a conference on theology, politics, and peace, cosponsored by Emory University and the Carter Presidential Center in Atlanta. The conference atmosphere was electric. The featured speaker was Jürgen Moltmann, a well-known German theologian from Tübingen University. From his own experience as a young man in Germany during the Nazi era, he developed a theology of hope that seeks a political engagement within a Christian framework, exactly the type of theology and political action that was missing during the Nazi era.

With its concern for promoting justice and peace, Moltmann's perspective engages some aspects of liberation theology. One difference between these theologies is how they engage Jews. While for liberation theologians, Jews are distant, for post-Holocaust political theology, Jews loom large in the European, especially German, mind. This sensibility makes it difficult for political theologians to deal with the Jewish question as it is today. In an ironic twist, it is easier for Moltmann and his fellow German theologians to deal with Jews who are absent than to deal with living Jews, especially dissenting Jews in conflict with the broader Jewish community. Dead Jews of the Holocaust paradoxically allow them to mourn the victims of the Holocaust in a way that they can control. For them, Jews are always the innocent victims. Therefore, they are excused from dealing with the culpability of the Jewish community in the present.

To protect, develop, and project these images, European Christians try to limit their interaction with Jews to biblical texts and historical events, primarily in remembrance of the Holocaust. Israel is also an event, but one devoid of analytical categories. Israel is simply seen as a logical outcome of the Bible and the Holocaust. Coupled with the Christian sin of anti-Semitism, the Jewish story is more or less summed up, and the discussion then moves on to Christian themes.

Moltmann is one of these Christians who keeps Jews, especially dissenting Jews, at a distance. For years many German Christians refused to meet with Palestinians visiting Europe. When the uprising made it impossible for them to ignore Palestinians, they were usually silent about the Palestinian experience. As Germans, they simply could not speak about Israel in a negative way after the Holocaust.

Yet Moltmann and other German theologians were hardly alone. Walter Brueggemann, the American Protestant biblical scholar, writes book after book on the Hebrew prophets, applying their message to the Christian community of our day. His interpretations are tremendously insightful, yet it is also true that he veers far away from any discussion of Jewish life. I wonder how he can avoid the most obvious of questions that relates to his own work on prophetic criticism and the Jewish relation to the land. Again his great love and feel for Jewish texts does not bring him to interact in a critical way with Jews of his day. Loving the biblical text does not mean loving Jews. It may even be a way of distancing himself from flesh-and-blood Jews. Is this great scholar also afraid of a possible rebuke from the Constantinian Jews from whom he seeks permission to narrate his theology?

After being greeted by David Blumenthal, the major person in Jewish Studies at Emory, I delivered my luncheon address. I began with the change of title. Because of the uprising, my new title was "The Palestinian Uprising and the Future of the Jewish People." As I announced the title, there was a hush in the room, and, though luncheon noises usually continue through such addresses, I experienced a deep and abiding silence.

With the title announced, I spoke about my experience teaching Christians and how I often wondered how Christians related the history of Christianity to their children. With the good parts, do they tell the bad: the early persecutions carried out by Constantinian Christianity, the Crusades, the globalization of Christianity through colonialism and imperialism, the history of anti-Semitism culminating in the Holocaust? I then shared how Israel's brutal repression of the Palestinian uprising made it impossible for me to communicate the Jewish story to my children the way it had been told to me as a child. Our role in history had changed from victim to oppressor. I wondered aloud if Judaism can be passed on in such a compromised way.

From the biblical narrative to the present, difference is always at the center of the explanation of what it means to be Jewish. Now that we are creating victims, we are no longer different. If we want to replicate and embrace a history that looks more like Christian history, then we should tell this to our children in the same way that Christians should inform their children of Christian history. Since most Jews think Christians should be ashamed of their history—I certainly think this—shouldn't we also be ashamed of the history we are now creating?

At the close of my address, I read a haunting statement by the German Roman Catholic theologian Johannes Baptist Metz and then paraphrased it to deal with contemporary Jewish life. Metz said, "We Christians can never go back behind Auschwitz. To go beyond Auschwitz by ourselves is impossible. It is only possible with the victims of Auschwitz." I added, "We Jews can never go back behind empowerment. To go beyond empowerment by our self is impossible. It is only possible for us together with the victims of our empowerment, the Palestinian people." Perhaps this confession is my way—and perhaps the way for Jews in general—to find healing after the Holocaust.

My talk was welcomed with silence, and then with deafening applause. I responded to questions. After my first response, a voice next to me said that he wanted to respond to my address. It was Blumenthal. I pretended not to hear him and went on. A moment later I felt him tapping me on the leg, insisting.

Since no respondent had been scheduled, and since I understood from the invocation he gave that he felt he was the only Jew in the room and would probably try to "correct" what I had said, I resisted his intervention. Nonetheless, after a few minutes he forced his way to the podium and began to respond, announcing his credentials in Jewish Studies and his unqualified support for Israel. He then held out his hand to me as some kind of gesture. I refused and told him never to do that to me again. Then I turned and walked away.

As the luncheon ended, I noticed that I was being escorted out of the room by some friendly Emory professors. When I inquired about the need for such an escort, they crowded around me and continued taking me through the crowd. Evidently they were concerned for my safety.

President Carter had brokered the Camp David agreement with the Israeli prime minister Menachem Begin and Egyptian president Anwar Sadat in 1978. This was the first crack in the Middle East stalemate and was widely applauded in the Jewish community. He had also initiated the establishment of the United States Holocaust Memorial Museum in Washington, D.C., by forming the first commission to study and promote its construction. Elie Wiesel was chairman of this commission. More than a few commentators thought that Carter initiated the museum partly to assuage the hurt feelings of the Jewish community for Andrew Young's contacts with the PLO as the United States ambassador to the United Nations and for other Middle East policies that Jewish leadership felt favored the Arab world, which included the sale of AWACS to Saudi Arabia.

The day after I spoke, President Carter hosted a luncheon and I was included. When I walked into the room, I realized that only the major speakers and a few dignitaries were invited so that fewer than a dozen would attend. The table was small and rectangular, so the seating was close. We had assigned seats, and I found my place directly across from Carter, mere feet from him.

When, after about an hour, Carter began speaking with me, he asked me to tell him about some of my recent writing. When I told him of my book on a Jewish theology of liberation, he took out his pen and wrote the title in his notepad. As he did so, he asked me some of its main themes. Carter listened intently and told the others around the table they should as well. He then spoke about his own dealings with the Israeli government over the years. I knew Israel could be tough, but Carter's recitation of his dealings with Israel and their betrayal of many of the signed documents the two governments had negotiated clearly bothered him.

In private, at least, his disappointment was palpable. The Jewish leadership in America fared little better in Carter's analysis. Though he supported the state of Israel and recognized the need for Jewish empowerment, his feelings were almost bitter. There was reason to be. More than a few thought that Jewish leadership had much to do with Carter being a one-term president. No matter the continuing accolades in recent years, the loss of a second term clearly bothered Carter some eight years later. When almost two decades later he published a major work on the deteriorating situation in the West Bank and titled provocatively *Palestine: Peace of Apartheid*, he was assaulted by the Jewish establishment. The assault was more than politics: he was accused by many of writing a blatantly anti-Semitic book. Was this because he named the Wall being built around the Palestinians as "apartheid" policy?

A Political Double Standard in the Academy

Campuses are often rough places for Jewish dissenters. With the uprising in full bloom, the Hillel movement across the country mobilized to shut down speech critical of Israel. The usual pattern of my university appearances during the uprising, however, engendered engagement on a much deeper level. Even when protest groups came to my lectures wearing matching pro-Israel T-shirts, and matching looks of disdain on their faces, some in the group would break away from their original charge.

Unfortunately, the Hillel movement, ostensibly on college campuses to assist in the evolving identity formation of Jewish students, has taken on an ideological tone over the years. Instead of welcoming and honoring diversity among Jews, it has increasingly become a point of division among Jewish students. Those Jews who have critical understandings of Israel are turned away and carry the stigma of being uninterested in the Jewish community or having distinctly anti-Jewish sensibilities. Jews who are pro-Israel in an unthinking way are promoted as the "authentic" Jews on campus. This, of course, influences other identity groups on campus, as they experience "authentic" Jews as militaristic and against free speech.

Outside of Hillel, I encountered Jews struggling to find a positive identity in solidarity with other ethnic and religious groups on campus, including Palestinian students. For these students to cooperate with each other would mean they were risking the approbation of their respective communities. A Jewish college student engaging and working in solidarity with Palestinians and vice versa represents much more than a personal exploration. It is a life choice with implications beyond the college milieu, one that holds out perhaps the singular hope for peace in the future.

I learned that the University of Michigan college newspaper, the *Michigan Daily*, reprinted an article of mine that emphasized the need for Jews to come into solidarity with the Palestinian people during this time of crisis. A firestorm ensued. The Hillel rabbi wrote a letter to the president of the university suggesting that the editors of the newspaper be reprimanded, while students held demonstrations on both sides of the issue, some supporting the newspaper and its editors, others demanding their resignation. When I arrived on campus, I was amazed to learn that the editorial staff was divided equally between Jews and Palestinians.

Though the Hillel center was speaking vigorously on one side of the issue, few other voices were heard in public. The school's large Jewish faculty provided little guidance on the Israeli-Palestinian issue. The students asked me why I thought that the Jewish faculty refused to engage in discussion. What they wanted from me was what they were not receiving from their own teachers: guidance, a vision, a show of support, permission to struggle with and develop their own perspectives.

The Palestinian students were clearly atypical college students. They were afforded an opportunity to study in order to develop the skills of leadership in different fields and move the struggle from the streets to the creation of their state. I found them amazingly generous, especially in their relations with the Jewish students. They listened patiently when Jewish students told them of their own fears and those of their parents. In the American context, listening to Jewish fears about security and the possibility of another Holocaust is simply second nature. Seeing Palestinian youth listen to these fears is quite another thing.

I spent two days on campus, surveying the landscape and lecturing, but most of my time was spent counseling these young Jews and Palestinians. It was the first time that I was involved in this intense interaction with students, at least in a self-conscious way, and I began to understand that part of my role was to help young Jews and Palestinians find their way and survive a choice they had already made. Still, I was sad that there were few if any Jewish adults on campus who would be there for the Jewish students when they needed guidance and advice, or even a listening ear.

As my stay came to a close, a Jewish student asked me if I was a rabbi. This was after a long conversation, late into the night, one that involved her and her Palestinian boyfriend. I simply said no, and I thought little at the time about her question: "Would you be a rabbi for me?" It was late, and I told her I would see her and her friend in the morning.

11

An Unexpected Blessing

Edward Said's
Religious Secularity

M y travels brought me more into contact with Palestinian and Muslim
groups and, ultimately, to one of their few role models, Edward
Said. Before he died in 2003, Said was a professor of English at Colombia
University in New York City. He was known throughout the world for his
groundbreaking work on the colonial relationship between Europe and the
Middle East. Defining this relationship as "Orientalist," Said claimed that
for hundreds of years the West had defined the East in its own image. The
East was "other," sensuous, backward, of ancient greatness and present-day
corruption.

The power to define goes hand in hand with military power, so that
political colonialism is often followed by scholarly and academic colonialism. Said charged that academic colonials continued long after military
colonialism ended. In discussions about the Middle East in Europe and
America, Orientalism remains important.

Translated to Arabs and Jews in the present, Said thought that Arabs
and Palestinians are "other" to the West and therefore seen as different.
Though in their ancient greatness they are respected, in their present corrupted state they are demeaned and feared. Uncivilized and seething, their

ethical and intellectual capacities impaired, Arabs (and Muslims in general) should be kept at bay. The opposite, the Jews in Israel of European background, are, like the West, civilized and ethical. Under the threat of barbarism, Israel needs the support of the West.

Said's argument is much broader than the Israeli-Palestinian conflict, and he often separated the two. Yet his own background as a Palestinian and his increasing fame as a speaker and writer on the conflict made it impossible to divide his work so neatly. With the first Palestinian uprising, Said became the foremost Palestinian commentator in the United States, indeed internationally. As was often the case in this conflict, he was also infamous. There seemed to be no way to be one without the other.

His book *The Question of Palestine* became an instant classic and for good reason. In it, Said analyzes the search for a Palestinian identity in historical and philosophical terms. Part of this search is an independent one—who Palestinians are as a people within the context of the birth of new nations after colonialism. The other part lies within the context of the formation of Israel as a state on Palestinian land—what Palestinians can say about themselves in this situation of loss and occupation.

Said thus locates Palestinians within the broader currents of world history and the more narrow confines of the Israeli-Palestinian conflict. The situation is further complicated by the fact that while a significant number of Palestinians remain within what is now Israel and what might one day become a Palestinian state, Palestinians are also dispersed outside of Israel and Palestine, in the Arab world, and also in Europe, Latin America, the United States, and Australia. Palestinians within their historic homeland and in the Diaspora must struggle together to find their identity as a people.

Like most important authors, Said states the obvious that has yet to be articulated: Israel was not created on vacant land, nor is the Israeli-Palestinian conflict between a historic people and an indigenous collection of individuals without a history or identity. In short, Said writes as a member of and on behalf of a people who, like Jews, have a history and, again like Jews, have a stake in the land. In denying the possibility of a Palestinian identity, Israel and Jews in the Diaspora deny the authenticity of the Palestinian struggle against occupation to create their own state. In fact, from the Palestinian side, it is Jews and Israelis who have to prove their case for belonging to the land and justify taking over Palestinian land and identity.

For the first time in print and in English, Israel and its supporters, Jewish and non-Jewish, were faced with a powerful assertion of the wrong that had been committed against a nation and a people. The Palestinian people also had a right to their place in the world. They had a right to struggle for that place and in fact were obligated to do so.

Said's book offered a Commanding Voice. Like Emil Fackenheim's 614th commandment, the commandment emanating from the Holocaust to survive and to flourish, Said brought to Palestinians within their history a mandate for their future. There are many differences, of course, between Said and the proponents of Jewish Holocaust theology. Though Christian in background, Said was a confirmed secularist and abjured religion except as a cultural force. Unlike Fackenheim and the other Holocaust theologians, there is no struggle with God in Said's writing. Rather, the struggle is to constantly create a humanism worthy of the name.

For Said, the failures we experience as humans are our own. In the present context, the loss of Palestine is a human failure and a diminution of Palestinians and the larger human community. The re-creation of Palestine is a human endeavor that will enhance both.

Said makes no special claim for the Palestinians, and here again he counters the Jewish understanding of chosenness. The Palestinians are rooted in Palestine as any collective has roots in a particular place. Palestinians can make no claim beyond that. Nor can any other people. Jews can and have developed a particular sensibility about themselves. However, they cannot use that against others. Even Jewish suffering, a suffering that Said affirmed and was sympathetic to, cannot be used to justify the dispersion of another people. The complications of any people's journey must be worked out internally and in fraternity with others. No one community is special, at least not any more special than other communities.

Said claimed a people's dimension to Palestinian history because of their communal experience in the land through history. A culture had developed that was distinctively Palestinian. Since the world denies this distinctiveness, and because of the recent loss of their homeland, Palestinians are also in danger of losing their identity. The present struggle against occupation is not to negate Israel. Rather, it is an attempt, in a difficult situation and exigent circumstances, to find again who Palestinians are as a community.

Yet Said counsels against thinking that any identity, including Palestinian—and by extension Jewish—is fixed. It is this very notion of a fixed identity, an essentialism regarding Jewish identity, that has been used as the intellectual and emotional justification to drive Palestinians out of their own homeland. Palestinians have to struggle against this Jewish essentialism. However, if in this struggle Palestinians adopt the same understanding of their own identity, they endanger their own moral and ethical standards, imposing upon themselves the very trappings of essentialism they struggled against in its expression in the state of Israel.

An identity that is in flux adapts to different situations and, while retaining some foundational aspects, assimilates new cultures and religions without fear of being dominated by any of them. For Said, the challenge of a Jewish and Israeli culture on Palestinian land is one that has to be joined as other challenges of cultural and religious intrusion have been met in the long history of Palestine. In the end, Palestinians, but also by implication Jews, should see the present as an impetus toward integration and transformation rather than positing two immovable forces that cancel out each other. At this point the victory of either community can only lead to disaster, politically and culturally.

The flux of communal identity opens the possibility of dissent. Indeed, as I read Said, I was also finding an entire history of Jewish dissent that had never been gathered into a conceptual framework. The world as a whole knew little about this dissent, and Jews in particular knew even less. I found most of the material buried in out-of-print memoirs and writings that once had an audience until they were buried under the avalanche of Holocaust remembrance and unquestioned support for Israel.

Dissent on the Question of Zionism

I appreciated the form of dissent articulated by Roberta Feuerlicht and Earl Shorris, both writing in response to the Lebanon war in the 1980s. Now I was drawn back into history to explore other dissenting voices.

While Martin Buber's sense of mystery in *I and Thou* had been absorbed into the Jewish mainstream, his stance on Israel and the Palestinians had been neglected. In his time, Buber argued the need for a Jewish home in Palestine. He argued this before his forced emigration in 1938 from Germany to Jerusalem and after his arrival in Jerusalem until the formation of Israel in 1948. After the formation of Israel, which he accepted as fact rather than ideal, Buber hoped for a reconciliation of Jews and Arabs in a binational state or in a confederation framework.

From the turn of the twentieth century, Buber was a Zionist. Yet the Zionism he espoused was an alternative to state Zionism. Buber's Zionism valued Palestine as the historic homeland of the Jewish people and as the cultural and spiritual center of the Jewish people worldwide. It did not seek the status of a nation-state, and he was decidedly against the formation of a Jewish state. Rather, Buber thought the Jewish homeland should be situated in Palestine with the Arab population and encourage mutual relations and exchange. Otherwise, the possibility and hope of Palestine would be drowned in arms and bloodshed.

The nation-state was seen by Buber as a false community that revolved around a distorted spirituality. In true community, the spiritual center is embraced as a Thou. Therefore, there is a voluntary quality to community and a freely given assent. The spirit itself draws a community around it, and those so drawn together live a community life characterized by mutual respect and justice. In order to remain true to itself, the community is small in population but intense in terms of commitment. The material aspects of life are important and take on significance when oriented around the spiritual.

In terms of societal organization, Buber was a decentralist, regional thinker. He was ambivalent toward the emerging industrial global economic order. For Jews to be involved in the modern enterprise of state building and economic industrialism would be to assimilate to the world. Buber saw this as following and becoming like other nations. Jews have always been called to be different, unlike the other nations. With the ongoing experience of the violence of nations, did Jews really want to be part of this world order?

Jewish survival was indeed a question, and Buber argued that Jews could not witness to the nations without a homeland. That homeland only made sense in the historic homeland of the Jewish people, where the people Israel was formed and where the formative experiences of the Jewish people took place. Buber's ideals were constantly under attack, contested by the ongoing World War II, Arab resistance, and Jewish projects for statehood. Nonetheless, he stood firm. What was at stake was nothing less than Jewish destiny.

If the reality around him was violent, it did not keep Buber from thinking and acting. As a scholar, Buber wrote long essays on a variety of topics ranging from the Bible to the history of ideas. As an activist, he wrote manifestos and broadsides. He did not mince words, and his most biting attacks came against Jewish leadership in Palestine. He was specific in his targets, naming names and events. When, in the war to create the Jewish state, a massacre of Arabs was carried out at Deir Yassin, he condemned it as a "stain" on Jewish history.

After the creation of Israel, Buber regularly lectured the political leaders of the state on their violation of ethics and morality. He did this in writing and in person. A memorable event, recorded for posterity, was the debate Buber had with the first prime minister of Israel, David Ben-Gurion. Among other things, Buber reprimanded Ben-Gurion for Israel's refusal to allow Arab refugees to return to what was now Israel. Were we not once refugees ourselves? Buber asked. He even lectured those outside the Jewish community, including Mahatma Gandhi, who in 1938 had counseled non-violent resistance to the Nazi regime.

Another Jewish dissenter came to my attention, this time an American rabbi, Judah Magnes. Though not nearly as well known or accomplished as Buber, Magnes became the first chancellor of Hebrew University. Like Buber, Magnes was a spiritual Zionist who saw Palestine, and especially Jerusalem, as necessary to reinvigorate Jewish identity and the Jewish contribution to humanity. As an American, Magnes did not know the desperate sense of loss of place that Buber and other European Jews were experiencing.

Magnes came to Palestine because, in his view, the Jewish witness in the world was on the verge of taking another positive step. Like Buber, Magnes believed that Palestine was important as a center for Jews, but he had a more positive sense of the reciprocal relationship of the Jewish community in Palestine and other Jewish communities around the world. Instead of one detracting from the other, the Jewish homeland in Palestine and the Diaspora are interdependent. One without the other is less than both together.

Magnes was also a binationalist. He believed that Jews and Arabs should live together in Palestine and that the creation of a Jewish state would unnecessarily and inappropriately divide the Jewish and Arab communities. Just before his death in 1948, Magnes traveled to Washington, D.C., and personally lobbied Secretary of State Marshall and President Truman in hopes that the American government would refuse to recognize the coming declaration of an independent Jewish state. Among other things, Magnes argued that instead of such recognition, President Truman should send American troops to Jerusalem to prevent the division of Jerusalem and the Holy Land.

Magnes's private meetings with the secretary of state and the president were bold in their content and moving in the pleas he made. As strong was his article in the important and widely read journal *Foreign Affairs*. Here he argued for a federation of the Arab countries that would include Palestine and the Jewish homeland within it. In this article, Magnes counseled that time was running out for a Middle East affected by post–World War II stability. Time was also ticking for the hope that Jewish settlement in Palestine would be beneficial for Jews and others.

The reasons to keep silent in Buber's and Magnes's time were plentiful. The Holocaust was taking place. After the Holocaust, the security of the Jewish community in Palestine was tenuous. The creation of Israel was only recently achieved, and Israeli military dominance, needed to maintain the state, was nowhere near what it would become in the ensuing decades. Could direct, unequivocal dissent be afforded in that context? The lobbying of non-Jews, especially in political positions that had the power to affect the outcome of the creation and sustenance of Israel, could be seen as bordering on treason.

The Jewish tradition of dissent is only briefly alluded to in *The Question of Palestine*. Yet Said's sense of identity formation as fluid with only loosely defined borders contrasts directly with both Buber and Magnes. While both consider the need for Jewish integration into the Middle East as essential, neither considers the possibility of that integration moving beyond relations with collectives.

Though Buber and Magnes see Jews as set apart, they did not see this as divisive. Nowhere in their writings or public statements do they subscribe to a citizenship for Arabs and Jews in Palestine that compromises the particularity of the Jewish community. However, despite their pleas for the end of Jewish violence and concern for the Arabs of Palestine, they did not see Jews and Arabs as equal. Both Magnes and Buber saw the Jewish presence in the Middle East as a force for uplift in a backward area of the world. In short, both had a colonial mentality. In Said's parlance, both were Orientalists.

The combination of Buber and Magnes being quite progressive—radical from our perspective—and Orientalist is intriguing. It also provides a warning to Jews that even placing our best foot forward on Israel demands a critical dialogue partner outside our community. This warning is compounded with something even more disturbing. How many Jewish leaders today know of Buber's resistance to the creation of a Jewish state? How many understand his reasons for that opposition? At least Buber's name is known. When I mention Judah Magnes to Jews, I am usually met with a blank stare. In one encounter, a local Jewish federation accused me of making up these names and positions.

The Limits of Jewish Progressives

It was through the published results of my research on Jewish dissent that I met Edward Said. After reading an excerpt from my book in a Palestinian-American journal, he wrote me a short letter telling me how much he appreciated my ideas.

A few months later I met him in person at an event sponsored by an Arab-American group in Chicago. Said was a handsome and charismatic man, and when he arrived at the dinner to address the mostly Palestinian audience, he was greeted like royalty. I watched as he entered the hall. People hushed and made way for him. They were caught between wanting to rush and greet him and feeling they were in the presence of a man who, out of respect, should not be approached.

That night he spoke of his travels to South Africa, at that time still locked in the struggle against apartheid. By then it was apparent that the apartheid regime would fall soon; it was only a matter of time. For those in the anti-apartheid struggle, the Palestinians represented a still-embattled people who mirrored their own struggle.

Said was greeted as a world leader, an intellectual who articulated the hopes and aspirations of his own people. For the Palestinians, Said was in the same league as the soon-to-be-released Nelson Mandela. Said was fascinated with the people he met in South Africa and inspired by their disciplined struggle. Did this hold out hope for the Palestinians? Would the South Africans and Palestinians be liberated together?

In our conversations through the years, it was clear that Said had a great respect for Jewish dissent. It pained him that the Jewish community, so known for thought and analysis, had become so "stupid" on the issue of Palestine. Said understood the horror of the Holocaust and often lectured Palestinian and Arab audiences on their need to recognize the Holocaust and the Jewish fears that sprang from the history of anti-Semitism. In some Palestinian and Arab venues, this theme struck a discordant note. Regardless, Said persevered. He did not want to repeat the denial of the other that had so negatively impacted his own people.

In our meetings, I never experienced a tinge of anti-Semitism. His anger was about the displacement of his own people and the devastation it had caused. He wanted it to stop and for Jews and Israel to admit the wrong that had occurred. At the same time, he continually warned his own people that anti-Semitism was the path of people who refused to think. It was a dead end emotionally, philosophically, and ethically. He abhorred anti-Semitism. When anyone within his hearing approached that level, he quickly and forcefully condemned it.

Yet he could also pursue Jews who legitimated the diminution of Palestine and Palestinians. Foremost among his targets were Michael Walzer, the Jewish ethicist, and other Jewish liberals who wrote about the ethical imperative and conveniently justified Israel's behavior against the Palestinians. Said's ability to embrace and also criticize Jews was a complexity many Jews chose to ignore. Because Said wrote little about Jews and because of the general Jewish prejudice against Palestinians, most Jews knew only of his criticism. Said was a target; never before had the post-

Holocaust Jewish narrative been challenged with a competing Palestinian narrative. The prejudice toward Palestinians included an assertion that Palestinians lacked intellectual ability. With Said, Jews and others had met their match.

In my own experience, I came to understand Said's impatience with Jews who posited ethics in theory and practice yet excused Jews and Israel from both, or as was more often the case, those who developed an ethical theory that excused Israel or defined Israel's behavior as an allowable diversion from ethical theory. This was Said's criticism of Walzer, the veracity of which I experienced directly.

I met Michael Walzer before I read Said's ongoing and combative discourse about him. It was in Jerusalem, in 1987, and he chose to offer a diatribe against an as yet unpublished book on a Jewish theology of liberation. He was so angry that he was shaking throughout his response. For Walzer, Jews were the oppressed. In his mind, we are still oppressed today.

This approach was undercut when Said, in response to Walzer's take on the Exodus narrative, identified himself as a Canaanite. Though the Jewish story is powerful and full of complexities, Said points out that there are also victims of that story then and now. Said demands his and his people's place in the narrative, that their voice be heard rather than suppressed, and that a counternarrative be raised. Said wanted to give voice to the victims of the Exodus narrative in the biblical story and in the creation of the state of Israel.

Clearly, Walzer wasn't listening to Said or to me. Walzer, like Hartman, had become a darling of the Christian liberal establishment. After hearing Walzer's response to me, I thought that his warning was addressed more to Christians who might find my thought attractive than it was to me. I was quite young, and Walzer was a seasoned and respected scholar. Perhaps his outburst was a warning to Christians and an attempt to shut me down. After his onslaught, perhaps I would change my analysis, cutting off the rough edges or, because I was fearful of the consequences, stop speaking and writing on the issue. Whatever his intention, his response did alert me to the assumptions of much of contemporary Jewish thought. He was clearly out of touch with the facts on the ground—in the Middle East and in his own life.

In light of Said's sparring with Jewish intellectuals, two more progressive Jews, the brothers Boyarin, Jonathan and Daniel, challenged Said to a dialogue. Though neither was an ardent Zionist, they argued that the Jewish narrative undergirding Israel could be moved in different directions, perhaps one day toward peace and justice. They argued that while Palestinian suffering legitimated Said's argument, both sides of the conversation should be respected and given their integrity.

Said's response was as forceful and as critical as his response to Walzer. The Boyarins' plea to leave the Jewish narrative intact asserted a symmetry between the Jewish and Palestinian narratives. While the Boyarins assumed this was a positive step, Said argued that without equality on the ground, a proposal of equal narratives is only a subterfuge, one possibly more dangerous than the assertion of Jewish superiority. With the assertion of superiority, Palestinians know where they stand. A surmised equality with no basis in reality is disarming and therefore dangerous.

Said's response to the Boyarins served a larger purpose. He was putting Jewish progressives who separated themselves from Jewish liberals on notice that their own analysis was wanting. For Jewish progressives, Palestinians have been wronged—though this wrong is limited to the occupation and settlement of the Palestinian territories won in the 1967 war. Israel is at fault. Jewish liberals argue from the perspective of Israel as a liberal state that should not engage in illiberal policies like the occupation of the West Bank and Gaza. Israel is justified and good, but the occupation is sapping its strength and moral standing in the world. In a sense, the occupation is beneath Israel's ethical standards. Of course, the Palestinians are mostly at fault for not immediately and completely embracing the idea of a Jewish state. Still, Israel should rise above this opposition to resume the Jewish ethical standard.

Jewish progressives criticized the liberal position because they thought it was an attempt by the Jewish establishment to hold back criticism of Israel and stake a position on the moral high ground without engaging in real action to solve the problem. The progressive position is more critical, at least from their perspective. The occupation and settlement of Palestinian land after the 1967 war are wrong. The policies of the Israeli government to destroy the Palestinian uprising are wrong. Pretending that the Palestinians are always and everywhere at fault is misleading. The pretense that Palestinians, while existing as individuals, do not have a collective will and destiny is an example of Jewish leadership placing their heads in the sand. A new engagement is necessary with the Palestinian people.

Are these positions so different? Said thought not, and having been asked into the dialogue by the Boyarins, Said relished pointing this out. In the end, both positions were patronizing toward the Palestinian people and would, if unchecked, lead more or less to the same political situation. Certainly this had been true over the last decades. The internal arguments between Jewish liberals and Jewish progressives had yielded nothing but more misery for the Palestinians. If Jews were going to change course, Said felt that a deeper engagement was essential. Meanwhile, the Palestinian uprising was being crushed. Palestinians were being imprisoned by the thousands. The number of martyrs grew by the day.

Constantinian Judaism Triumphant

As the failings of Oslo became clear, my feelings of separation and isolation deepened. Critics of my work operated from a predictable perspective that, in my view, trivialized the Holocaust by trivializing the suffering of the Palestinians. They were so outraged by the very challenge to their categories that their ability to reason, even to have a measured civil disagreement, was impaired.

Said was a voice of sanity for me, and perhaps because I saw him infrequently, our meetings took on a special poignancy. I recall being with him at a conference in Paris that he chaired and his curiosity about a book I had coedited that featured Palestinian Christians speaking their stories about suffering and hope. As a determined secularist, Said had little time for religion, but as our small group gathered around the seminar table for further discussion, he kept paging through the book while I spoke. Later when I finished, I asked him if he would like my copy, and when he nodded eagerly, I placed it before him. I wondered then if the great cosmopolitan intellectual might be interested in recovering part of his own Christian roots.

In 1997, after Said was diagnosed with a life-threatening illness, a deeper connection evolved. One day I received a letter asking me to lecture at a conference honoring him. Though Said would battle his illness for years to come, it was then thought probable that he would die soon after the conference was over. He was standing in the back of the room when I announced the title of my lecture: "Edward Said and the Future of the Jewish People." That a Jew would honor Said might be in the realm of the possible. One might relate Said's thought as a critic of Israel and thus to Jewish history as Jews embody it. But could Said be seen as a fellow traveler, as one who accompanies Jews into the future, helping correct and even guide us?

My own sense was that Said functioned as a contemporary prophet for Jews, warning us that our newfound power had become a form of idolatry and that the reduction of Palestinians to permanent refugees and to homelessness that precluded their continuance as a culture and a people violated Jewish ethics and justice. Isn't this the message, albeit directed at the internal workings of the people Israel, of the prophets? And since through the return of Jews to Palestine and the formation of the state of Israel we had created injustice for the people of the land, aren't Palestinians now, in a practical and ethical way, part of Jewish history and polity?

Though ostensibly outside the Jewish community, Said was speaking from within. He was a victim of Jewish power yet living among Jews in New York City and traveling with Jews around the world. Like dissenting Jews, he was feeling the brunt of an empowered Judaism in America and Israel; he also was working and in solidarity with Jews of Conscience. Constantinian Jews and Jews of Conscience were locked in a civil war, and Said was on the mind of both sides. Over the years Said became indispensable to the Jewish civil war. In this case he was a fellow traveler, perhaps even an honorary Jew.

As we moved toward the twenty-first century, I began to meet Jews of Conscience all over the world. A division could be seen within the Progressive Jewish movement between those Jews like Michael Lerner and Arthur Waskow who had led opposition to some of these policies, and other Jews who felt that such opposition was covertly a part of the support for the main thrust of Israeli policy. Jews of Conscience were beginning to drop the balancing act that characterized progressive Jewish movements, on the one hand criticizing Israeli policy and on the other insisting that Palestinians were also wrong, their leadership corrupt, and their radicals in need of discipline.

With the al-Aqsa uprising that broke out in September 2000, the Jewish narrative took another turn. A civil war broke out within the Jewish opposition. Jews of Conscience began to realize that the stakes were higher, the issues more serious, and that the leadership of the progressive movement was suspect. They felt the very heart of contemporary Jewish life to be corrupt in a way that transcended the chasm between the establishment and anti-establishment sides. An increasing number of Israelis began to voice these perspectives as well.

Said was part and parcel of this civil war on the Jewish left, moving easily and in step with Jews of Conscience. One of the elements of this split was the realization that making Judaism and Jewish history central to the discussion of Israel/Palestine was itself a mistake or, with the passing of time, an archaic fall-back position. Israel is established as a Jewish state. Does the continuing expansion of the state have anything to do with things Jewish or simply the injustices that all nation-states, when they have the opportunity, partake in?

Is Israel—now—a special case that needs special pleading, or is the assertion of special status part of the problem? If, as Palestinians insist, human and political rights are universal, Israel can be indicted, indeed chastised and punished, like any other nation. Is this the end of the public and private sense that as Jews we are somehow different? Now Israel, shorn of its halo, stood only slightly higher than the corruption surrounding it. By 2000, even this small distinction was challenged. And this was before the election of Ariel Sharon as prime minister. It was before the use of helicopter gunships against defenseless Palestinian refugee camps, towns, and cities. It was before the building of the Wall that surrounds and ultimately will ghettoize Palestinians in the West Bank.

With the Wall—composed also of barriers and fences and built in the West Bank so Israelis can live normal lives there as the injustice continues—the assertion of Israel as a refuge for Jews or a light unto the nations, even its relation to the Holocaust, is gone. But how does one argue Jewishness without the category of uniqueness, however that is defined? From the beginning of Jewish history, chosenness has been central to Jewish identity. Over time, chosenness had been defined and redefined in a variety of ways, often depending on the situation that Jews found themselves in. Though the initial sense of chosenness found in the Torah seems straightforward, in fact it was already being contested. Were Jews chosen to be an established and powerful nation, or were they chosen to embody a society of justice that would become a beacon to the nations around them?

The entry into the land heightened the stakes of this internal struggle over self-definition. When the time of Jewish sovereignty ended at the beginning of the Common Era, the question of chosenness assumed a new and almost frightening level. If part of Jewish chosenness is to inhabit a land promised by God to the people Israel, was this promise now abrogated? Were the chosen now unchosen?

The rabbis argued that, though seemingly contradicted by the geographic and political reality of dispersion, the initial promise held. Undeniably difficult and with many hardships ahead, the Diaspora itself was the other side of chosenness; it was a time of waiting and understanding what might bring us back to the land. In our time, chosenness has been reinterpreted in the context of Holocaust and Israel. Jews are singled-out in suffering and in the creation of a Jewish state. This singled out condition is in line with Jewish history, and like that history, the Holocaust and Israel are unparalleled.

But through the 1990s, the singularity of this condition was challenged. Palestinians asked these questions out of existential need, as the narrative of chosenness reduces their claims as an equal and beleaguered people. If Jews occupy the high ground, then the occupation of the Palestinians, both in the inception of the state of Israel and today, can be justified. For Palestinians to fight the occupation of their land is therefore also heightened to a battle of the people of God against those who defy God. This is why their struggle is defined as terrorist when the aggression against them could easily be seen as legitimate.

I knew that Said was correct on this issue. Whatever Jews wanted to think about themselves, they could not use that self-identification against others, in this case the Palestinians. Chosenness is a religious marker for Jews; it cannot be used to justify a political program. Clearly Jews accept this principle when used against us. It is difficult to find a Jew who accepts the Christian self-designated mission to affirm a Christian America or even the use of law to coerce non-Christians to listen to Christian prayers. The religious sensibilities we abhorred when they were used against us, we now employed for our own political aspirations.

I was entering a conundrum. Could I affirm that Jews were indeed chosen but that this chosenness had to be disciplined in the political realm? Or was it the marker of Jewishness to use this designation, however articulated or disguised?

This struggling was intensified by the question of conspiracy. It seems that the question of chosenness and the idea of conspiracy are twinned in the public mind. To almost any Jew, this sounds like a modern equivalent of medieval anti-Semitism. Jews are everywhere and in cahoots, especially when they work for their own self-interest and disguise it as public good. As I often heard it on the lecture circuit, Jews are in control and controlling against the best interests of the general population. The cleverness of the Jews makes it possible for such a small minority to manipulate and deceive the majority. Jews are powerful, and they use that power for their own benefit. Don't Jews control the media and the Congress? How else could one explain the amount of money given to Israel vis-à-vis other, needier countries? And how could one explain the silence on Israel's transgressions except through Jewish control of the media, the economy, and American political life?

Over the years, I have encountered these conspiracy theories in different parts of the world—especially related to Jewish "influence" in history and today. In the post-9/11 world, they seem to be everywhere. This is true in parts of the Arab world. In 2006, when I traveled to the American University of Cairo, I was surrounded by conspiracy theories about Jewish control of the world and claims that suffering in the Holocaust was exaggerated. Sometimes in European and American movements supporting Palestinian rights, I find the same understandings. At times it is blatant, other times hidden from view. People who seem quite rational and cordial are all of a sudden visiting Holocaust deniers in prison. Errant e-mails surface speaking of "J-town," ostensibly short for "Jerusalem" but intended as

"Jewtown." Biblical theorists, such as the late Michael Prior, trumpet the violence of the "Old" Testament and blame Christianity's colonialism on Torah texts. I have known political scientists who refer to a particular member of the United States Senate as "our senator from Tel Aviv."

I grew weary of responding. There is no Jewish conspiracy. Yet to deny Jewish influence is absurd. Of course this influence is earned and exercised within the full parameters of democracy open to all persons. Though my answer was rational, I began to realize that there was also an anger behind it. In the end, it was defensive, in part hiding behind a rhetoric that was increasingly outmoded. I was also shielding the Jewish community even as I was criticizing it, holding it open to critique yet also deflecting that criticism. I was not ready to say, and in a definitive way, that we were no better than any other people. If I admitted that not only for this present time but for all time—that given the same contexts we are no better than any other religion or community—my ability to articulate Jewishness might come to an end.

In a sense, this is where Edward Said was heading, and Jews of Conscience had little choice but to admit he was correct. Those who say no to oppression have to say no to each and every case, and those who say yes to justice and ethics have to confront the claim of specialness that divides one from another.

I was being persecuted by the very same Jewish power that others were calling conspiratorial. I felt it at every turn of my own life. And yet there were Jews who considered that what I was thinking and writing confirmed their own sensibilities. While sharing ideas and ideals with all who seek justice, there remains a particular sense, a Jewish sensibility, a conviction that I and other Jews have found almost a homecoming within a deepening exile.

I realize that any such homecoming can only occur within exile. Without a home there can be no exile. A sense of homecoming, no matter how brief and contested, implies an enduring connection. Perhaps it is Constantinian Jews who have left the essentials of Jewish life, and Progressive Jews, arguing the details of dissent within the Constantinian framework, have also left.

I wonder if Jews of Conscience might be a remnant, destined either to disappear or to become the nucleus of a new community. I also wonder if Jews of Conscience will give rise to a new community and whether that community will identify as Jewish, or whether their ideas and aspirations might simply merge with others of like mind, forgoing an identifying marker or perhaps creating a new one.

Does it matter if the designation "Jewish" is lost? If it survives and even flourishes in its Constantinian sensibility, which no doubt it will, does that represent a triumph?

An Unusual Rabbinic Ordination

One of my last meetings with Said was that fateful Jerusalem conference in 1998 where I debated Rabbi Abraham Milgrom about the contemporary meaning of the biblical Jubilee and saw my Palestinian friend Naela Ayaed for the last time before she was murdered.

Despite his adamantly professed secularity, in several articles Said had referred to me as a rabbi. Then just before the Jerusalem conference, in a speech broadcast on a progressive radio station in New York, I again heard Said refer to me as a Jew of Conscience and with the title Rabbi Ellis.

Each time I read or heard this designation, I was mildly surprised and secretly delighted. Increasingly over the years, that designation had been applied to me without my knowledge and sometimes after I specifically told the person I was not a rabbi. This constant appellation started a thought process within me. What does it mean to be a rabbi? Is it simply a case of ordination? Ordained rabbis are often silent on the injustices we are now committing and even attempt to silence dissenting Jews. Are they rabbis?

Said forced my reflection to another level. However, it did pose a problem. I did not want others to think that I was posing as a rabbi. So, knowing that I would see Said at the conference, I was determined to correct his understanding. I had to tell him that I was not a rabbi.

I first saw him at a distance. He was being introduced to speak, and I could see that his physical condition had deteriorated significantly from a few years earlier. In fact, at the conference he looked worse than he did in the year before he died. His illness had made him susceptible to colds and flus, so he had been advised to simply deliver his lecture and leave. Human contact made him vulnerable.

I gave up on the idea of speaking to him about such a mundane matter. In fact, I didn't think I would have any personal contact with him at all. And then through happenstance, our paths crossed. He greeted me warmly and, despite the people around him who cautioned him about his health, took some time to talk with me.

After a few moments, I broached the issue. I thanked him for ordaining me to the rabbinate but mentioned that in fact I am not a rabbi. Always the stickler for accuracy, Said apologized. Then he continued: "Marc," he said, "to me a rabbi seeks wisdom and speaks for justice, and you do that." He paused. "For me you are a rabbi."

And with that, Said, the handsome prince now gaunt and near death, the great secular thinker who, if the truth be known, hated religion, embraced me—as a person, a Jew, and a rabbi.

12

Reading the Torah Out Loud

Reclaiming the Text
in an Age When Israeli
Star of David Helicopter
Gunships Fly

Survival is necessary. It also carries its own demands. The prophetic in its religious and secular garb, employed for so long in Jewish life to criticize those who oppressed us, has diminished, the remnants disciplined. Jewish articulation continues apace in the service of community empowerment and, over the years, turns its ability to admonish those who offer a critical eye when that empowerment extends beyond our need for survival and begins to disempower others.

Reading the Torah and the prophetic writings, one can hardly escape the reality that the entire vocation of the people Israel is endangered by these external and internal threats and that, in the end, the internal violations could actually trigger the collapse of Israel and her deliverance to enemies. Anyone who reads the Exodus story or the later struggle over kingship or the still later words of Isaiah or Jeremiah must recognize that the judgment of God on Israel is an ever-present possibility.

After our arrival in the Bible Belt in the late 1990s, my oldest son, Aaron, came home from school one day and asked if we could read the Bible together. Because of my stances on Israel and the Palestinians, we found it difficult to participate in local synagogue life. Aaron had never attended Hebrew school and only occasionally synagogue services.

Nonetheless, and perhaps even more so because of this fact, our home was filled with discussions about the meaning of a Jewish life, often with guests prominent in theological circles that crossed international boundaries and religious affiliations. In the mornings, we prayed together as a family, and on Friday night we celebrated Shabbat with prayers, candle lighting, and a special meal. Yet, though the essentials of Judaism were emphasized, the reading of the Bible was lacking. In response to his query, I asked Aaron two questions: Did he want to read the entire Bible? And why did he want to read the Bible?

The answer to the first question was yes. The second had to do with discussions by his peers that almost constantly referred to biblical literature. I suspect there was a deeper curiosity as well, introduced by the culture around him that continually challenged why he was Jewish rather than Christian and the desire to get to the sources from which Judaism evolved. Perhaps he felt the need for a deeper grounding.

So we began, from the first words to the last, a marathon in which each night I read page after page to a youngster who prodded me on when I was tired and especially when I thought he might have had enough of the Bible for the evening. As with any new adventure, the enthusiasm of beginning soon reaches a point where endurance is essential if the enterprise is to continue. I was worried that this point might be reached quickly, especially when we encountered the rough going of tribal relations, extensive lineage, and ritual detail surrounding the Tent of Meeting. These details are usually swept aside in standard compilations, but Aaron was keen on all of them. To my surprise, so was I.

Like all readers of the Bible, Aaron and I encountered it within our own context. It is in the era when Israeli Star of David identified helicopter gunships fly, controlling and displacing a defenseless people, and Jewish leadership demands the end of Jewish dissent. It is also the time when Jews of Conscience struggle toward articulation. It is the time of an ending and a new beginning.

Within empowerment, what was once a source of hope, the Torah—as I began to refer interchangeably to the Hebrew Bible as we started reading nightly—has become a battleground. There is an internal war over biblical interpretations between Settler Jews and Progressive Jews, each emphasizing aspects of the Torah narrative that buttress their own political positions. Could the Torah help Jews of Conscience move beyond the impasse that both Settler Jews and Progressive Jews represent?

Much of this posturing neglects a central aspect of Jewish life, the covenant. The covenant has grown to be an important category in my own life and reflection. What can we say about the covenant in our brokenness and in our power, especially in the abuse of that power? Jews of Conscience, most of whom make no religious claims at all, are, at least in my understanding, embodiments of the covenant. Do religious folk have it all wrong, assigning the unassignable to themselves and claiming what cannot be claimed as if they own the covenant?

Is There Violence at the Heart of the Jewish Covenant?

Part of the violence among those who claim the covenant seems to revolve around a need to secure it, as if the covenant can be owned. In this way the Bible is the deed of ownership. But since those who originally claimed the ultimate powerful God, Egypt, were blinded by the advent of this covenant with the Israelites, another unexpected appearance could occur, challenging the claim of the covenant through the question of justice.

Irving Greenberg and his investigation of the Third Era of Jewish history raise important questions about God and the covenant. There is a movement from the silence of God in the Rabbinic Era to horror in the Third Era. Since there is little speculation about God in the Jewish tradition, God's silence is not decisive. Rather, it encourages questions about God, questions that take on meaning within an ongoing engagement with the covenant.

Greenberg sees the rabbis' call to increased covenantal responsibility as an affirmation of the human drama. A deep agnosticism is one of the beauties of the Jewish tradition. At least at the time that I began writing on the covenant, agnosticism allowed me room to affirm being Jewish without having to make a decision about God. Could it be that once in history, the covenant, a *traveling* covenant, was not only free to roam where it needed to but also free of God?

The Third Era of Jewish history, with the establishment of a Jewish state, calls for the end of wandering. In light of Emil Fackenheim's introduction of survival and support for the empowerment of Israel as the 614th commandment, to call for a new wandering is to court excommunication.

Could there also be excommunication for the violence of ethical standards, such as demolishing Palestinians' homes, assassinating their elected political leaders, and firing missiles into crowded civilian areas? To do this we would need a 615th commandment: Thou shalt not demean the Palestinian people.

Each night before bed, Aaron and I settled onto our living room couch and read the Torah (in the beautiful Jewish Publication Society translation).

Unfamiliar with the text, Aaron picked up on the obvious uncorrected parts of the narrative, beginning with the two creation accounts in Genesis.

God's demand that Abraham should sacrifice Isaac and God's wrath in the destruction of Sodom and Gomorrah—accompanied by complete submission to the will of God and by a fierce and stubborn argument about God's understanding of justice—are softened by the promise to Abraham and Sarah that, despite their years, they are to conceive a child.

The reversals are many, and the God who promises Abraham a land and a nation delivers, although with many twists and turns. Aaron found the stories fascinating: Abraham's passing Sarah off as his sister; the struggle between the brothers Jacob and Esau; Jacob's wrestling with God until dawn.

The story of Joseph is captivating. His interpretation of dreams and his ability, as a foreigner, to develop a master plan for the survival of Egypt in a time of plenty and then famine are patterns that run through Jewish history. But the great drama of Joseph's life, before and after his rise to power in Egypt, is his reconciliation with his brothers and father. Though successful in Egypt, he remains, at least in his own mind, a foreigner; his last request is that his remains be taken from Egypt and buried near his father in the Promised Land. Yet Joseph's success—paradoxical for the reader, in the narrative providential—sets the stage for the increase of the Israelite population, their eventual enslavement, and the reappearance of God in their struggle for liberation.

That struggle consumes the bulk of the Torah, and the drama, already intense in the birth of a people and the record of its sojourn, intensifies. Aaron found these stories of liberation more complex than the Passover recitations. They were exhilarating. They were also troubling. God seems absent from the scene and then suddenly reappears. As with Abraham in the confrontation over the righteous in Sodom and Gomorrah, God is independent, making his own judgments, at times listening and rethinking his conclusions by paying attention to the questions of justice and suffering.

God hears the cries of his people and reintroduces himself as the God of Abraham, Isaac, and Jacob; the text has God remembering his own promise to Abraham. Because of the suffering, God is reenergized. In the text, the God appearing in Egypt is the same God who spoke to Abraham. Yet Aaron asked the obvious question: Is this in fact the same God, or is the narrator bridging a gap in oral and now written history?

Like Abraham, Moses is stunned by God's address to him. In exile from the royal palace and his native Egypt, happily married, Moses receives God's message and the command that he return to his homeland and lead his people out of bondage. As in the earlier narratives, God is presented here as a complex figure, a bundle of contradictions exaggerated by his absolute power and his need to work through human beings.

Aaron was of course thrilled with the choice of his namesake to accompany and speak for Moses. Later, in the golden calf episode, Aaron is chastened, and my son felt let down. Yet as I pointed out to him, all of the biblical characters are flawed and fall short. Ahead of us, Moses is denied entry into the Promised Land, a denial that even the most sophisticated biblical scholars hardly justify.

Reading the Torah narrative out loud, I was determined not to intervene on behalf of God or the Israelites and not to preclude Aaron's questions or comments. When Moses descended from Mount Sinai only to find revelers around the golden calf and the slaughter of thousands of Israelites ensued, Aaron was upset with Moses and with God. He referred to the God of those passages as a "dictator God." I agreed.

Yet again the dictator God is followed by a God whom Moses challenges. This challenge is about justice. It is also about God's reputation and compassion. God threatens to wipe out the Israelites and begin again with Moses, now modeled on Abraham as the progenitor of a people. But what would liberation mean after such a slaughter? God would become a laughingstock, a scandal to his own power and purpose.

The covenant comes and goes in offering and acceptance. Initial covenants to Abraham and Noah are invoked, then suspended, appearing again in their own respective lifetimes and reappearing under somewhat different terms. God goes back and forth, and so do the people. Both obey and disobey the terms of the covenant, rendering the contract changeable.

Brilliantly, and of necessity, the rabbis tame this instability by distancing the voice of God. In the process, the prophetic quality of the narrative is reduced if not eliminated altogether. The very narrative Aaron and I were reading is safely tucked inside the Ark of the Covenant, covered with beautiful cloth and insignia. The ritual is replayed daily with prayers prayed before the Ark, then the Torah scroll is taken out, read in portions with the rabbi's commentary, then covered and placed back in the Ark with the appropriate prayers. Is there any religion that does not tame the prophetic, arguing that the prophetic *was* rather than *is*?

A Dark Vision

When I see the Torah scrolls in the Ark of the Covenant, I reflect on how the religious overtakes the prophetic. In an age of Star of David–identified helicopter gunships, it seems a form of idolatry to raise the Torah scrolls as a weapon against the prophetic need to challenge the community to justice. Each time I see the curtains of the Ark open, I envision that the Torah scrolls will be absent. After all, the covenant refuses to consort with injustice. Instead of the Torah scrolls, helicopter gunships must be in their stead. What we do, we worship.

During the time of our reading, I traveled to Manchester, England, for a series of lectures, and, unbeknownst to me, at the end of one of my lectures I was scheduled to attend Shabbat services at a local synagogue and then, at the meal afterward, speak to the congregation.

Toward the end of the day, a rabbi appeared carrying reams of papers purporting to analyze my positions on the Israeli-Palestinian conflict. After initially complimenting me on my prophetic stance, now he spoke about my distortions of Judaism and Israel and the unrepresentative status of my beliefs. Once in the synagogue, the rabbi and I were seated with the congregation facing the Ark, and I became fixated on it. For some reason I became absolutely convinced that when the curtains were open the Torah scrolls would be absent. In their place would be a helicopter gunship.

It was a dark vision. The helicopter gunship I imagined was shorn of its ugliness. Instead of its menacing look, with its protruding machine guns and missiles, it assumed a ritualistic gloss. In my imagination, it glistened with a fresh layer of silver paint. The helicopter gunship was worthy of veneration.

The congregation would be amazed as they laid eyes on this powerful object that secured Jewish identity in a menacing world. I was disappointed when my vision did not materialize.

When I speak of this dark vision, some find it troubling. Indeed it is. Is my vision more troubling than the behavior the vision illustrates? Of course the easiest way to banish this imagery is to change the policies that give rise to it.

In my view, transformed religious imagery is hardly restricted to Jews. I also envision the eucharistic wafer shaped like a nuclear weapon, or with special crusader imagery. Perhaps an alternating series of events in Christian history can be featured, the Crusades for sure, but also the slave trade, the colonialism of 1492, and beyond. And in the mosques, along with prayers for peace should be inscribed slogans of conquest and hate. Islam means to submit. Muslims can submit to a God of peace, but they also can submit to a God of violence and empire. While Muslims should not be singled out, they are not exempt. Why live one way and pray another? Shouldn't we pray what we are?

These images haunted me as Aaron and I continued to read the Torah out loud. To be fair, perhaps the Ark of the Covenant should have the Torah scrolls, a helicopter gunship, and symbols of Jewish contributions to civilization—art, literature, and medicine, for example—so the diversity of Jewish life is reflected there. This would broaden out the imagery and illustrate the choices we have made and could make again. The drama of the giving of the covenant in the form of the Decalogue—with various compositions presented at different times—is central, but the events after the people's acceptance of the covenant are equally important. And often disappointing.

I also had another vision, of our history after the Torah's inclusion in our liturgies. At the proper time we would read from the book of Exodus, but we would also read from the "book of Palestine." Like the book of Exodus, the history would be long and complicated with many twists and turns. Both books would include struggle and achievement. Both books would also include episodes we as Jews would rather bury and forget. The book of Palestine would include our long and difficult history in the land. It would also include our cleansing of the Palestinian Arabs, the extension of Israel, and the Wall that ghettoizes them. Of course I would suggest this also to Christians and Muslims, Christian reading alongside the New Testament what I would call the Historical Gospels: the "Gospel of Constantine," the "Gospel of 1492," the "Gospel of Colonialism," and the "Gospel of Treblinka."

Rebellion is never far from the surface, and God's anger is only assuaged by Moses' special pleading. The Israelites are tempted by the other tribes' indigenous religious systems. Still, Moses, through trial and tribulation, brings the tribes together around a memory of common suffering and mutual responsibility. The promise is a land flowing with milk and honey. Yet where is this land, and why the delay in arriving there?

Then, at last, the land comes into view. The inheritance is finally at hand. In a terrible twist, the generation that wandered in the desert is denied entry, and Moses, the great leader, is allowed only to glimpse the Promised Land. It is with Moses' last days that the epic journey in the wilderness—and the book of Deuteronomy—comes to an end.

Moses' last days are recorded in surprising detail, and his last words, a farewell testimony, are long and powerful. As it will be done by others in Jewish history, here for the first time in a pattern that remains to this day,

Moses recalls the entire history of Israel. That history is already shaped; it is articulated here in the form in which it will be remembered and passed on to the children generation after generation.

After reciting this history, Moses calls the people of Israel to his side and speaks: "Take to heart all the words with which I have warned you this day. Enjoin them upon your children, that they may observe faithfully all the terms of the Teaching. For this is not a trifling thing for you: it is your very life; through it you shall long endure on the land that you are to possess upon crossing the Jordan." And then, in the land of Moab, short of the Promised Land, Moses dies and is buried. He had been allowed to survey the land he would not enter.

On the steppes of Moab, the people mourn his passing for thirty days. Joshua, son of Nun, already anointed by God and Moses, will lead the Israelites into the land. Moses is gathered unto his people—a beautiful description of the meaning of death in the Torah—and buried. As Deuteronomy tells it, Moses is buried in a place that is unknown to the people, then and now. Linking Moses with the exodus from Egypt and citing his intimate relationship with God, the Torah seals the prophetic: "Never again did there arise in Israel a prophet like Moses—whom the Lord singled out, face to face, for the various signs and portents that the Lord sent him to display in the land of Egypt, against Pharaoh and all his courtiers and his whole country, and for all the great might and awesome power that Moses displayed before all Israel."

That night, after finishing Deuteronomy with Aaron, I felt spent. As a child living in south Florida, I experienced ferocious hurricanes that are punctuated by the absolute, eerie stillness of the eye of the storm. It is precisely because the end of the biblical narrative is really only the beginning that the Torah is ultimately so powerful. If the narrative was not alive, if Moses had indeed been the last prophet, the readings would lack urgency and depth.

The Torah is more than an ancient classic text. The end of the Torah is like the eye of the storm. There is a before and an after. The sadness over the death of Moses—the very injustice of God's refusal to allow Moses to lead his people into the Promised Land—was highly charged for us as Jews. But what of the discontinuities in the Bible and beyond, the obvious editing and compiling of the text? The Bible is fragmented and unfinished. It is also complete. The power resides in its message and our encounter. Shakespeare pales in comparison, and Shakespeare's characters appear limited and circumscribed. With them the tragic element of life is the only crossroad to be faced. The biblical drama faces squarely that tragedy with a choice and a God who opens a future.

By reading the Torah out loud as a continuous narrative, we challenge ourselves and also the rabbinic interpretative model that informs Judaism. Though the breaking apart of the narrative informs the rabbinic tradition, it also limits the reach of the biblical story.

While the cultic aspects of Israel and the rabbis seek stability, in the Torah the journey is incomplete, the outcome still in doubt, so that even the settling of the covenant in the temple in Jerusalem seems precarious. After all, the commandments of the covenant are always shadowed by the people's abrogation of them, and the kings of Israel are constantly in danger from the prophets. David is confronted by Nathan, and later Isaiah and Jeremiah rail against—and even condemn—the monarchy and the people.

If the Deuteronomic announcement of the end of the prophetic is misplaced, the rabbinic placement of the Torah in the Ark of the Covenant in the synagogue is even more problematic and disturbing. The Torah scrolls locked in the synagogue can become the very locus of idolatry, the very possibility of which the original Tent of Meeting attempts to guard against.

Reading the Torah out loud reinforced some of my views on why Jews—especially Jews of Conscience—have fled the synagogue. What connection can these Jews, who embody aspects of the prophetic, feel with a Torah that, especially when read in the synagogue, is stripped of its volcanic irreverence for power and its emphatic disdain for the abuse of power?

The liberation of the Israelites is always shadowed by their failure to embrace their destiny. This is true because the *question* of liberation—what it means to be free, just, and within God's framework of life and destiny—is as central to the biblical narrative as the fact of liberation.

It was in the context of our reading the Torah out loud that Martin Buber's understandings of the Bible became relevant to me. In the end, they seem more important to me than either his understanding of Thou or his argument for a Jewish homeland in Palestine. Perhaps better stated, Buber's conception of the Bible is key to these other understandings. It is the basis for his understanding of God and the land and the encounter that both presume if the genuine spirit of the people Israel, a spirit so important to Jews and to the world, is to be renewed.

For Buber, the moments of relation between God and the person, God and Israel, recorded in the Torah are models for our own encounters today, so that the Torah is neither definitive nor a source for truth or dogma. But religion can substitute the encounters of the Torah for our own, thus excusing us from the task of encountering the world ourselves. Excused from our uncertainty, we are unable to move forward.

Religion teaches us that we should look to the Bible for success, yet every movement and major figure of the Bible is, more or less, a failure. Yet for Buber, worldly "failure" is the secret route to redemption. This is especially true of the prophets. The tender mercies promised an errant people upon their return to justice and God are deeply rendered because the failure is evident. Isn't this the reason the prophetic announcement of Israel's reconciliation with God is always to come about in the future?

Even then the reconciliation is fraught with anxiety. Moses' last statement makes this proclamation as strong as is found in any part of the Torah. Announcing his imminent death and the mourning that will follow, Moses yet predicts the shortcomings of his people. It is, as Buber rightly notes, a decision that is before the people: "See, I set before you this day life and prosperity, death and adversity. For I command you to this day, to love your God, to walk in his ways, and to keep his commandments, his laws, and his rules, that you might thrive and increase, and that the LORD your God may bless you in the land that you are about to enter and possess. But if your heart turns away and you give no heed, and are lured into the worship and service of other gods, I declare to you this day that you shall certainly perish; you shall not long endure on the soil that you are crossing the Jordan to enter."

When we read the Torah out loud, the journey of the Israelites is ours. Nevertheless, the Bible as end precludes our beginning. The prophet turns toward God and humanity, and though both the prophet and the people fail, there remains the chance to turn and begin again. At least for Buber, the turning is unmediated and without reward, except that in the turning the meaning of life is found. The choice to turn—and thus the choice to turn away—is before us. Our destiny always hangs in the balance.

But how can my own personal beginning—in the drama of a people, no less—be found in the Torah? I asked this question as Aaron and I ended Deuteronomy and began Joshua. How could this drama, for Buber an unending drama, be mine and not mine? How could I be there in the narrative and here reading it at the same time? How could the Torah be so compelling and not definitive? How could I enter the Torah and not be overwhelmed by it? In a way, I felt the biblical voice speaking to mine. Is that because I was reading the Torah out loud?

Is There Justice in the Land?

As we read, Aaron asked about the relevance of the seemingly endless specifications of atonement sacrifices and purity regulations of the Levitical codes. It was difficult to argue with his sense that we might skip them and rejoin the text of the wandering Israelites. What relevance did the tribal demarcations have, each positioned for entry into an allocated area of the Promised Land? Then there were the warnings throughout the Bible, increasing as the approach to the land drew near. The ominous possibility of the Israelites' becoming what they had left in Egypt or the Canaanite society they were entering is a dire threat.

This cycle of liberation, separation, possession, and the fulfillment of God's promise is shadowed by the possibility of exile, the Jewish equivalent of hell. The Promised Land is a place where purity is emphasized in detail, as the people Israel will encounter are themselves polluted. This is why the land is to be cleansed by Israel under God's leadership. It is a holy war that Israel is called to by God.

God's evolving nature through the Bible is a problem. Once Canaan is reached, the situation becomes so grave that the very annihilation of the people is threatened by God. For the most part, the tender encounters, even Jacob's wrestling with God, are a thing of the past. As Israel begins its journey into the wilderness and later enters the land, a militant God is at the lead. Rather than visitations with his chosen witnesses and leaders, he is now a disciplinarian who visits often in wrath. Nevertheless, God and justice are joined together in the land. Could I then, reading the Bible out loud, oppose the reentry into the land for which the modern state of Israel stands in the minds of many Jews?

The proponents of Israeli policy simply point to the land as promised to the Jews. The biblical narrative is clear on this question. The land is promised to the Israelites. The people already in the land have polluted it, and because of this they will be conquered and dispersed, if not annihilated. The land is being cleared, and Israel, with God's help, will clear the land for God's people. The clearing provides a territorial base for the fulfillment of Israel's destiny. However, there is tremendous difficulty ahead, as the purification of Israel and the land is fraught with the danger of human and pagan debasement. The clearing of the land is shadowed by the threat, invoked on numerous occasions and carried out on several, that because of its own violations, Israel will be cleared off the land. God will be in charge of that clearing and the prophets will announce it to the people.

When the certainty of the promise is announced by some Jews, especially the settlers in the West Bank, there is little mention of the corollary threat. The stakes are high. The motivation for Baruch Goldstein and Yigal Amir comes from these biblical sources and from rabbinic interpretations that highlight these sensibilities. If I read the Torah out loud, should I then be with Goldstein and Amir? And how, if I side with Rabin against them, can I also be critical of Rabin's participation in the origins of the state of

Israel when he and others cleansed the Palestinian population from the land? When I do support the state of Israel in its existence today from the perspective of the Holocaust rather than the Bible, is my support coming from my Judaism or from a secular humanism that recognizes a history of Jewish suffering and the need to secure Jews from that threat?

Can the Torah speak for itself, without today's agendas? Can it remain as it was and also be present to us in an important way? The simple reading of the Bible had an effect on Aaron and me, as if the words read out loud were already imprinted on our subconscious. The many arguments for interpretation—rabbinic, progressive, feminist, or otherwise, all having integrity within their own sphere—appeared beside the point.

The application of the text seemed, at least in specific ways, also to be beside the point. Neither Aaron nor I was looking for guidance on the issues of homosexuality or abortion. The Promised-Land theme, so central to the narrative, did not for a moment quiet our unease about Israeli policy toward the Palestinians.

Peoplehood is central, and indeed the Promised Land is meaningless without it. Yet even so, the personal, at least in the voice of the prophet, is elevated above both the community and the land. Or perhaps better stated, the prophet embodies the future of the community and the land. For without the prophet, the people are lost and the land is polluted. Tragedy awaits when the prophetic voice is neglected or stilled. So the gathered community at Sinai and the expectant communal entry into the land are only the canvas for a larger struggle for conscience and justice. It is a struggle that runs through the Bible and has never ended. This is the struggle that Aaron and I heard in the Torah narrative as our own, to be lived now, in our context.

There are passages that relate directly to conscience. Many of them are spoken to Moses by God, and they appear over and over again in Leviticus and Deuteronomy. They are commands from God and function as a way of informing individual and collective conscience. The repetitions themselves are a way of teaching, providing a framework that is lasting and formative.

The teachings are practical, dealing with the actions of the Israelite and the people Israel. Even when they reference God, they are about doing right and good rather than exercises in speculation and power. They also tend to include the stranger as citizen, the "other" as related to Israel, so that otherness is neither definitive nor abused. Thus the particular, while emphasized, reaches out to the universal, until it is often unclear where the boundary lies between the Israelite and the foreigner, or whether it should or must remain.

This confusion is itself a trajectory within the Torah, or perhaps it is no confusion at all. In the Exodus many foreigners left Egypt with Israel; the

Israelites themselves are made up of tribes that are only partially integrated in the desert wanderings. The divisions of culture and special vocations among the Israelites continue as the people cross the Jordan.

So, in Leviticus 19, God commands Moses and the people regarding the harvest: "When you reap the harvest of your land, you shall not reap all the way to the edges of your field, or gather the gleanings of your harvest. You shall not pick your vineyard bare, or gather the fallen fruit of your vineyard; you shall leave them for the poor and the stranger: I am the LORD your God."

Moses also instructs the people: "When a stranger resides with you in your land, you shall not wrong him. The stranger who resides with you shall be to you as one of your citizens; you shall love him as yourself, for you were strangers in the land of Egypt: I am the LORD your God." Citizens, here defined as the Israelite and the foreigner, have mutual responsibilities; they seem to possess a joint destiny.

They also bear the blame for disobeying God's commands, as in Leviticus 24: "And to the Israelite people speak thus: Anyone who blasphemes his God shall bear his guilt; if he also pronounces the name LORD, he shall be put to death. The whole community shall stone him; stranger or citizen, if he has pronounced the Name, he shall be put to death."

God commands: "You shall have one standard for stranger and citizen alike: for I am the LORD your God." Then, in the discussion of limiting punishment in Exodus 21, a "fracture for fracture, eye for eye, tooth for tooth."

The sabbatical cycle is also emphasized. On the seventh day, seventh year, and fiftieth year, the call for rest and freedom is heard. Wealth and power are to be redistributed. This was my response to the scholarly invocation of Rabbi Milgrom, when he spoke so movingly about the Jubilee year in 1998. Yes, to the redistribution of land, wealth, and power—to Jew *and* Palestinian throughout the land.

This one standard is the trajectory of the Torah, reinforced by the Prophets and a return to parts of the narrative before the Exodus. Though by the time of the Exodus it is clear that peoplehood and the land will be foremost, and the origins of the narrative will be seen as foreshadowing, the personal address to the individuals of the Bible remains central.

Moses' entry into Pharaoh's palace is dramatic for the confrontation that will ensue; it is dramatic because we have followed the arc of Moses' life from his birth, awakening, and exile to his encounter with God in Midian. The moment is even more poignant because of the earlier history that found Joseph in Egypt, followed by his needy brothers and father. Those before Jacob, stretching all the way back to Abraham, had wrestled with and followed the commands of God. We find the soul of Judaism in Jacob, the God-wrestler and traveler, broken by the loss of Joseph and then reunited with him in his later years. This is why Martin Buber counsels that while the outer shell of Judaism involves the Law, the soul of Judaism is pre-Sinai.

Practicing Exile Then and Now

The Torah speaks at length about exile as both the threat and the reality of exile move through its pages from Genesis to the Prophets. Yet there is always the return, a return of God to the creation and the people, as well as a return of the people to God and the land. Exile is harsh, the return sweet.

So it is with Joseph's last request to have his bones carried from Egypt to the Promised Land. The request would seem logical and perfunctory rather than gripping and almost a surprise. Why indeed would someone so loved and respected—so important to the history of Egypt—want to be buried in a relatively unknown and unimportant land? Why would he choose Hebron over Egypt, an insignificant outpost over the glories of empire?

For Joseph, the Promised Land is the place where he will be reunited with his ancestral family, gathered, like his father, to his people. Joseph does not anticipate that it is in that land that the very unity and purpose of Israel will be tested over and over again. Being gathered to one's people in death is one thing; living among the people is another.

Since Joseph dies before the need for liberation, he is spared the Exodus wanderings and trials that plague Israel in the land. The experience of betrayal by his brothers is devastating and personal. At least initially, Joseph does not understand his trauma as related to the future of Israel. He resolves his abandonment by recognizing, mostly in a personal way, God's providential presence.

Joseph "practices" exile in Egypt. He retains his particularity within the context of service to others. His private drama is, for the most part, hidden from the people he helps govern. When it is exposed, when Joseph can no longer hold in his emotions after recognizing his brothers, the guards around him who hear his weeping and Pharaoh, who is told of Joseph's family reunification, are elated. Joseph's personal joy is celebrated as is his service to society.

The exile from the Promised Land would be quite different. Injustice and idolatry are the main causes of exile, and God's wrath is predicted and then experienced by the people.

It is more complicated for Israel to practice exile after the land is defiled. The land is promise. The land is dangerous. Israel's witness is tied to the land; for most of Israel's history, it will live outside the land. Since Israel lives outside the land, exile is the place of Jewish life and, paradoxically, the place from which commentary about the land is developed. The land is romanticized as the reality of life in the land is downplayed.

Though the synagogue liturgy features lament and loss in relation to the land, the lament itself romanticizes the land to the extent that the punishment that presages exile is almost forgotten. Thus lament is soon without context. Where once the land was concretely hungered for and struggled for, now it is spiritualized. In the wilderness, manna from heaven is survival. Later, in exile, it becomes a miracle. Here is found what remains unstated in the Torah: once exiled, the people lament from afar. Offered the chance of return to the land, few accept.

There comes a time when the exile is no longer exilic and the very naming of life as exile is a misnomer, and perhaps now it is counterproductive. Today there is an exile within the return to the land in the form of Jews of Conscience. Can that exile link with the exile outside the land? If exile is not exilic in the biblical sense of the term, do Jews need to change their language, prayer, and understandings about Jewish life? Would this then contradict the biblical narrative, rendering it superfluous, archaic, and even dangerous? Reading the Torah out loud may then be irrelevant and confusing, well beyond the modern one-dimensional critique of the narrative as patriarchal and a purveyor of violence.

Perhaps this exile is really a new Diaspora shared with many others in exile from different cultures and religions. If this is true, again the biblical narrative is thrown into question, at least the way Jews have read the Torah through the years, as our own, for us and no one else.

Of course, Christians have claimed the Torah as their own as a precursor to the New Testament, reading the Torah as their Old Testament. It could be that the Torah is not exclusively for Jews or Christians, with a strict continuity and ownership through a claimed inheritance. Perhaps the Torah simply is—a complicated, assembled, and interpreted story of a journey that breaks off, as it were, in midsentence.

Bury Arafat and Sharon Together

In the latter part of 2004, as Yasser Arafat lay dying, I was again reading the Torah out loud, this time with my youngest son, Isaiah. Aaron was a freshman at college, and Isaiah, seven years younger, eagerly awaited our evening readings. A week before the news of Arafat's deteriorating health was made known to the world, I received a video on the Wall that Israel was continuing to build in the West Bank. We had just finished reading all of Leviticus, hard slogging for an eleven-year-old.

Isaiah wanted to view the video with me. He watched with complete attention and then went up to his room to listen to music. A few minutes later, I called him down to talk. We sat on the same couch where we read the Torah. I talked to him about my own perspectives and asked him how he felt about the video.

As we talked, Isaiah came closer and put his head on my chest, then began to cry. They were the same soft tears that had come when we first read of the death of Abraham. Isaiah had wanted Abraham to live forever. He also wants everyone, including Palestinians, to live peaceful lives.

Children pick up on things. They know that some Jews would prefer me to be somewhere else and that my life has been punctuated by Jews who question my integrity and character. This was my first direct talk with Isaiah about these matters. Can we as Jews claim our Jewishness and oppress another people? How can we speak of ethics and wall in a people, effectively ghettoizing them, as we ourselves have been ghettoized? Isaiah's intuitive sense is that our behavior is wrong, that it cannot be justified, and that change is needed. Isaiah, like Aaron, with his integrity and conscience trumps the very best of our theologians—and our leadership.

My own sense is that most Jewish youth have the same intuitive sensibility that Aaron and Isaiah have, and that most Jewish education today is structured to discipline that intuition, infect it with doubt, and then reverse it. To do this, Jewish youth have to be convinced that the Palestinians are unlike us, with sinister motives and an inability to think ethically. They are taught to believe that the Wall is needed to protect us from "them" because they cannot live in peace with us.

The difficulty in teaching Jewish children this lesson is that it is inherently counterintuitive to children's sense of justice and equanimity. The children surrounding them in school in America, regardless of race or ethnicity, seem more or less the same. Can Palestinian children be so different?

Reading the Torah out loud, we find a bundle of contradictory paths: on one side, toward peace and hospitality, on the other, a violence toward the other that is unremitting. As with Aaron, I provided Isaiah with very little commentary as we read. Like the rabbis, Isaiah interprets the text or, more importantly, interprets the movement of the text within the challenges of his own life. He is, like his older brother, choosing a way of being Jewish.

Isaiah was very interested in the dying Arafat. His illness was a mystery, and speculation about the impending funeral abounded. Palestinians wanted the burial site in Jerusalem, making their claim to Arafat as a national leader and East Jerusalem as the capital of the soon-to-be Palestinian state. Israel wanted nothing to do with this, of course, and initially suggested Gaza as the burial site. The haggling was over symbolism and power. Meanwhile, Palestinians continued to live under occupation. The Wall continued to be built.

My mind recalled the dramatic moment, almost a decade before, when the widow of Yitzhak Rabin, Leah, invited Yasser Arafat to come to her home and sit *shiva* for her husband. He had done so, sans military uniform and *kefiyah*. Absent was Benjamin Netanyahu as Leah Rabin would rather have her husband's "enemy" in her home than her own countryman, a Palestinian Arab Muslim rather than an American-Israeli Jew.

There was little reflection in the news media about what barriers both Leah Rabin and Arafat had crossed to meet in her home that day. Given the blow to the peace process struck by the assassination, Arafat's appearance was, from a political perspective, courageous. More than politics was involved. Sitting with a family who has lost a loved one so unexpectedly and in such a brutal manner is not easy even for a practiced politician. Palestinian culture, unknown to most Jews in or outside of Israel, has a traditional depth to it, a closeness to the basics of life and religion. I had traveled for years among Palestinians. Sheer politics could not have been the entire story.

Yet who among Jewish commentators could see this depth, feel and breathe it, and thus recognize the possibility that there was more to Arafat than politics? Rabin was a lifelong politician, yet in his death the personality and struggles of Rabin as a man were emphasized. Was it impossible for Arafat to have this other side to him as well?

Now he lay dying, and I wondered if there would be any similar gesture by any part of organized Jewish life in America or Israel or by individual Jews. I remembered the admonition in the book of Exodus that "when you encounter your enemy's ox or donkey wandering, you must take it back to them." Even when dealing with someone we despise, we must act justly and fairly. It can be argued that the true measure of our ethical commitment is whether we treat our enemy justly and fairly. Also in Exodus: "When a stranger resides with you in the land, you shall love him as yourself, for you were strangers in the land of Egypt." Even for Jews who see Israel as our homeland and Palestinians as strangers, the reckoning is clear.

Though I longed for a gesture that went far beyond the understanding of Arafat and the Palestinians as enemy and stranger, the most basic decency demanded a gesture that moved beyond politics and recognized the inherent dignity of a leader and his people.

During this time of waiting, I had a dream, and I awoke with a statement that echoed in my mind: "Bury Arafat and Sharon together." The statement was clearly formed, almost like a command. But what could it possibly mean? Arafat was dying; at the time, Sharon seemed to be in good health. Clearly they would not be dying at the same time. Of course the very notion of a joint burial was scandalous—and to both sides.

A family plot—husband and wife, later to be joined by children—enfolds a shared life and destiny, lived in a mixture of love and difficulty, embrace and storm, now at rest. Certainly Arafat and Sharon embody their respective people's desire for justice and nationhood. To their peoples, each is a hero; each is a villain. The two spent their entire lives fighting one another, so the very image of the "other" and the people he represents is one of mutual hatred. Each needed the other to fulfill his own destiny. Why not join them in death as they were joined in life?

For Palestinians, the preferred place for Arafat's burial—as a Muslim and national leader—was Jerusalem. Israel would have none of it. The struggle brought to mind God's refusal to allow Moses into the Promised Land. God did grant Moses a view of the land. Is this the same kind of view that Arafat had of Jerusalem, a short distance away in Ramallah?

Moses was buried outside the land. Both Aaron and Isaiah thought this extremely unfair. Moses' sin at the waters of Meribah seemed trivial in comparison to his long-suffering and bold leadership. Like Moses, Arafat longed for the land and Jerusalem. It was a scandal to deny him the place in Jerusalem in death that he was denied in life.

Upon Arafat's death, there was no reciprocation of his mourning for Rabin with Leah Rabin. The separation in life between Jews and Palestinians was accentuated in the death of the only leader the Palestinians had ever known—a final humiliation borne by the Palestinians, added to the endless humiliations visited upon them by Israel, but also a marked declamation of the violence that now enveloped Jewish life.

Arafat was as fascinating in death as he was in life, a bundle of contradictions, and certainly not afraid of using violence on behalf of his people. Sharon was hardly different, nor were any of the prime ministers in Israel's history. The Israeli minister of justice, Tommy Lapid, responded to the possibility of Arafat's burial in Jerusalem by declaring, "Jewish kings, not Arab terrorists, are buried in Jerusalem."

A lifelong Israeli peace activist, Uri Avnery, responded that Menachem Begin, "a terrorist who became 'king,'" was buried in Jerusalem. For Jews, Begin was a hero, one of the founders of the state of Israel. For Palestinians—and indeed the Lebanese and even some Jews inside and outside of Israel—

Begin was a terrorist and a war criminal. Many of the same people feel this way about Sharon. Should he be denied the same burial afforded Begin in Jerusalem?

Avnery saw a double standard at work and more. Quoting from Proverbs 24—"Rejoice not when thine enemy falleth, and let not thine heart be glad when he stumbleth, lest the Lord see it, and displease him"—Avnery lamented the "disgusting filth" that poured out of the Israeli media in the days after Arafat's death. It made him ashamed to be an Israeli. But Avnery did not simply point this out from a distance. He and others of the Israeli peace group Gush Shalom attended Arafat's funeral and wrote from that vantage point. Avnery lamented that decades of occupation had left Israeli society "bestialized" and "bereft of even common decency." Avnery's eye-witness account was an elegy not only for Arafat, a man he had known and negotiated with for decades, but for Israel, the nation he had also helped build.

For Arafat and the Palestinians, the Promised Land is Jerusalem as it means full equality with Jews in Israel/Palestine. Perhaps one can consider in biblical terms the Palestinian insistence that Arafat's burial place in Ramallah is temporary. Was Arafat like Joseph, his last desire that his bones be carried out of Egypt and buried in the land? It seems that only Star of David helicopter gunships can deny this dream. Of course when Joseph died, the reality of liberation was far away. It was a promise, a future when the pharaohs had forgotten Joseph, and God, witnessing the agony of the people, returned to them.

In the Torah, God's return to the people is beautifully rendered: "A long time after that, the king of Egypt died. The Israelites were groaning under the bondage and cried out; and their cry for help from the bondage rose up to God. God heard their mourning, and God remembered his covenant with Abraham and Isaac and Jacob. God looked upon the Israelites, and God took notice of them."

Could God also, in another time and context, take notice of Palestinians—and those Jews struggling with them for a joint future in the land, a land of so much violence and promise?

Epilogue

Standing Up

Mourning is the great equalizer. A path of sorts, one that beckons to all of us. Also darkness and death. If we knew in advance that we would all be buried together, friends and enemies, would that change our perspective on how we live together? A shared darkness and death. Would that force us to concentrate on light, the light we find and share together?

Twenty years after I wrote *Toward a Jewish Theology of Liberation*, I was invited to keynote a conference in Israel exploring its future. Aaron, now in his second year of college, traveled with me. This keynote in Israel was a first for me. I was honored and pleased. Just months earlier I had also been honored by an invitation to keynote the Society of Jewish Ethics from Rabbi Elliot Dorff, the society's president. Rabbi Dorff is one of the premier scholars of ethics and Jewish law in the Conservative movement, the movement I was trained within. Earlier, Rabbi Dorff had offered an extended—and positive—promotion blurb for the third edition of my *Toward a Jewish Theology of Liberation*. I was also pleased when Susannah Heschel, the daughter of Abraham Joshua Heschel, did the same thing. Both Dorff and Heschel hold endowed chairs in Jewish thought and theology at the University of Judaism and Dartmouth respectively. Was the

Jewish community finally getting the message that something was clearly wrong in Israel?

My writing on Jewish theology began in earnest as Aaron was coming to life. Now we were traveling to Israel together. A year earlier, Aaron had traveled on his own to Israel and spent a summer with an Israeli NGO that helped to rebuild Palestinian homes in the West Bank that had been demolished by Israel. Rebuilding a home was, for Aaron, a fulfillment of the biblical injunction to live a just life. To do unto others as you would have them do unto you. It was also a way of seeking to repair lives that had been broken by violence. It was a token expression to be sure. The rebuilt home would soon be destroyed again.

This time we were traveling to Israel together, father and son. Our travels first took us to Jerusalem and the surrounding areas. As always, travel in Israel and Palestine is invigorating. The beauty of the land captivated us. We spoke with Jews and Palestinians late into the night.

Aaron and I stood together at the Western Wall, the remains of the ancient temple, and the Apartheid Wall, the wall that encircles the Palestinians in the West Bank. The first wall stood for our suffering and dispersion, the second for our return and our power.

As we crossed into the Palestinian cities of Ramallah and Bethlehem, we stood in the long lines of the checkpoint terminals. Thoroughly modern, with only the hint of the human, it was a horrific experience.

We waited with the Palestinians, who were herded like animals, awaiting permission to cross to and from Israel. Loudspeakers shouted out instructions. The noise levels and scrambled tones made it difficult to discern the language spoken, let alone the orders being given. I suspected that this jumble was purposeful. The terminals were constructed to disorient and humiliate. We read the sign placed by Israeli authorities on the Wall as we entered Bethlehem—"Peace Be upon You"—in Hebrew, Arabic, and English. Was this also a purposeful play on words and religion?

It was an incredible message the Palestinians were receiving. And, during our travel, Aaron and I received that message as well. The message was for Palestinians *and* Jews of Conscience. Was it like other messages in Jewish history, messages in other people's histories as well, that the oppressed should feel lucky and well? After all, things could be worse. At least the crossing terminals were modern and clean.

Aaron and I traveled to Israel just months before the Israeli-Lebanon war in the summer of 2006. The destruction and death of that war were immense, especially on the Lebanese side. Israel also was hit and hit hard. Hezbollah rockets and missiles repeatedly struck within Israel. During this time I wrote a diary every day. I had the sense that something momentous was occurring. Lebanon was burning. So was Israel. Could the Holocaust theologians be right in predicting that Israel might indeed fall? And what was the responsibility of Jewish leadership if indeed this did happen? The thought was too grave to consider for long. It remains in the back of my mind. Surely if this happened Lebanese and Israelis would be buried together. How much better it is to live together in peace.

This was also the time when the Iranian president Mahmoud Ahmadinejad began his diatribes of Holocaust denial and his expressed desire to wipe Israel from the face of the earth. It was silly talk—and dangerous at the same time. This kind of rhetoric exemplified what was wrong in parts of the world and also played into a post-9/11 frenzy coming from America and Israel. Though such words played a domestic role in Iranian politics, the expression of Holocaust denial and threats against Israel was and is despicable.

The summer war over, I traveled to the Philippines. I looked forward to this trip because I had many Filipino students when I taught at Maryknoll in the 1980s. Perhaps this would be a relaxing journey, one that could take my mind off the future of Israel, Jews, and Judaism.

What I found was the opposite. Traveling with pastors, I was introduced to the continuing suffering of the Filipino people. In the last few years, more than seven hundred extrajudicial killings have been reported, most of them attributed to the government and the military. The killings are part of the government's war against "terror," collateral damage in the post-9/11 world. Of course, most of the destruction after September 11 has little to do with the event itself. It is difficult to relate the struggle of peasants and laborers for their rights to land and a living wage with terrorism.

Before I left the Philippines, I read about the murder of Bishop Ramento, a bishop in the Independent Catholic Church. Ramento, a defender of peasants and workers, was killed as he slept, stabbed to death. The second day I was in the country, I met with a pastor, Reverend Billie Austin, who had been shot twice, once in each leg, for his work with the people. He had escaped death and now was given sanctuary by the bishop of his diocese. Still, he was convinced that he would be killed "as Christ was." The next day I met with a labor leader whose union had been on strike against the Swiss multinational Nestle for the past five years. His two predecessors had been murdered.

Speaking to a person who has been shot and another who is marked for death is sobering. What does one say without coming off as an idiot, speaking about hope where there is only gloom or praying, as some of my traveling companions did, as if somehow prayer addressed the solitude of these committed and hunted men?

I was asked to speak to the gathered union members and then privately with the union president. Gathering my courage, I asked the labor leader what the past months had taught him—about the struggle of labor, about politics, about God. For him, the God question was the most easily answered. He simply responded that some pastors were journeying with him and the union struggle. Therefore, God was present.

So simple, I thought. And yet also sophisticated. Sophisticated beyond the twists and turns of theological reflection in which we toss events up in the air and wonder what God has to say about them. On the firing lines, concentrated thought is crucial. It tends to eliminate abstractions and maneuverings with regard to God. The desire to criticize God. The need to save God.

Can God be saved? The Philippines is like so many of the countries I have visited, ravaged by and for the affluent, indifferent to the poor, all in the name of progress. Progress for the affluent is often equated with God. For many years I have thought that the major religion of the world is modernity. All other religions either serve modernity or are irrelevant. At least, much of the time it seems this way. In the Philippines, the connection is palpable.

Over the years, my own thinking about God has shifted. Some time ago I felt the God of History take leave of me. As if that God is no longer relevant. At the same time, I experienced a deepening sense of God's presence. Paradoxical on the most immediate level, on another level it now seems consistent. As my exile took shape, my birth community became more distant to me. My lived community became the exiles around me, Jews of Conscience some of them, but also others from different backgrounds who were exercising their conscience. They were in exile too. Exile is the gathering point where we meet.

Exile within and from political and economic empire. Also exile from the Constantinian religions that link with empire. Exile from empire creeds and empire doxologies. Exile from Christianity as the only way to God, a Judaism formed around the Holocaust and Israel as our chosenness, Muhammed as the final prophet.

The flow of particularity and universality continues apace. I find that the journey does not have an essential destination that is preordained. Perhaps there is no destination, only a committed life lived as fully as we can. Here the question of fidelity lived trumps doctrinal and historical differences that divide us. Or the divisions, once seen as definitive boundaries, now hinder our fidelity. I have been faithful as a Jew. Could I have pursued that fidelity to its fullest without the witness and support of others who are not Jewish?

A new spirituality takes the maps of our lives—the maps of our fidelity —seriously. Dorothy Day, Gustavo Gutiérrez, and James Cone—could I have been faithful without them? Perhaps others can say the same about Jews of Conscience. I doubt that it is possible to be a faithful Christian today without Jewish witnesses of the past and the present.

This is more than the familiar trope that brings religious Jews and Christians together to combat secularism, the great Satan that allows a restorationist kind of Christianity and a Constantinian Judaism to join forces against political and religious dissent. In our time, dissent is necessary to break through religiosities that support and enable empire.

Restorationist Christianity, a variation of Constantinian Christianity, abounds. Hidden behind the smiles and well-pressed suits is an anger about the world and what it has to say about the violence of Christian history. Restorationists seek to whitewash that history with a philo-Semitism and a hatred against Muslims. To do this, they seek to resurrect a Christian-American empire. "Onward Christian Soldiers" is their watchword. Like Constantinian Jews, they hold court regularly. In this era, they are even glad to rotate judges, Constantinian Christian and Constantinian Jew being interchangeable.

Perhaps the defining religious question is the struggle for community against empire. Don't those who practice empire in essence have the same religion? Those who practice community also have the same religion. The symbol structures are different to be sure. Still, it is fair to say that Jews of Conscience are closer to Christians or Muslims of Conscience. Christians and Muslims of Conscience are closer to Jews of Conscience than they are to their Constantinian variants.

God can flee and be found—at the same time. The prophetic in our time experiences this. The traditions we come from are shattered. Shall we pretend they are whole? The God within those traditions is also shattered. Shall we pretend that God is whole, as God was presented to us, naming our community, Jew, Christian, or Muslim, as the chosen ones, the ones with the straight and narrow path that we must follow to the end, lest fire and brimstone await us?

The Constantinians of every religion who believe in these divisions or, whether they believe in them or not, enforce them publicly for political reasons are the very same ones who persecute dissenters in every tradition. They brings us political assassinations, expropriation of lands, multinationals with little regard for their workers, wars without end—all blessed by the Star of David, the cross, or the crescent. Shall we follow these unbroken religions that break everything in their paths?

We carry our fragmented traditions into exile, with the parts of God that remain, experiencing in our time the willingness to *Stand Up* and be counted. In this framework a new covenant is found. A covenant without the promise of redemption, rather the promise of a journey without end that, in spite of everything, including the absurdity we experience of being persecuted by the religious authorities, believes that there is meaning. In living this journey of promise, there is community. Even and especially when we seem so alone.

We experience the pre-Sinai prophetic as we search, wander, and explore. We respond to the human and God without preconception and without a religion that is easily trumped by God's address and our response. Hearing God, we turn, sometimes leaving where we are, journeying out, wrestling with blessing and materiality to be sure, but on the move, learning, destinations unclear, knowing that we are unfinished, as is God. God is present, shorn of a systematic theology. God cannot be found in systems, boxed and wrapped, or passed on as a holiday gift certificate for you and yours.

In the Philippines, the seminary that hosted me made a decision to grant sanctuary to peasants who were being thrown off the land by the owners, who attend Mass regularly. When asked what I thought of this idea of sanctuary, I immediately congratulated them. The offer of sanctuary seems to be obvious, as the seminary has land and a commitment. The peasants are displaced, now without land. Still, the offer carries a danger for the peasants—the military knows where they are—and for the seminary community—the military sees this as defiance of their authority, as a form of disobedience.

By providing sanctuary, seminary students and professors alike are defying the law. By harboring those defined as security risks to the development plans of the wealthy, they place themselves at risk. The wealthy are seen as the ones blessed by God. Thus, in the minds of the wealthy and the churches that minister to them, the seminary, by defying the state, is betraying the economy and God. In this understanding, church folks who declare sanctuary for the displaced, such as the peasant organizations and labor organizers, become enemies of God. The penalty is death.

In this Constantinian court, sanctuary-granting Christians are criminals. Is this court that tries the seminary community, more or less, the same court that tries Jews of Conscience? As we are hauled into court, is it important to flash our badges of identification, Jew, Christian, or Muslim, as if the court, taking note of our particular affiliation, will somehow exempt us from punishment? Or should we present our identification as a demonstration to the court that our traditions do in fact continue unabated, proving a power beyond the present, so that others might take notice and resist as well?

What would that notice show? That our religious affiliations are strong enough to withstand the scrutiny and power of self-appointed leaders? Or is the notice taken as a declaration of our willingness to give everything to the present, simply because we are compelled to do so, without regard to the court's assumed jurisdiction or an agenda to prove anything? Sanctuary means simply to *Stand Up* for all who are in need, as we are in need.

Sanctuary may be the bedrock of the new Diaspora, prompting the development of a creative spirituality that can help guide those within it. Sanctuary here is broadly considered, applying wherever we are, being for one another, and raising questions about what this means in political, material, and spiritual terms. Since sanctuary is for all, regardless of geographic or birth affiliations, it makes little sense to wear these backgrounds on our chest or to ritualize them in exclusive ways.

Sanctuary is shelter from the storm that the prophet Isaiah so beautifully renders. It is also movement within the storm to broaden possibility and life. All of our traditions have aspects of sanctuary; they have also, all of them, historically or in the present, created the need for sanctuary. Left intact or articulated as such, the future continues to be a time of power and dislocation. Jews needed sanctuary; Christians created that need. Christians offer sanctuary; Jews are creating the need for sanctuary. Muslims offered sanctuary for Jews; Muslims now create the need for sanctuary. While we remember and celebrate those within these traditions who offered sanctuary, those who stood up for those in need, almost all of those we remember in this way stood up against the powers that be within their own tradition. When will we learn the lesson, that the intact power brokers of Constantinian Judaism, Constantinian Christianity, and Constantinian Islam have and will hand over those who *Stand Up*?

Standing Up, we are a community. With a tradition. Looking for a renewal of our birth traditions, pretending that the exile isn't permanent, is a recipe for the augmentation of the very traditions that persecuted the prophets then and persecute them today. Shall we remain part and parcel of this simply because we fear the exile we live and explore, the unnamed terrain like the pre-Sinai essence of the people Israel? This exile terrain might just be the essence of all, no matter the rubrics that we were born with.

We are like Job, Joseph, and Jesus, with others in between and after, being with and for others, walking down the road, wondering about life and

God, questioning and doing. Is there anything more in life? What more can we expect or hope for without crossing that line into power and idolatry? The line that has been crossed so often. Even now, in the courts of all religions where the prophets are handed over.

This handing over is also a tradition. Shall we count it a privilege to stand in the same place where others have been handed over? The place where we might, one day, be handed over as well?

Being handed over is never a pretty sight. And certainly not something to be sought. Every culture has its way of handing over dissenters, some, as in the Philippines, for death. In America among Jews and Christians, character assassination and loss of jobs and status are the norm. Dissenting Muslims may be next, handed over by a community in search of mainstream American respectability. Dissent has its context. Penalties are also contextual.

This means that theology honed in dissent is also contextual. Perhaps it has always been this way. Theology is the search for a relevant way to speak about God.

But how do we speak about God in a context where God is used to discipline the prophetic and where the prophetic dare not make claims on God that it cannot obviously support? The prophetic today is with/out God. The prophetic may be like the covenant: having come into the world, it now remains and takes on a life of its own. The prophetic, like the covenant, journeys wherever it needs to. Thus religious seekers travel to wherever the covenant is, remaining there and seeing what they are called to do. Here is the only ground from which to speak about a God who was and is, and the traces of God's presence that remain, those traces illumining our lives. In this way we also illumine our times without dissipating the darkness. The darkness remains. There is also new light.

The prophetic in a time of darkness refuses false light. It refuses to posit light where there is none. It also refuses to declare that there is no light in the darkness. The task is to gather light where light is clearly there and where it is hidden. Aren't the prophets, then and now, the ones who gather light?

Gathering light in the end is the light found in mourning. Morning light appears each day, dissipates, comes again, and becomes the light that remains at the end of the day. Morning light is a memory that has to be passed on. Lest we mistake mourning and darkness as an end that has no after, light exists even in the darkness.

Darkness and light, the great struggle that every generation wrestles with. Shall we throw our lot in with history and continue that struggle, to wrestle light from darkness?

Here the prophetic is clear. The bearer of bad tidings is also the bearer of light. If only Israel—and now all people—will listen. That listening is within and across barriers and boundaries. Indeed, the crossing of boundaries, of power, economic class, geography, and religion, is the vocation of the prophet. That is why the prophet is so controversial, an in-house critic who also speaks to the world and calls the people Israel and everyone who can hear to a new dispensation. Here particularities are questioned and affirmed even as they become more deeply themselves and something else.

The prophets call Israel to its origins and, doing that, also calls Israel beyond itself. The prophets call Israel to itself and also to something that Israel has only been in potential, a light unto the nations that will one day be with all the nations.

There is nowhere in the Torah that Israel's light is exclusively and eternally only for Israel. Light seen, light gathered, is light for all. We are all called to the prophetic light that embraces all who struggle and hunger for justice and compassion. This is the light we have, the context in which other questions arise, questions of purpose and hope, the ends of life as well as the living of it. So justice and compassion are less answers than the context in which other questions come to the fore and in which spirituality, so important to justice and compassion, moves to another level. The context for questioning is important, as is the formation of a community where the context promotes learning and sharing. Mutuality then characterizes our journey, one that limits and cultivates our aloneness. Aloneness becomes the place from which the next step of the spiritual quest is prepared.

The prophetic is a solidarity that allows solitude its rightful place. Neither solidarity nor solitude precludes the other. Rather, they work together to encourage us to find light where there is light, especially when darkness surrounds us.

Like the biblical Job and through the eyes of Gustavo Gutiérrez, we struggle for the light that comes with justice and compassion. We too ask what innocence is and why the innocent suffer. Martin Buber also is with us on the journey, noting that the prophetic is indigenous to Israel but hardly confined to any people or time. A true ecumenism they model, Gutiérrez and Buber, grappling, searching for the inner circle of prophets and becoming part of that tradition in our time. They are also calling out with *Christ in the Breadlines* (etched by Fritz Eichenberg, a Jew who was also a Quaker), Dorothy Day, and the Catholic Worker as inspiration.

Does the prophetic call us, all of us, regardless of where we hail from and what traditions formed and exiled us? The prophetic call is found beneath, around, and through the fragments, the debris, the junk that has accumulated, all that blocks the light and makes darkness seem as if it is our fated destiny. Which it might become if we don't dig our way out, by ourselves but also with others.

Those others, in history and today, through their own journey, are here with us. Shall we inquire and distinguish where they have come from, what religion they were raised within, what culture they have experienced as their own? Or shall we recognize the fact that we have arrived at the same place, our common struggle, and view later the beauty of diversity, that we have come from near and far, being other to each other, only after we realize that the joint struggle brings each one of us nearer than near?

Light gatherers. *Standing Up*, we create a new way of life. Together.

One day we will read the Torah out loud together—*Standing Up*.

Bibliography

Attek, Naim. *Justice and Only Justice*. Maryknoll: Orbis, 1989.

Attek, Naim, Marc Ellis, and Rosemary Radford Ruether, eds. *Faith and the Intifada: Palestinian Christian Voices*. Maryknoll: Orbis, 1992.

Blumenthal, David. *Facing the Abusing God: A Theology of Protest*. Louisville: Westminster John Knox Press, 1993.

Borowitz, Eugene B. *Liberal Judaism*. New York: Union of American Hebrew Congregation, 1984.

———. *Renewing the Covenant: A Theology for the Post-Modern Jew*. Philadelphia: Jewish Publication Society of America, 1991.

Boyarin, Daniel, and Jonathan Boyarin. "An Exchange on Edward Said and Difference II: Toward a Dialogue with Edward Said." *Critical Inquiry* 15 (Spring 1989).

Buber, Martin. *Eclipse of God: Studies in the Relation between Religion and Philosophy*. San Francisco: HarperCollins, 2000.

———. "Genuine Conversations and the Possibilities of Peace." *Cross Currents* 5 (Fall 1955).

———. *A Land of Two Peoples: Martin Buber on Jews and Arabs*. Edited by Paul Mendes-Flohr. Chicago: University of Chicago Press, 2005.

———. *The Prophetic Faith*. New York: Collier, 1985.

———. *Two Types of Faith*. Syracuse: Syracuse University Press, 2003.

Buber, Martin, J. L. Magnes, and E. Simon, eds. *Towards Union in Palestine: Essays on Zionism and Jewish-Arab Cooperation*. Jerusalem: IHUD, 1947.

Chmiel, Mark. *Elie Wiesel and the Politics of Moral Leadership*. Philadelphia: Temple University Press, 2001.

Cone, James H. *A Black Theology of Liberation: Twentieth Anniversary Edition*. Maryknoll: Orbis, 1990.

———. *God of the Oppressed*. New York: Seabury, 1975.

———. *Martin and Malcolm and America: A Dream or a Nightmare*. Maryknoll: Orbis, 1992.

Day, Dorothy. "Catholic Church Has Defended Jews during Times of Stress." *Catholic Worker*, December 1938.

———. *The Long Loneliness*. New York: HarperSanFrancisco, 1997.

Dorff, Elliott N. *Love Your Neighbor and Yourself: A Jewish Approach to Modern Personal Ethics*. Philadelphia: Jewish Publication Society of America, 2006.

———. *The Unfolding Tradition: Jewish Law after Sinai*. New York: Aviv, 2005.

Dorff, Elliott N., and Louis Newman, eds. *Contemporary Jewish Theology: A Reader*. Oxford: Oxford University Press, 1998.

Edwards, Herbert. "Black Theology and Liberation Theology." In *Theology in the Americas*, edited by Sergio Torres and John Eagleson. Maryknoll: Orbis, 1976.

Fackenheim, Emil L. *God's Presence in History: Jewish Affirmations and Philosophical Reflections*. New York: New York University Press, 1976.

————. "Jewish Values in the Post-Holocaust Future." *Judaism* 16 (Summer 1967).

————. *To Mend the World: Foundations of Future Jewish Thought.* New York: Schocken, 1982.

Feuerlicht, Roberta Strauss. *The Fate of the Jews: A People Torn between Israeli Power and Jewish Ethics.* New York: Times, 1983.

Finkelstein, Norman. *The Holocaust Industry: Reflections on the Exploitation of Jewish Suffering.* London: Verso, 2000.

Forster, Arnold, and Benjamin R. Epstein. *The New Anti-Semitism.* New York: McGraw-Hill, 1974.

Greenberg, Irving. "Cloud of Smoke, Pillar of Fire: Judaism, Christianity, and Modernity after the Holocaust." In *Auschwitz: Beginning of a New Era?* edited by Eva Fleischner. New York: KTAV, 1977.

————. "The Ethics of Jewish Power." *Perspectives.* New York: National Jewish Resource Center, 1981.

————. "The Interaction of Israel and the Diaspora after the Holocaust." In *World Jewry and the State of Israel*, edited by Moshe Davis. New York: Ayer, 1977.

————. "The Third Great Cycle in Jewish History." *Perspectives.* New York: National Jewish Resource Center, 1981.

Gutiérrez, Gustavo. *A Theology of Liberation History, Politics, and Salvation.* Translated by Caridad Inda and John Eagleson. Maryknoll: Orbis, 1988.

————. *Las Casas: In Search of the Poor of Jesus Christ.* Translated by Robert Barr. Maryknoll: Orbis, 1993.

————. *On Job.* Maryknoll: Orbis, 1987.

————. *The Power of the Poor in History.* Translated by Robert Barr. Maryknoll: Orbis, 1987.

————. "Toward a Theology of Liberation." In *Liberation Theology: A Documentary History*, edited and translated by Alfred Hennelly. Maryknoll: Orbis, 1990.

Handelman, Susan. *The Slayers of Moses: The Emergence of Rabbinic Interpretation in Modern Literary Theory.* Albany: SUNY Press, 1982.

Hartman, David. *Conflicting Visions: Spiritual Possibilities of Modern Israel.* New York: Schocken, 1990.

————. *A Living Covenant: The Innovative Spirit in Traditional Judaism.* New York: Macmillan, 1985.

Heschel, Abraham Joshua, Abraham Rattner, and Susannah Heschel. *Israel: An Echo of Eternity.* Woodstock, Vt.: Jewish Lights, 1997.

Lapide, Pinchas, and Jürgen Moltmann. *Jewish Monotheism and Christian Trinitarian Doctrine.* Philadelphia: Fortress Press, 1981.

Lerner, Michael. *The Geneva Accord: And Other Strategies for Healing the Israel/Palestine Conflict.* Berkeley: North Atlantic, 2004.

————. *Israel/Palestine: A Path to Peace and Reconciliation.* Berkeley: North Atlantic, 2003.

————. "Israel's Choice: Either Transfer a Million Palestinians or Get Out of Gaza." *Tikkun* 8 (January–February 1993).

————. *The Left Hand of God: Taking Back Our Country from the Religious Right.* New York: HarperSanFrancisco, 2006.

Levinas, Emmanuel. *Difficult Freedom: Essays on Judaism*. Baltimore: Johns Hopkins University Press, 1990.

Linenthal, Edward T. *Preserving Memory: The Struggle to Create America's Holocaust Museum*. New York: Columbia University Press, 2001.

Magnes, Judah. *Dissenter in Zion: From the Writings of Judah L. Magnes*. Edited by Arthur A. Gordon. Cambridge: Harvard University Press, 1982.

———. *Like All the Nations?* Jerusalem, 1930.

Miller, William. *Dorothy Day: A Biography*. New York: Harper & Row, 1982.

———. *Harsh and Dreadful Love: Dorothy Day and the Catholic Worker Movement*. New York: Liverwight, 1973.

Moltmann, Jürgen. *The Crucified God: The Cross of Christ as the Foundation and Criticism of Theology*. Minneapolis: Fortress Press, 1993.

———. *The Gospel of Liberation*. Waco: Word, 1973.

Niebuhr, Reinhold. "Jews after the War." *Nation*, February 21 and February 28, 1942.

Pappe, Illan. *The Ethnic Cleansing of Palestine*. London: Oneworld, 2006.

Perlmutter, Nathan, and Ruth Ann Perlmutter, *The Real Anti-Semitism in America*. New York: Arbor, 1982.

Roskies, David. *Against the Apocalypse: Responses to Catastrophe in Modern Jewish Culture*. Cambridge: Harvard University Press, 1984.

Roy, Sara. *Failing Peace: Gaza and the Israeli-Palestinian Conflict*. London: Pluto, 2006.

———. *The Gaza Strip: The Political Economy of De-development*. Washington, D.C.: Institute of Palestine Studies, 1995.

Rubenstein, Richard. *After Auschwitz: Radical Theology and Contemporary Judaism*. Indianapolis: Bobbs-Merrill, 1966.

———. "Buber and the Holocaust: Some Reconsiderations on the 100th Anniversary of His Birth." *Michigan Quarterly Review* 58 (Summer 1979).

———. *The Cunning of History: Mass Death and the American Future*. San Francisco: Harper & Row, 1975.

———. "Homeland and Holocaust: Issues in the Jewish Religious Situation." In *The Religious Situation: 1968*, edited by Donald Cutler. Boston: Beacon, 1968.

———. Journey to Poland." *Judaism* 15 (Fall 1966).

———. *Power Struggle: An Autobiographical Confession*. New York: Scribner, 1974.

———. "Reflections on Power and Jewish Survival." *Jewish Frontier*, May 1980.

Said, Edward. *After the Last Sky: Palestinian Lives*. New York: Pantheon, 1986.

———. *Culture and Imperialism*. New York: Alfred Knopf, 1993.

———. "An Exchange on Edward Said and Difference III: Response." *Critical Inquiry* 15 (Spring 1989).

———. "An Ideology of Difference." In *The Politics of Dispossession: The Struggle for Palestinian Self-Determination, 1969–1994*. New York: Vintage, 1994.

———. "Michael Walzer's 'Exodus and Revolution': A Canaanite Reading." *Grand Street* 5 (Winter 1986).

———. *Orientalism*. New York: Vintage, 1978.

————. *Peace and Its Discontents: Essays on Palestine in the Middle East Peace Process*. New York: Vintage, 1996.

————. *The Question of Palestine*. New York: Vintage, 1979.

————. *Reflections on Exile and Other Essays (Convergences: Inventories of the Present)*. Cambridge: Harvard University Press, 2002.

————. *The World, the Text, and the Critic*. Cambridge: Harvard University Press, 1983.

Shakah, Israel. *Jewish History, Jewish Religion: The Weight of Three Thousand Years*. London: Pluto, 1994.

————. "The Jewish Religion and Its Attitude to Non-Jews." *Khamsin* 8 (1981).

Shorris, Earl. *Jews without Mercy: A Lament*. Garden City, N.Y.: Doubleday, 1982.

Staub, Michael E. *Torn at the Roots: Jewish Liberalism in Postwar America*. New York: Columbia University Press, 2004.

Swidler, Leonard. "The Dialogical Decalogue." *Journal of Ecumenical Studies* 20 (Winter 1983).

Walzer, Michael. *Exodus and Revolution*. New York: Basic, 1985.

Waskow, Arthur. *From Race Riot to Sit-In: 1919 and the 1960s*. New York: Doubleday, 1967.

————. *Torah of the Earth: Exploring 4,000 Years of Ecology in Jewish Thought*. Woodstock, Vt.: Jewish Lights, 2000.

Wiesel, Elie. *Against Silence: The Voice and Vision of Elie Wiesel*. Vol. 2. Edited by Irving Abrahamson. New York: Holocaust Library, 1985.

————. "At the Western Wall." *Hadassah Magazine*, July 1967.

————. *Dimensions of the Holocaust*. Evanston, Ill.: Northwestern University Press, 1977.

————. *The Gates of the Forest: A Novel*. New York: Avon, 1967.

————. *A Jew Today*. New York: Vintage, 1978.

————. "Jewish Values in the Post-Holocaust Future." *Judaism* 16 (Summer 1967).

————. *Night*. New York: Hill & Wang, 2006.

————. "Your Place Is with the Victims." In *Bitburg and Beyond: Encounters in American, German, and Jewish History*, edited by Ilya Levkov. New York: Shapolsky, 1987.

Wilmore, Gayraud, and James Cone, eds. *Black Theology: A Documentary History, 1966–1979*. Maryknoll: Orbis, 1979.

Wyschogrod, Michael. *The Body of Faith: Judaism as Corporeal Election*. New York: Seabury, 1983.

Index

Other Fortress Press titles from Marc Ellis

Practicing Exile
The Religious Odyssey of an American Jew

Paperback
180 pages
$18.00
978-0-8006-3443-8

Unholy Alliance
Religion and Atrocity in Our Time

Paperback
240 pages
$15.00
978-0-8006-3080-5

O, Jerusalem!
The Contested Future of the Jewish Covenant

Paperback
208 pages
$20.00
978-0-8006-3159-8

MARC H. ELLIS is University Professor of American and Jewish Studies and Director of the Center for American and Jewish Studies at Baylor University. One of today's foremost Jewish theologians, he has also taught at Maryknoll School of Theology and Florida State University and served as a Senior Fellow and Visiting Scholar at Harvard University. A pioneer in Jewish liberation theology, he is author of many works, including *Toward a Jewish Theology of Liberation* (1987), *Beyond Innocence and Redemption* (1990), *Ending Auschwitz* (1994), *Unholy Alliance: Religion and Atrocity in Our Time* (Fortress Press, 1997), *O, Jerusalem!* (Fortress Press, 1999), and *Practicing Exile: The Religious Odyssey of an American Jew* (Fortress Press, 2001).